BEST OF

Prairie Schooner

PERSONAL ESSAYS

Edited by Hilda Raz and Kate Flaherty

University of Nebraska Press, Lincoln and London

© 2000 by *Prairie Schooner*
All rights reserved. Manufac-
tured in the United States of
America. ⊖ Library of
Congress Cataloging-in-
Publication Data. Best of
Prairie schooner : personal
essays / edited by Hilda Raz
and Kate Flaherty. p. cm.
ISBN 0-8032-8982-0 (pbk.: alk.
paper) 1. American essays –
20th century. 2. Authors,
American – 20th century –
Biography. I. Raz, Hilda.
II. Flaherty, Kate.
PS681.B47 2000
814'.508–dc21   99-086691

Contents

Introduction

The small biographies in *Best of* Prairie Schooner: *Personal Essays* suggest there are very few writers who would claim "essayist" as their main vocation. Maxine Kumin is an award-winning poet, as are Jonathan Holden, Miroslav Holub, Ted Kooser, and Linda Pastan. Wright Morris, Valerie Miner, and Robin Hemley are novelists, Alberto Ríos and Judith Ortiz Cofer are fiction writers and poets. Nancy Willard is a biographer, novelist, poet, and writer of children's books. Virginia Faulkner was an editor and critic. Only a handful of the authors here choose nonfiction as their primary genre, although even in that group there are some, like Jo Ann Beard, who suspiciously call their essays "stories" from time to time, which confuses the issue further.

All of these authors and more have come together in *Best of* Prairie Schooner: *Personal Essays,* a companion to the *Best of* Prairie Schooner: *Fiction and Poetry,* to be published in 2001 to celebrate *Prairie Schooner's* seventy-fifth anniversary of continuous publication. In its early years *Prairie Schooner* contained occasional memoirs and many scholarly essays, but in the past twenty years the magazine has included at least one or two personal essays in each issue. *Prairie Schooner,* like other literary magazines, shows a wider interest in literary nonfiction, a genre that has grown exponentially in the latter part of this century. Although the essay form is hardly new, as Phillip Lopate says in *The Art of the Personal Essay,* "The personal essay's suitability for experimental method and self-reflective process, its tolerance for the fragmentary and irresolution, make it uniquely appropriate to the present era." All of the elements Lopate describes are here in these pages.

Jo Ann Beard's essay on the women in her family flows like a memory, skipping effortlessly from a small-town summer parade to a wedding reception on the farm to an Eric Clapton concert to the bedside vigil for her mother, dying of cancer. Valerie Miner follows her relationship with her mother through a series of memoir vignettes, separate and distinct, yet all part of a whole. Judith Kitchen's words are brushstrokes creating an impressionistic portrait of her struggle to accept her father's death, and even her essay's form asserts her belief that time swallows all facts and reality, leaving only metaphor and image. Judith Ortiz Cofer writes of her education by eavesdropping in the parlor of her grandmother's home in Puerto Rico, where the afternoon she describes represents all afternoons, just as the one planting season Maxine Kumin describes in her essay is all planting seasons, where experience has taught her to do what she can to plan, and plant, and nurture her garden, and then delight in the unexpected, for it will always come.

Robin Hemley follows a more traditional story line as he remembers a particularly difficult time in his childhood when he had convinced himself he was a jinx, responsible for the deaths of both his father and two of his boyhood friends. Stephen K. Bauer writes of his childhood spent fishing and how fishing ultimately became his escape from a life he was unable to face as he shuttled between his divorced parents, feeling oddly excluded from the families they'd created with others. David Haward Bain makes a pilgrimage back to the city of his birth, Camden, New Jersey, and ties in his memories with the colorful history of the town, now in desperate shape, and the life of Camden's most famous hometown boy, Walt Whitman.

Other selections focus on the relationship between personal history and writing, as Jonathan Holden invites us to see how his connection with his twin brother has shaped his poetry, the ways his brother's coming out as homosexual in their teen years made him come to terms with his own sensitivity to and acceptance of alternate lifestyles. Nancy Willard describes how a cousin's death forces her to ask what her obligations are, as a writer, to record personal tragedy. Wright Morris explores his identity as a Western writer and exposes the links between his life experiences and his novels. Ted Kooser mulls over the ethics of "lying" in poetry, considering the balance between desire for aesthetic and emotional power with the responsibility to be honest in the telling of any story that can be perceived as autobiography.

Best of Prairie Schooner: *Personal Essays* is testament to the revival of the personal essay, as the authors in these pages connect with the reader on the most intimate levels, "speaking directly into your ear, confiding everything from gossip to wisdom," as Lopate describes. In this collection, the authors are revealing their magician's tricks, pulling the curtain back to let us see what makes their stories, what makes their poems, what makes their lives. As we share these essays with you – the best of *Prairie Schooner*'s exemplary history – we hope you too will find these essays moving and powerful, wonderful, instructive, and most of all, a delight to read.

Best of *Prairie Schooner*

Jicama, without Expectation

There never blows so red the rose,
So sound the round tomato
As March's catalogs disclose
And yearly I fall prey to.

This, my first published poem, appeared on the Home Forum Page of the *Christian Science Monitor* in March of 1953. Forty years ago, in a handkerchief-size suburban backyard dominated by a huge maple tree that admitted very little sunlight, I raised half a dozen spindly tomato plants and first made the acquaintance of the fearsome zucchini. Burpee's was my catalog of choice back then; indeed, I doubt that I knew any others existed. The prolixity and seductive lure of today's catalogs almost exceed my desire to leaf through them. It is not roses I seek; I am in search of the perfect vegetable. Open-pollinated, disease-free, all-season producer, easy to harvest, fun to cook, and heaven to eat. What cultivar is this, as yet unborn?

I have lived long enough to see the sugar snap pea survive its trials and move into the glossy pages of Harris, Stokes, Shepherds *et al.* I have seen the great viney winter squashes shrink into manageable bush types. A white eggplant has swum into my ken, as have seed potatoes, and giant onions that spring up from seed in a single season. The red brussels sprout has arrived. There is an ongoing revolution in the pepper world: orange, red, yellow, chocolate, and now white peppers are all said to be possible.

Lettuces of every hue and configuration have all but obliterated the boring iceberg head, and Japanese vegetables are so numerous that they now command their own category in the catalog. Central and South American varieties are not far behind, although I have only this winter tried to jump-start jicama, a delightfully crunchy root I first met on an hors d'oeuvres platter in Texas ten years ago. To my surprise, it has a vining habit and will want something comforting to twine itself on.

Climbers of the leguminous persuasion, from heirloom shelling-out beans to a strain of leafless peas, all do well in our soil. Frankly, I am deficient in the pepper department. *Capsicum*'s pod-like fruit mostly just sit and sulk in my central New Hampshire garden, although the long green Buddhas, which I haven't deliberately planted in a decade, continue to volunteer in all the wrong places. As do Oriental poppies, broadcast by unseen birds. These refuse to be transplanted into some other location but dot themselves among the carrots and beets at will.

For just shy of twenty years now I have been gardening in the same spot abutting the forest out of which emerge such menacing outlaws as raccoons and woodchucks, skunk, deer, and black bear. I long to have my garden closer to the house where it would be less subject to depredations. The dogs could keep an eye on it there. But our hilly farm yields only this distant tabletop for garden a hundred yards above the house and barn, and it must serve. The earth dries out slowly there, backed by our pond. But it stands open to full sun and yields eight hundred pounds of produce in a decent season.

Substantial credit for this prodigious yield goes to the *New York Times*, which arrives Monday through Saturday in the mailbox at the foot of the hill, courtesy of the RFD mailperson and her jeep. On Mondays or Tuesdays the *New York Times Book Review* comes via the same route. I don't subscribe to the Sunday edition, partly because it weighs too much to carry half a mile north, and partly because I fear it would usurp every Monday to work my way through it.

It makes no difference that the news is a day late when I carry it up the hill, usually on a horse, sometimes on foot. For breadth and depth of coverage, the *Times* has no peer. Certainly no other newspaper can match, inch for inch, its thick accretion of words, stacked and ready at all seasons in the mud room.

In March, when I start seedlings in flats on top of the refrigerator and dryer, little cutouts of wet newspaper line the trays and help hold in the moisture. New York City's ten best Szechuan restaurants underlie Johnny's new hybrid pepper seeds, which seem to take forever to wake up and grow. My almost-antique celery seeds that have not failed in four years lie atop Charles Schwab's ad for how to open an IRA account. Germination rates may exceed interest again this year.

A little later in the growing season such directly sown vegetables as beets and green beans are also mulched with "All the News That's Fit to

Print." Once the individual plants are well organized with their second set of true leaves showing, I enclose them, tearing slits in three or four thicknesses of paper to fit around the whole plant.

This is tedious and time-consuming, but pays off mightily in shutting out weeds and preserving the soil temperature that suits each variety. Green beans, for example, like warm soil, but want to be mulched before summer's full heat strikes. While kneeling to put paper around them, I can catch up on an enormous range of topics that eluded me when they were current events. If it's windy, though, I have to hurry and weight down the papers with mulch.

A vegetable garden just below a pond, just inside a field bordered by hundreds of acres of forests, clearly needs to be fenced and refenced. To keep down weeds that take tenacious hold in, around, and through the original buried chicken wire fence and the later additions of hardware cloth, screening, and other exotica thrown into the breach when emergencies arise, fat sections of the *Times* are stuffed into the gaps and pleats, then mulched for appearances' sake.

All around the outer perimeter, whole sections of the newspaper lie flat, weighted and stained with handy rocks. Before I climb over a stile of poplar chunks and into my garden, I sometimes stop to marvel at the Roche Bobois furniture ads, the gorgeous lofts in Chelsea, the halogen lights and sunken marble baths of the back pages. Here where tomatoes overgrow their cages and Kentucky Wonders climb chaotic tepees of sumac branches, I admire engineered closets and beds that fold up into walls.

My corn is not sown here, but in an inviolate space facing south in the uppermost and hottest pasture. A year's worth of book reviews, exactly the correct width when opened out, serves as carpet between the rows. And an opened-out page folded into thirds slips between individual plants, once they're six inches high. It's an Augean labor, but only needs to be performed once. Hay and/or sawdust mulch covers the paper, and nothing further is required except to eat the ears when they're of a size. No, I misspoke. Just before the corn really sets ears, I need to energize the two strands of electric fence that keep raccoons at bay.

Next April, when a general thaw makes it possible to turn the garden once again, nothing much is left of the *New York Times*. A few tatters with mysterious pieces of words on them are in evidence, but, thanks to thousands of literate earthworms, not enough remains to construct even a minimalist story.

Cultivating a garden satisfies at least some of my deep yearnings for order. Everything else has a ragged sort of shape to it. In an old farm-house, cobwebs cling to exposed beams. Pawprints muddy the floor. Doors have to be propped open with stones, the stair risers constructed two hundred years ago are amateurishly uneven. Wisps of hay ride indoors on our sweaters. It's a comfortably down-at-the-heels atmosphere. Sometimes, guiltily, I think of my mother, who would never have tolerated this welter. But the garden is composed of orderly rows and blocks of raised beds. Weeds do not penetrate the deep mulch. Serenely, plants grow, blossom, set fruit. All is as workable as Latin grammar: *Amo, amas, amat* among the brassicas; *hic haec, hoc* in a raised bed lively with parsnip foliage.

You cannot justify a garden to non-believers. You cannot explain to the unconverted the desire, the ravishing need, to get your hands into the soil again, to plant, thin, train up on stakes, trellis onto pea fence, hill up to blanch, just plain admonish to grow. From Pliny to Voltaire, from Thomas Jefferson to St. Exupery, gardening has been an emblem of integrity in an increasingly incomprehensible world.

There is an intimacy to the act of planting as tantalizing as possessing a secret. Every seed you sow has passed through your fingers on its way from dormancy to hoped-for fruition. "Trailing clouds of glory do we come," Wordsworth wrote. Thus come the little cobbles of beet seeds that separate when rolled between your fingers, the flat, feathery parsnip ones that want to drift on air en route to the furrow, the round black dots that will be Kelsae onions, fat and sweet by September, the exasperatingly tiny lettuce flecks that descend in a cluster and the even harder-to-channel carrot seeds.

Some of my seed packets are a decade old, but they've lost little vigor. Stored out of season in an unheated closet, they have amazing keeping qualities. But consider the lotus seeds found under an ancient lake bed in Manchuria. Carbon-dated at eight hundred years old, they grew into lotus plants of a sort that had never been seen in that particular area. Such extravagant longevity makes me hopeful that we humans too will ever so gradually advance into new forms, a higher level of lotus, as it were.

A few years ago, early in May, while upending a wheelbarrow load of horse manure onto the pile, I noticed some splayed green leaves emerging along the midriff of this sizeable mountain. They were not poke or burdock. They had a cultivated look. By tacit agreement my husband and I began to deposit our barrow loads on the north face of the pile.

By mid-June the south slope was covered with a dense network of what were now, clearly, squash leaves. Male blossoms, visible on their skinny-necked stems, were popping up and a few bees were already working the territory. *Let this not be zucchini,* I prayed to Mother Nature.

Around the 4th of July, green swellings could be seen at the bases of the female blossoms. The solo plant had overrun the manure pile and was now racing along our dirt road, uphill and down. Every few days I policed the road's edge and nipped back each of the brash tendrils that thought, like turtles, to cross the right-of-way. Thwarted in this direction, the heroic squash began to loop upward, mounting a huge stand of jewelweed in its eagerness to get at a telephone pole.

Well before Labor Day we knew what we had: Sweet Mamas of an especially vigorous persuasion. About ten of these pumpkin-shaped winter squashes were visible from the mountaintop. Several looked tableready.

We watched and waited, despite several frost warnings, secure in the knowledge that the warmth of the pile would protect this crop from an early demise. A two-day downpour flattened some of the luxuriant foliage; we could see that the plant was still setting fruit, heedless of the calendar. After several sunny days when things had dried out a bit, I poked around a few of the giants at the top of the mountain. They had orange streaks and some of the stems were cracking.

Harvest time was at hand. I began yanking the vines hand over hand, as if coiling the ropes of a seagoing vessel. In all we garnered thirty-five beauteous volunteers. Not a single squash bug anywhere. No chipmunk toothmarks, no tiny gnawings of mice or voles. It seems that even the lowliest creature disdains a manure pile.

We compost all our garden and table scraps, from elderly broccoli plants to orange peels to onion skins. The simplest method is just to dig a hole anywhere in the brown mountain, deposit the leavings, and backfill with a few shovelfuls of the usual. Leftovers disintegrate in a few days; sometimes I catch a glimpse of grapefruit rind or eggshell not fully digested. I re-inter them without a backward glance.

Late November is manure pile demolition time on the farm. As much of the mountain as can be moved manually or by machine is returned to the gardens, pastures, and riding ring. In the course of upending and hauling, some ancient Sweet Mama cotyledon must have been stirred to germinate. I like to think of the seed lying there through several seasons before the right combination of sun and warmth, moon and rain awakened it.

Early in October, in Geese Go South Moon, leaves rain down with a muffled sideslipping sound. Dust motes spin in sunlight like flour sifting in puffs onto the beginnings of batter. For the horses this season is heavenly. We haven't had a killing frost yet. All of our fields are open to them, and they wander like sleepwalkers from one area to another grazing intermittently, sometimes standing for long thoughtful moments silhouetted against the backdrop of forest or granite outcropping.

This is the season when tails at last become superfluous. The biting insects have fled, migrated, died off, or entered hibernation. Except for the usual small ectoplasms of gnats that still hover in quiet air, all is benign and salving in the ether. Gone the vicious little trapezoidal deerflies that draw blood from animal and human. Vanished too the horn and face flies, bots and horse flies. The ubiquitous black flies, that penance of the north country, never quite disappear but they are greatly diminished. And this summer's long tenure of mosquitoes appears to be over.

We are in the briefest and most beautiful moment of stasis. Along the perimeter of the pastures, fall flowering asters, tiny blue florets with yellow centers, flourish. A few late blackberries go on ripening, daintily pursued by the greedy broodmare, who rolls back her lips in order to nip them off, one or two at a time, without getting pricked by thorns. The Jerusalem artichokes, harbingers of frost, are in bud and threaten to open in today's sunlight. Toads in the vegetable garden, deprived of their prey now, have begun retreating to the woods after a long and profitable summer. Mushrooms appear everywhere – two brain puffballs in the dressage ring, little pear-shaped lycoperdons dotting the pine duff like misplaced miniature golf balls, smoky hygrophorus clustering in the dark corners of the pine grove, and in the rocky acre allotted the ewes, brickies – hypholoma sublateritium – spring up, breaking their gray cobwebby films. The chanterelles we prized and ate all summer are gone, but clusters of honey mushrooms at the base of decaying oaks are now ready. Sometimes, traversing the woods on horseback, we spot a full bloom of oyster mushrooms swelling on the trunk of a dying tree. Foraging for mushrooms has its own visceral pleasures: we reap where we did not sow, paper, mulch, or water.

The war against the thistles continues. Day three of eradication, extirpation, elimination, waged by me with a large serrated bread knife and by my helper with a presharpened posthole shovel. I bobble along on my knees, repositioning the kneeling pad that was a birthday present, scraping my knuckles against the inside of these thistle-proof deerhide gloves. I infer from what I see that the thistle is a biennial plant. The great green overlapping swords I am digging up – though seldom does the entire taproot come with the plant – will be the stalk and flower of next summer.

The dried vicious pickets we can pull out, thereby scattering ten thousand new seeds for the future, are no threat for the immediate season. While we're about it, we yank any surviving nettle plants, which ovines will eat if desperate.

Nothing on this farm ever reaches the desperation stage. The several ewes who summer here, leaving their home pasture to the newly weaned lambs, make little single-file trails, over to the pond, behind the pond to the woodlot, thence along the fence line back to the rockpile, and in the heat of the day, into the run-in shed where they lie on green pine sawdust in a flaccid heap like dirty laundry. We are their sabbatical. They arrive sheared and anxious in May and go home in October woolly, plump, and totally at ease, to be bred once again.

In the garden broccoli continues to bud, the Kentucky Wonders still put up beans, and the cauliflower plants left unpulled have, to my wonderment, made multiple tiny new heads. We've pulled and dried and braided our onions. Carrots too cannot stay in the ground, as voles and mice begin to nibble them. Two years ago I left parsnips in their bed to winter over and found not a trace of them by spring; last winter I pulled and scrubbed them, dried them off, and froze them, on the theory that they sweeten in the frozen earth if undisturbed. My theory proved itself, for we ate them with relish all last winter in soups and stews.

Kale, brussels sprouts, leeks, celery root, and three purple cabbages remain. Two five-gallon pails of tomatoes, last of the line, are ripening on the porch. A small group of gargantuan zucchini, somehow overlooked, have already been converted into zucchini bread and/or grated, salted, squeezed dry, and frozen to be sneaked into next winter's recipes a little at a time. They blend unnoticed in winter soups and are barely discernible when spread on pizza dough before the sauce and toppings are added. The freezer is packed with the summer's haul of strawberries, raspberries, peas, corn, green beans, and aye the rest. Part of me – the weary part – longs for frost. The other, frugal self is happy to receive each day's reduced provender.

November 15. Now I am removed by a thousand miles from my farm and garden. A wet snow is falling in central Illinois, locus day and night of mournful diesel whistles at grade crossings. Here, the campus grounds are littered with crabapples and I find myself mourning that no one cared enough to gather the harvest and make jelly. I think of my own shelves full of blueberry, strawberry, elderberry, and grape jams, and the fifteen gallons of blackberries waiting in the freezer for a January nor'easter so they can be cooked into "that tar-thick boil love cannot stir down."

There are still brussels sprouts to be picked and half a dozen daikons to be pulled, but otherwise the garden is done for. And with it the unremitting labor. Dilled green beans and bread-and-butter pickles crowd the storage shelves, abutting bottles of decorative purple-pink chive blossom vinegar. Mint, tarragon, and dill plants are drying in paper bags hung from the porch rafters.

Visitors to the farm fall into two categories: the urban admirers, nostalgists who long, but only in their imaginations, for gardens to tend, and The Others, who see this as madness. It's not cost-effective, they remind you. Look at the money you spend for seed, blood meal, Dipel, whatever. Look at the fencing (which is now deplorable and needs to be redone). On the other hand, nothing we eat has been drenched with pesticides or fertilized with chemicals. There's also the deeply Calvinist satisfaction of knowing you have earned by the sweat of your brow this delicious feast of fresh asparagus, new spinach, sweet corn, either harvested in situ or now, at this season, brought up from the capacious freezer in the cellar.

"The poet," Thoreau wrote in *A Week on the Concord and Merrimack Rivers*, "is he that hath fat enough, like bears and marmots, to suck his claws all winter. He hibernates in this world, and feeds on his own marrow."

December. Home again, to bountiful snow. Such good cover we can open the fields again, as soon as hunting season passes, to the horses to wander at will. This is the Moon That Parts Her Hair Right Square in the Middle, so styled because of the shortest day of the year and the welcome beginning of longer days. December and the arctic months that follow belong to the writer in a leisurely way, to read, think, scribble, declaim aloud, and develop a dozen fantasies of fulfillment. In January's Help Eat Moon – stay inside; too cold to do anything else, so eat more – and February's Moon of the Eagle and Hatching Time of the Owl I will suck my claws.

Ruminating in February, I read through a stack of old *Smithsonian* and *Natural History* magazines, my favorite provender. When I lift my eyes to the hills that surround us, all visible activity is suspended. This could be a glacial prehistoric era but for the two woodstoves radiating a hospitable warmth indoors and the two domesticated wolves several times removed dozing on the hearth. As I muse on the tenacity of the life force – the mice and voles unseen, running along their narrow tunnels under the snow, deer bedded in a hemlock grove far from any road – I come upon an article about suspended animation. The technical term is cryptobiosis. Brine shrimp, which flourish in brackish water that other plankton cannot tolerate, manage to survive even after the ponds dry up. They stop consuming any oxygen at all and simply encyst their embryos until conditions improve. Researchers have carbon-dated some cysts they retrieved from sediment found to be ten thousand years old. Amazingly, several of these hatched when placed back in water. I am comforted, and it is not a cold comfort; it cheers me to learn that certain kinds of brine shrimp reproduce by parthenogenesis and have persisted without male assistance for millions of years. This is less a feminist statement than an affirmation of reproductive forces.

Now we have arrived at Groundhog Day, an increasingly trivialized ceremony in this epoch of electric lights and central heating. Once, it was an event that pledged the faith of human beings in the approach of the vernal equinox. Early Slavic peoples celebrated a holiday that translates as "butter week," when, as an act of sun-worship, they devoured mountains of the pancakes we know as blini or blintzes, slathered with melted butter. Preparing, chewing, and swallowing were meant to ensure halcyon days to come with abundant crops, golden marriages, and sturdy offspring to till the fields. I like this story much better than Pennsylvania's Punxsutawney Phil, dragged out of hibernation and paraded before the television cameras to make the feature page of every newspaper in the east.

We have forgotten that we celebrate the coming of the growing season. Most of us are so far removed from the acts of cultivation that we would be unable to recognize a tepee of horticultural beans at twenty paces. But we are evolved from East African hominids that once subsisted on a totally vegetarian diet. This line of herbivorous pre-humans possessed incredibly powerful chewing teeth about five million years ago, but the species did not last. Our molars and pre-molars have shrunk, our craniums have enlarged, and we are less-robust omnivores, and what has it profited us?

It's fascinating to realize that the formal notion of agriculture, of actually sowing, weeding, and reaping plants from the soil for human uses, is only about ten thousand years old, a mere blip on the screen of human/pre-human history. We seem to have evolved in response to varying temperatures, "successive cooling plunges," anthropologist Elisabeth Vrba calls them. Wet forests gradually shrank into dry grasslands and then climatic upheavals probably reversed this action several times. Rainfall amounts and geographical boundaries tend to isolate animal populations, limiting the exchange of gene pools. These smaller groups may then diverge to permit the development of new species, or they may simply die out – more's the pity – as did our very early vegetarian ancestors. I read that the biosphere is "a living layer, stretched thinly over the globe, responding rhythmically to the beat of the earth" and I think of the holes we are poking in this thin curtain that sustains us. What new species will evolve once we have destroyed the atmosphere we require in order to breathe? What new brine shrimp will we become?

This past winter I've had a sleigh at my disposal, a little two-seater built by the Excelsior Sleigh Co. of Watertown, New York, around the turn of the century. At some time in the past hundred years an importunate horse's hoof has kicked a crescent-shaped hole in one side of it, but this in no way limits its serviceability. With new shafts and a few mended braces, it's sturdy enough to drive across the fields and, before the plow arrives, down the road as well. Twice we sojourned with it to Vermont to attend festive sleigh rallies that looked like events recorded by Currier and Ives.

When conditions are optimal – about six inches of snow over hard-pack – going sleighing is as exhilarating as the daredevil belly flopping runs of my childhood. Down the steep of our backyard that connected with the Kellys' driveway, around Devil's Elbow and out onto Pelham Road we flew, perilously side by side, in Germantown, Pennsylvania, long ago.

My half-Arab, half-Standardbred gelding loves to pull. Once he overcomes inertia and the sleigh begins to glide, he finds it all but effortless to keep it skimming. I have to hang on tight; I drive him with the reins on the lowest (most severe) slot of his Liverpool bit. In summer with the two-wheel phaeton, I can trust him with just a snaffle. The term mercurial accurately reflects changes in equine temperament according to the vagaries of weather. When the mercury plunges, their exuberance rises proportionately, and vice-versa. In winter our horses are very shaggy, volatile, round-bellied from free-choice good hay. By midsummer, freed of those heavy coats and in regular work, they are sleek, supple, almost obedient.

There's a place we love to go, on horseback or by phaeton and now by sleigh; it's a protected stretch of wetlands under federal jurisdiction, crisscrossed by a network of driveable trails. Weekdays we are usually the only travelers. The dogs go with us, sprinting into the woods to follow some elusive scent, bounding back to catch up with us around the next bend. In winter we cross-country ski here, too, along paths that weave through managed stands of red and white pine, hemlock and some few larches. Only an occasional patch of sunlight makes its way here. The prevailing northerly wind is deflected by the abundant growth. The stillness is so palpable I would risk calling it holy.

Rhythmic hoofbeats and arrhythmic sneeze-snorts echo like gunshot in these vasty rooms. Although I have never seen the taiga, I think it must look like this, with a three-abreast hitch of caribou flying over the tundra, outstripping their wolves. We seldom raise any wild creatures here as there is very little understory for browsing, but once, around a bend in the trail, we came upon a magnificent coyote, well-nourished, tall at the shoulder. There was barely enough time to admire him before he was gone. Oddly, our dogs never picked up his scent but continued their dilettantish feints around the bases of trees up which a few sparse squirrels had scampered.

These are the best of days. At noon when the temperature peaks in the twenties the fresh powder of last night's little snow squalls squeaks under our skis or runners. My horse is shod with borium caulks on all four feet. In front he wears snowball poppers, pads designed to keep the snow from balling up in the concavity of his hoof known as the frog. He is surefooted and a little too eager! We fly along in an extended trot until he wears down the edge of his enthusiasm and will come back into my hand.

Is it dangerous? Of course. A spill in cart or sleigh is far more fraught with peril than an unceremonious dumping from the saddle. The horse's life, too, is at risk when he's in the traces and upsets. But I mind the trail, squint in a sudden stretch of sunlight, settle into a long easy trot on the flat, and ask him to walk the last mile back so he can cool out without chilling.

In March the lambs – singles, twins, and triplets – begin to be born to various small-farm and hobby-farm breeders. The professionals who raise lamb in quantity for the market breed early, risking losing some newborns in order to have table-lamb, as they call it, in time for the Easter trade. It's baby chick and rabbit time, too, most of them destined for oblivion in eight to ten weeks. Goat farmers are happy to have infant bucks on hand for the Greek Orthodox Easter market in Boston, where roast kid is considered a delicacy.

I can't blink these facts, but I'm grateful I don't have to participate in them. By and large, the small breeders raise their animals for slaughter in a far more humane fashion than the animal factories of agribusiness. Around here, veal calves are not confined in slatted cages in the dark, chickens scratch in capacious barnyards and are not debeaked, sows farrow in full-size pens or in the open. Does it matter how they live, since they are all going to die to feed us? I think it matters mightily, not only because these uncrowded creatures need not be shot full of antibiotics to survive to marketable size, but because how we treat the animals in our keeping defines us as human beings.

April is punctuated by the geese going over, baying like beagles in the dawn sky. Our hundred maple taps run grudgingly around midday, then seal up tight until the next day's warmth releases them again for a few hours. Traditionally, George Washington's birthday is the first acceptable date to go out with brace and bit and bore holes in pre-selected trees. This year, blizzards and relentless cold delayed the start a good three or four weeks. Sugaring-off time depends on the freeze-thaw cycle of March and early April. This hasn't been a good run compared to last year, but the deep snow cover is prolonging it clear to the end of the month, which is unusual. Things have a way of balancing out, a fact it has taken us thirty years here to accept. Drought one season, monsoon the next.

For the first time in our long tenure here, the spring peepers have been all but inaudible. True, we've had a slow, cold spring, but except for a few tentative pipings, no evidence of *hyla crucifer*, whose high, shrill whistle ordinarily raises a deafening chorus every night during mating season. Some nights I've even closed the bedroom window on the lower-pond side to reduce the noise pollution. Now I find myself straining to hear that high-pitched stridulation.

Reflecting back on last summer, the population of bullfrogs in our upper pond, normally abundant enough to keep our dogs busy startling them off their sunbathing perches, seemed to have diminished. There were sporadic late-afternoon jug-a-rums announcing the locations of various kings, but the usual clumps of tadpoles in the shallows sprouting forelegs and gradually absorbing their tails were greatly reduced.

The salamander density seemed undisturbed, especially in the red stage on dry land when they are known as efts, a useful Scrabble word. The salamander is voiceless, so far as I know, but consider this lyrical outburst from my sobersides bible, the *Complete Field Guide to American Wildlife, East, Central and North*, by Henry Hill Collins, Jr.: "The cries of the ancient frogs may well have been the first voices in the springtime of the Age of Land Vertebrates. For millions of years before the coming of the songbirds, the calls of various frogs and toads must have been the most musical sounds on earth."

Another mystery is the absence of great blue herons from the rookery in our secret beaver pond a few miles away. For years we've gone on horseback every few days beginning at the end of April to keep tabs on this enormous nursery, where a dozen or more nests decorate the tops of dead pine trees still rising from their flooded bases. So far this year, no activity is evident. No crying and flapping, no ack-ack-ack of hungry fledglings, not even any tardy parent brooding over her eggs. Are we simply in a new cycle of birth and decay, have the herons relocated to a better, even more remote pond, or is the culprit man-made: acid rain?

Still, the geese go over barking in formation, the rusty-hinge sound of the red-winged blackbirds announces that insects are once again abroad. Tongues of snow retreat in the woods, the ubiquitous mud ebbs, pastures begin to green around the margins, fiddlehead ferns poke their spokes up through the woodland wet, and the first harbingers of spring, wake-robin trilliums, which will send up their distinctive burgundy blooms, announce the tidings with their earliest leaves.

Everything resurrects in May. Nettles first, followed by wild mustard, then dandelions and clover and tender grasses. The hardwoods flush faintly red with new buds, prelude to leaves. The willows sprout catkins, then laces of yellow strings. Wake robin is followed by bloodlilies, violets, lady's slipper, and the whole procession of miniature blossoms that dot the grudgingly greening pastures.

In the bird department, phoebes are the first to return after the blackbirds; I worry what they will find to eat before the air fills with insects. Robins next, then all smothered in a brief snowstorm. (I put out raisins and hope for the best.) Finches, both purple and gold, hung around all winter, as did the evening grosbeaks, but here come the song sparrows with their old-john-peabody, peabody, pea refrain, and finally the rose-breasted grosbeaks, spectacularly jousting at the feeders.

How joyous the first light is now, with all this territorial music! How lucky I feel to come awake to the overlapping hills and calls, a symphony of screes, caws, and warbles, many of them distinctive and recognizable, some tantalizingly elusive, even unknown. It is deliciously noisy at 5 A.M. Everyone is staking a claim. But what falls so happily on human ears actually reflects a tense struggle to survive and procreate. Life is not harmonious for the insectivores, it seems to me, who must sieve the air from dawn to full-dark for enough protein to sustain a clutch of nestlings. Prodigal nature dictates their stern routine: two, even three batches of babies in a season to guarantee the future of the race. In much the same way, nature sends down a deluge of volunteer dill into my vegetable garden, along with torrents of sprouting jewelweed, chickweed, lamb's quarters, and half a dozen extra-prolific others to bedevil the deliberately planted cultivars.

It's a penance of sorts to rise extra early and get the horses out on grass for a few hours before the wings of midges and black flies have dried. By 9 A.M. you cannot inhale outside without ingesting black flies. Even with face masks in place, the horses are driven wild by them and prefer to be in their stalls. We will endure black flies until the mosquitoes overtake them, but even this plague is self-limiting. In a few weeks, once the richest flush of growth has passed and with it the danger of founder from too much grazing, the horses will be out on grass all night. The cruelest pests – deerflies, horseflies, bots – are diurnal. Admittedly, mosquitoes raise welts on equines as well as humans, but they are more easily deterred with repellents and oily lotions.

One dawn's reward: a pair of loons crying their thrillingly demented cry overhead. That same week, wood ducks overnighting on the lower pond. The next morning a great showy splashing on the big upper pond. Two pairs of mallards, and later, one hooded merganser. What can you do with these treats? Like the winter's wild turkeys parading across the back lawn, the daily visitations by pileated woodpeckers, the late summer fawn still speckled with camouflage who bounded out of the tall grass like an enormous rabbit, these are honoraria to share with like-minded friends. We commingle our passions with a small band of other beast-bird-and-flower fanatics, like a secret cell of communists. Some of them have snapshots of moose, blurry because the photographer's hand was shaking with excitement, some have up-close black bear sightings, one has even come into the presence of a bobcat. Such events make us celebrities of a sort.

A Montana visitor in May, however, complained that the world of New England was far too verdant for her eyes. She could not differentiate the variations; all was a huge humid sea of green vegetation in her parched sight. Her retina longed to record the yellow and brown vistas of her native heath, the open plains and craggy mountains, canyons, and draws that comforted her.

Especially you know what not to rhapsodize about. Nothing rhapsodic about the enormous male raccoon who seems to have taken up permanent lodgings in the grain room of the barn. He sprawls over the cats' feeding shelf while they wait respectfully on the back sill, and it takes a snap of the lunge whip to drive him off. I am a bit leery, given the recent rash of reports of rabies in New Hampshire. All our animals have been vaccinated, but we humans are certainly vulnerable. Now I remove the cat dishes every evening hoping to deprive our adoptee of the easy pickings he seems to have come to expect. Bad enough to feed a flock of forty aggressive evening grosbeaks year-round. Am I destined to deliver cat kibble to the multitudes of masked bandits?

One afternoon our raccoon arrived just as I was feeding the cats. Abra growled, a sound I have never heard her utter before, and instantly decamped. I looked up into the coon's handsome feral face; he paid no attention to my shouts. I snapped the lunge whip at him but he stood his ground. The next crack caught him across the shoulders but hardly dislodged him. He retreated twenty paces into the broodmare's stall where she totally ignored his presence and went on eating. A raccoon that bold by daylight? We called the town's animal officer who offered us the loan of a Havahart trap.

"Take him at least ten miles from here, or you'll have him back next morning," he said. "Course, last time I did this, I got a skunk in the trap. If you catch a skunk instead, throw an old blanket over the cage before you pick it up so he won't spray." (Do I believe this will work? Not for one moment.) "Try peanut butter and if that don't get him, tuna fish."

Peanut butter didn't work, but the trap was sprung. We continue to reset it with various baits, but this fellow is apparently a graduate of Havaharts. He gets the goods and goes free. The cats and he seem to have agreed on a non-aggression pact. The dogs, too, have grown quite used to him; the horses treat him with total indifference. His hideout lies between the double walls that separate the broodmare's stall from the sawdust bin. He materializes and fades away as soundlessly as the Cheshire Cat. Often now I find him resting comfortably on the top ledge of that divider, eyeing the general proceedings. He is extremely handsome with his narrow feline face and foxy ears. I count five rings on his great tail.

Now I look over my shoulder before I open the grain bin, expecting the marauder to leap in unannounced. And as if raccoons weren't enough, Rilke, our mostly-German shepherd, came home from a trail ride today with ten porcupine quills in his face. Luckily, we were able to yank them out with needle-nose pliers while distracting him with dog biscuits. Dozens of other times with our other dogs, particularly with the handsome but ineducable Dalmatians we used to raise, we had to make emergency runs to the expensive open-all-night city-vet to have forty or fifty quills removed under total anesthesia. "The reason we don't learn from history," my poet friend Howard Nemerov once said, "is because we are not the same people who learned last time." Dogs, it seems, are never the same dogs who learned last time. Every porcupine, every skunk is newly imprinted on the brain pan, which then reverts to tabula rasa.

After a week of imprisoning one barn cat after the other in the Havahart – each seemed perfectly content there, having polished off a plate of tuna fish – our raccoon took the original bait of peanut butter. He slept most of the way to Mt. Sunapee State Park, lulled into slumber by the gentle motion of the automobile, leading me to suspect that he has made this journey before, but came awake at once when the trap door was opened. He snarled, leapt out, and shot up a tree. We hope we are permanently delivered of raccoon.

In mid-June we take our first delivery of next winter's hay, a hundred bales of first-cut timothy, insurance in case the second cutting, which we prefer for its better keeping properties, comes late or, heaven forfend, not at all. (There is always Canadian hay in an emergency, but the bales are wire-tied and the contents are coarser.) The farmer who supplies us is an old friend by now. He takes a proprietary interest in the well-being of our horses, especially my driving horse who took him for a few fast passes in the cart one day, and he is a source of rich anecdotes about the past in this corner of New England. His family has been here since, as he puts it, the back of the beyond. Steer are his specialty, but he also raises up a fine crop of local boys who hire on with him for summer jobs as soon as they are tall enough and strong enough. His work ethic is stringent but kind. Graduates of his school go on with better biceps and enlarged self-respect.

And so we grope our way into high summer again, into the time of strawberry-picking, followed by the first peas. If rain is bountiful there will be hundreds of coprinus mushrooms, our first available fungus, to make into soup. The green beans will ripen all at once, there will be too much broccoli, and when the yellow squash and zucchini begin to set fruit, there will be no sane way to cope with their overabundance. We will wait on the cusp of August for our first vine-ripened tomato. Turn around twice and they will be too many.

Just as we ate asparagus every night for three weeks when the crop gushed magically forth in May, so will we devour corn on the cob every night for those few weeks – if we're lucky! – at the end of August and into early September. A little melancholy will creep in when the corn is done. I know I will grieve as I stand there feeding the succulent shucks to the horses, as one does when a wonderful novel draws to its close. "What do I want of my life?" Stanley Kunitz asked in a poem. "More!"

Another year, please. Another year of the same. Hay in the barn, heavy snows, ten cords of dry firewood, split and stacked. Send in the black flies, let a new crop of nettles emerge, may the broodmare bring forth a healthy foal. Next year I promise to plant a smaller and thriftier garden. If I get another summer like this one, I vow to spend an hour every afternoon sitting by the pond or swimming in it. I will cultivate leisure as tenderly as jicama, which, by the way, made splendid vines and never cared to develop edible roots. I will grow jicama again, without expectation, simply to cherish it, along with the dogs and horses, the cats, even the raccoon, if he returns to raise a family, a not unlikely prospect.

For I too plan to stay.

Reading the Currents

T hrough the long winters I dreamed and prepared. The ground grew hard, snow fell and drifted, and the harbor froze. At night I read *Outdoor Life* and *Saltwater Sportsman*, and before sleep I imagined a broad silver fish leaping, lure clamped in its teeth, my legs shaking from the excitement of the strike. Often an early storm broke the harbor ice into jagged plates, but before long the harbor froze again, solidly. In eighth grade Social Studies I listed the fish I wanted to catch in the next season, separated into fresh and saltwater. After school I laid out my gear on the kitchen table, taking inventory. I sanded rust from spoons, sharpened hooks. Bought silver, blue, and black model paint to touch up chipped plastic minnows. On the coldest days, wind whipping, I walked to Northwest Outlet, wandered through the fishing aisles defrosting my glasses, and then moved along very slowly. I hefted Little Cleos, Daredevils, and Hula Poppers but bought very little, saving reasons to return. Cars skidded on the icy white streets, snowdrifts flowed across the harbor, covering inclines and ledges of ice, pushed on again by the wind. I practiced writing ocean and lake settings in my notebook, and described "that noble class of men that earns their living from the violent and tempestuous sea." Every day of thaw, the streets running with meltwater, proved a false sign. At some point in January I willed myself to stop paying attention to calendars.

For years, I did not associate fishing with pain or killing. I was aware of the life of a fish while it struggled and dove against the pressure I exerted, but once I'd pulled it from the water it quickly was reduced to a length and a weight, a snapshot, dinner. I never noticed the moment it died.

Fishing with my friend John, the night of his sixteenth birthday, his father only winked when he saw John loading a cooler with beer. Mr. Jordan went into the cabin to sleep and John and I took the boat out on Lake Ahmeek. We drank fast, kicking the empty cans back and forth. In complete darkness we trolled waywardly, rocking the boat with our lurching movements. When a fish struck my surface lure John cut the motor and the big fish leaped near the boat, raced away, diving. Though I wanted to concentrate, neither of us could stop laughing. John dropped a beer overboard, then upset the tackle box. I bumbled and swore and laughed, swaying in the tipsy boat, while John hit his head on the gunnel and cracked fresh cans for both of us, but the fish was still on all this time, pulling us toward the center of the lake.

I started to sweat, loosened the drag on my reel as the fish started a fresh run. John had found the flashlight, and swept the surface of the lake with the broad bar of light. Now he'd turned very serious, sitting with the long-handled landing net across his knees.

After a long time, after we'd been pulled almost all the way to the far shore, I began to raise the fish, gaining several feet at a time. I felt sick with excitement. When I had it in close, the fish must have seen the shadow of the boat, and it dove again and I let it go, knowing it would weaken soon. I pulled it to the surface again and John got the wide net under it and swung it into the boat.

We sat catching our breath, while the northern thrashed at our feet, its tail flicking away cans, slapping the boat bottom. John shone the light on its length, bony head caught in the plastic mesh. We cracked fresh beers and drank and drifted. We shone the light on the northern again, marveled at it. We began to tell the story of the catch, recalling the beer overboard, embellishing already. We drifted in the dark, pushed by the cool wind.

We were so tired by the time we reached the dock that we left our tackle and rods and cushions in the boat. Lacking even our usual common sense then, with no one around to tell us otherwise, we figured it would be all right to keep the northern alive all night. Kneeling at the end of the dock, I ran a stringer through the northern's gill and mouth, tied the stringer to a post. The fish flipped its tail on the surface and lay in the water. I wet my hands and walked up to the cabin with John, sleepy but wanting to think more about the catch, wanting another beer.

Early in the morning, awakened by the sun in my eyes, I remembered the fish, a feeling of accomplishment, pleasure. I pulled on a pair of shorts and went out, straight down to the dock, bending over the end, and all I found there was a fish head, tied at the gills, and stringy meat trailing down. I was more disappointed than horrified. I didn't think of the northern's death whatsoever, didn't picture the snapping turtles eating it alive.

Fishing with my family anywhere near made me uneasy. In my hometown of Superior, Wisconsin, on the western tip of Lake Superior, I considered the shoreline of Barker's Island my space, and I had an image of myself there which was violated by my family. My mother, her refined, slender hands patting my back as we stepped out of the car. My stepfather in his expensive Rockport walking shoes. I wanted them to see me make a great catch, wanted even more for them to sense my apartness, to perceive I'd made a bond with the place and with people who fished there every night, Indian boys with their handlines from the trestle. My parents should see the world I knew, feel sharply themselves that they did not know it, and admire me.

My mother's hovering presence embarrassed me, though. I was conscious of every elevated phrase she spoke, cringed to think of my fishing companions gaining a window to the living room of our house: dark wood and ponderous bookcases. My mother and sister walked along the railroad tracks back and forth behind where my stepfather and I fished. I could take only so much before I moved from my usual spot, only so much of the gathering of wildflowers and quoting from Shakespeare.

Whenever it seemed we might go fishing I checked out my stepfather's tackle, refilling the spool of line, oiling the reel. I didn't trust him to handle problems on his own and dreaded the familiar sight of him with tangles of line at his feet, calling me over to help. The proximity of his soft hands offended me. One night my stepfather caught a snake northern, too small to keep. From down the shore I saw him crouching on a flat rock, holding the fish by the gills and working the hook. Finally he put the fish down in the water in his gentle way, rinsed his hands. I couldn't imagine what he could want when I saw him walking toward me on the rise of the bank, and then I was confused, and humiliated, to see he was crying. He stood over me, squinting in the late sun, a little unsteady from drinks over dinner. Not caring who heard him, who saw him, he stood crying, wiping his eyes on the sleeve of his green corduroy jacket, and explained he couldn't stand it that the fish had died needlessly. It had swallowed the treble hook, now was dead. I looked behind him as he cried, probably seeming to sympathize, but actually steeling myself, thinking how much I hated this delicacy, watching cars passing up on the highway.

At age eight I fished for the first time, off Falmouth Beach, on Cape Cod. My father rented a cottage that summer, several months after my parents' divorce. He was harried and tense. After trying several babysitters for my sister and me, he finally imported his parents from Queens. My grandparents erected a yellow umbrella in the sand. My grandfather waded into the gentle surf wearing his black inflatable belt, and I kicked around at the margins of the beach, through the hot scruffy vegetation, for horseshoe crabs. I liked to parry with the exhausted ones, prodding them as they clawed the air. For long days my father was at work, and I occupied myself trying to find playmates, pushing along a boat with a red sail. My grandparents' functions seemed to be to remain under the umbrella by the water, to brush sand off us, to unwrap sandwiches. My grandfather slept and ate pretzels and drank beer, a salt orgy continuing day after day. Occasionally he would engage me in a strange game. He kicked a plastic stars-and-stripes ball across the sand and I ran to it, kicking it until it reached him again. He would only continue the game once I'd delivered the ball back into the umbrella's shadow. In the meantime, while I repeatedly kicked the ball wide or short or long, he stood watching with hands on hips. When I finally made a good kick there was no reward but another kick in another direction, further afield than before or into the water.

One rainy Sunday I lay on my bed, using a pencil and onionskin typing paper to trace a clipper ship from the seascape wallpaper. My father was watching a Yankees game on television, but at some point he brought me my rainslicker and told me he'd bought a fishing rod and thought we might try it out.

The rain was warm, flowing down my face. We walked across the parking lot, across the wet sand. He held the collar of my jacket as we walked out on a jetty, the slippery rocks pink and light and dark gray, speckled. The waves washed foaming into the spaces beneath us. I wanted to go right to the end, as far out as possible. The currents were whipping around the end of the jetty, tilting the red buoy. Between washes of the waves, I could see thick ropy weeds fanning out, brown and red, undulating. Mussels and barnacles on the rocks, a crab on the gray sand, and small fish darting toward it and away. I wanted to bring it all up before me, turn it over in my hands, pull it apart.

If that hook my father was tying worked I could hold a fish alive in my hands, touch the eyes and crescent slit of the gill plate. He tied a lead sinker above the hook, took a jackknife from his pocket, and then brought out a long white cardboard box. He told me we would use squid for bait, and opened the box and removed a purplish, sliding flexible tube of a body. Black bulging eyes, almost transparent tapered fins, and the tentacles he showed me had suction cups along their entire length. He cut off the head with one pass of the knife, made a slit in the body and spread it open. No blood.

"This is the backbone," he said, pulling out a clear strip, letting it fly off in the wind. I reached down and slipped my fingers across the slimy cavity. He cut a narrow triangle of bait and hooked it at the tip, slid it up the shaft of the hook, repeated the motion until none of the squid hung free.

"Watch me, Stephen," he said. He clicked down the silver bar of the reel, swung back his arms, and sent the weight and the hook spinning out in an arc. "I'm letting it sink," he said, after the splash. "Letting it settle." When the line bowed out in the wind, slack, he reeled in a few feet and handed me the rod.

"What do I do?"

"If something pulls, you yell."

I nodded tensely. He sat down behind me, packing his pipe, cupping his hands to light up. I stood straight in the rain, staring as far as I could beneath the streaked light on the surface of the currents.

Years later my father was still researching at the same laboratory at Woods Hole on Cape Cod every summer, and I had a new family, a troubling configuration of sister, half sister, two stepbrothers, new stepmother.

We stayed at 14 Devil's Lane, in a circle of cabins for scientists' families, three boys in one bedroom, two girls in the other. Down in the woods, with my notebooks and pens, I created simpler worlds. In one notebook I wrote admiring portraits of families fishing all day on the stone pier, cooking vats of menhaden soup. I called them "the husky Italians from Fall River."

In another notebook I recorded "Thoughts for the Day":

Early spring grass which is trod upon grows greener more quickly but does not grow as high.

Who is God? Is He the myth of trailing hope in a poor man's dreams or is He the pleasant reality of a rich man's existence?

It is hard to think of a thought for the day each and every day.

My big project, which I planned for every night, was a novel about slaves escaping by the Underground Railroad, called *A Taste of Freedom*. I felt virtuous, sitting on my bottom bunk writing while my stepbrothers read comic books or wrestled or made terrifically loud farting noises with their hands and underarms. Then in the morning I would go down to the woods and write on unlined paper, in tiny crabbed handwriting, over six hundred words to a page.

I also wrote settings of the places where I would be fishing later that day, or the next morning. I created places and then went to them, making notes on what I'd missed, urging myself to notice how the color of the sky affected the color of the water, signs of the tide shifting, the sounds of the wind.

My narratives were tributes to Hemingway. On the stone pier then, stoic and inscrutable, I would try to keep my dialogue terse, and hook into a fish that would be a worthy foe for my strength and steady resolve.

As I fished I recast my loneliness as moral detachment. For periods of the long nights alone then, on the stone pier, or at Barker's Island on prom night, I almost satisfied myself I was doing what I wanted. But even this near certainty gradually dissolved, especially if I wasn't having any luck, especially if the wind was cold. In the mournful foghorn, in the green flashing searchlight from Juniper Point, steady all night through, I finally read loneliness, and saw my own lack of backbone and importance. I fantasized that Elisa Goldman would come out there and find me. Seek me out. It would be just the two of us at the end of the pier, embracing, the waves engulfing us. We would be warming each other. I would be smelling her hair, her perfume. There would be no reason to fish again.

One morning when I was seventeen was memorable enough to sustain me through the summer. I was sleeping in my swimming suit, and when the alarm rang at 4:30 dressing only involved pulling on layers on top, T-shirt, hooded sweatshirt, jacket, baseball cap. I was out the door in ten minutes. The pavement cold under my feet, I walked away from town, toward Fey Beach. Down the curving road to a sandy path, under a trestle, through woods. To reach the private beach where the fishing had been best I had to cross a wide lawn with sculpted hedges. Holding my breath, tracking across the dew, glancing at the drawn curtains.

Blue water, flat beach, the sky starting to lighten. I assembled my rod, tied on a three-foot wire leader and a Creek Chub popper, a heavy lure meant to thrash on the surface like an injured fish.

The shock of the water on my feet, ankles, calves. The tide was low and I could go out far, slowly, up past my waist, soaking my clothes.

Casting, the line racing out. The water was almost motionless out there, ripples in sections, fanning out, and glassy, flat, barely-tilting calms. I let the popper float on the water a while, far out, then reeled in slack line and pulled my arms up sharply. The popper gurgled and splashed and now I brought it in fast, reeling and popping, as fast as I could. The sun began to rise and I cast and retrieved, toward ten o'clock, twelve o'clock, two o'clock – I imagined a girl coming over behind me,

Elisa Goldman with her almost-purple eyes, long muscular legs. I used to go over and over again the times I'd made her laugh and spend a few minutes with me. How had I done it?

While I imagined her asking me to see her that night, I slowed down at the end of a retrieve, the popper wiggling toward me only ten or twelve feet away. I started to lift the lure from the water and a fish bolted under it, rolled and raced away. My knees went warm. I swayed, but remembered to loosen the drag on the reel. The rod bowed and the reel sang, line stripping away. It jumped, way out there, broad and silver, twisting. A bluefish. It raced straight out and leaped again, higher, tossing its head to throw the lure. When it turned I could gain some line, and I increased the drag a little, leaning back, using the backbone of the rod against it.

I imagined being watched, still – How strong he is, how capable. She would be wanting to hold me. The aliveness of the fish traveled down my arms, though its force was diminishing. It lay on the surface, swimming sullenly, I imagined. It kept trying to turn but I was bringing it in, knowing I had to be ready, that when it saw me it would spook again and make a final run.

At the end of the fight I grabbed the leader and walked the fish to shore, letting it ride a wave to the sand. Big yellow eye, gill hardly moving, the green of the back subdued. Forked tail quivering. I pulled a loose stone from the jetty nearby, lifted the rock high and brought it down on the fish's head. Twice, and it was dead, blood coming from a cut on top of its head. I was shaking. I yanked the treble hook out of the side of its mouth and waded back into the water. I made several casts, not concentrating at all, mainly to feel the perfection of the scene. Wet, tired, happy boy. Tanned, strong hands. The sun up warm now, and behind him/behind me, the big silver fish lying on the sand.

After a while I went back to stare at the fish. The walk home along the road would be something to savor, more cars out now, people slowing and congratulating me. I lifted the fish in my arms; the tail was growing rigid and the colors were fading to gray on the sides. I walked straight back across the beach, noticing a man coming down to swim from a house a little ways down. A golden tan, but his face looked hung over. He took a stumbling running start and dove into the shallow water.

The bluefish was long enough that as I carried it by the gill its tail dragged in the sand. I could just see myself laying the fish across newspapers at the kitchen table, calling the family in to admire it. Up the three stone steps and across the big asymmetrical lawn, passing just beyond the shadow of the house. As I noticed curtains being pulled aside in a room upstairs, a door slid open. I started to run but two big dogs came around the corner. Black Labs.

"Hey," I said quietly. One jumped near my chest. They barked furiously, one to either side.

Someone called to the dogs and they stopped barking. We all looked toward the house. A woman in a long pink robe stood at the front door. She shook her fist at me.

"Next time I call the cops," she said.

"Sorry, I was only – "

"You've got no right. Get the *hell* off our property. Now. You have no right to be here." She stamped her foot and glared at me. "Bloody hell," she said, and ran her fingers back in her gray hair.

I started away and she whistled for the dogs.

"Get going," she said.

Glancing back at her, over my shoulder, I saw for the first time I was being watched, from a second-story window. A girl was watching me, smiling. She had long black hair, dark eyes, and I could see the tops of her bare shoulders. She must have been about my age. We watched each other for another moment, and then the woman shouted at me again and I turned and kept walking. I reimagined her face, thinking I saw more than curiosity. Her smiling but serious expression. I started to imagine her visiting me as I fished. Walking up the road toward home, I knew thinking of her would sustain me a long time. I didn't even think of actually trying to meet her but imagined that scene – our brief coming together as it had occurred already – was enough.

The shore on Barker's Island was never pretty. It was weedy, littered, the water chocolate colored or tea colored. Riding my bike down from the highway, I would turn down a long curving road and at the bottom, where the Island was straight ahead, with its gift shop, Vista Queen tourboat dock, public landing, I went to the left, along the railroad tracks. The concrete ended – first gravel, then dirt and cinders. To the left of the railroad bed, high weeds, wildflowers, and a hill up to the highway. To the right a narrow strip of brush dropping down to the shore of broken slabs of concrete, logs and brushy deadwood, and boulders. There was a trestle to cross, the water from a muddy culvert flowing into the lake, clouding it a deeper brown. Men and women going for carp or catfish stood at the trestle railing, drifting wads of white bread or pork rinds to the muddy bottom. I continued down the shore. The spots people claimed first were secluded pockets where there was room to spread your tackle out, a flat dry surface in the shallow water on which to stand. I poked along the shore until I found one. Weeds and wildflowers pushed through spaces of the broken shore. Clouds of gnats around my head, I would cast out again and again – a silver floating Rebel, a gold sinking Rapala, a Daredevil, a Krocodile, Hula Popper with purple speckled sides, a spinner from my Mepps Killer Kit. The rhythm of the casting, the constant wash of waves, breeze in my face, all broken only by a strike from a northern or walleye. On the way home, I stopped for donuts and coffee. If I had fish I would bring the cooler in, hoping someone would ask. I lingered there, too, arms propped on the counter.

I had the sense those long days of fishing of not having started to live yet. Someday I would be working, marrying, living on my own, but in the meanwhile – and I was pushing the "meanwhile" as long as possible – I was fishing. The endless rhythms of casting and retrieving, standing in the sun or rain, in the whipping wind off Lake Superior or in the spray on the stone pier, at daybreak and far into the night, even on Saturdays, when I could hear parties on Penzance Point, or watch couples my age and younger walking behind me. There was so much else I could be doing but I was reluctant. I was waiting, fishing, staring into the water, at schools of herring flashing, turning in unison, at searchlights crossing the water, at the ferry to Martha's Vineyard departing, coming back.

When I was twelve or thirteen I was playing hockey, skating and trying to catch a boy carrying the puck. As I leaned toward him, my tongue hanging out, straining, he swung his stick back for a slap shot. The blade caught me under the chin and I bit my tongue. Blood flowed down my throat, out of my mouth. It was warm against my neck and startling against the lightness of the ice. I filled my mouth with snow, held it melting there. The bleeding wouldn't stop so I went home. It was late afternoon and my mother and stepfather were both at work. In the bathroom mirror I saw I'd made a vertical slit all the way through my tongue. But I wasn't going to show anyone; I felt my parents couldn't be bothered. After the bleeding stopped I could feel my tongue swelling. I put myself on a diet of canned peaches, cottage cheese, soup that had cooled to room temperature. I hardly talked, but nursed my tongue, wrote notes to myself about the swelling and discoloration. I sat in school with all my concentration on the deep itch in the center of my tongue that couldn't be scratched. I dreamed of food – dreaming as I did while fishing for things I could say, wisecracks, confidences – and concentrated on healing and thriving.

During winters in Superior I tried to recreate the area where I fished all summer, off Woods Hole. In my notebooks I sketched the shapes of the shorelines there – Juniper Point, Great Harbor, the Hole where currents converged, Buzzard's Bay to one side, Vineyard Sound on the other. I wrote about wrecks on the rocks of the Hole, lives lost, hopes dashed. I wrote about rowing in the fog, chance encounters, boats lashed together while the lovers lay under the stars. I figured the anatomy of a wave, the play of light across the harbor, wind and current. At the library I found books describing the area. The Labrador Current from the north brings tuna, cod, haddock, mackerel, and herring, while the Gulf Stream from the south, veering off at the base of the Cape, brings sailfish, marlin, Portuguese Man-of-War, dolphins (both fish and mammal), moray eels. At the bottom of the Cape the currents meet, their ranges combining.

The town of Woods Hole was transformed to myth while I walked the streets and while I wrote about it, in summer two miles away, in winter half a country away. I made it into high drama, and believed it. The short main street – post office, drug store, boutiques and bars and restaurants, laboratory buildings – I made more grand. The Captain Kidd, with its dark wood bar and beery blast of air to the sidewalk, I made into a rough-and-tumble joint where the sailors – I meant merchant marines or commercial fishermen – came ashore to booze and fight. It was a point of pride that my father had brought me to play pool there when I was five or six, and when I wrote about it he wasn't drinking with other scientists but with grizzled men with an assortment of scars, clipped ears, foreshortened fingers, and elaborate scenes tattooed on their arms. They told their stories slow and understated, blue eyes dancing. Facilitated plenty by drams of ale. The street scene in my mind was endlessly interesting; dogs with bandannas tied around their legs, kids of scientists desperate with restless energy and desires, drinking late and going off in couples to dark beaches. The man who controlled the drawbridge I assumed, by his stupor, and by virtue of his closeness to "the sea," must have a fascinating story to tell. I wrote a tale of loneliness and rich adventure, watched his battles with tourists affectionately, and copied down the graffiti painted by boaters on the underside of the bridge.

I felt painfully excluded from the social scene and imagined myself above my peers. Of the entire milieu I made a morality drama. The rich and soft and greedy tourists. The coldly rational unfeeling scientists and their privileged but troubled families. The tough and unsentimental, hardworking and hardloving, noble sailors. I was hardest on my own peers, damning them for their petty conflicts, shallow attractions, casual drug use.

Most of all I made myself into myth. I was a transcendent being out there standing alone, a moral beacon in the darkness. I wouldn't want any part of their drinking around bonfires, their rides across the harbor, out, the sea a plaything to them to be used and thrown away like anything else, never feeling its power as they raced bouncing over the waves toward Middleground, toward Martha's Vineyard. Their drunken trysts. Their viperous intrigues. I exposed them, illuminating them harshly by my difference. I was going my own way. The tide surging in, flowing out, and I was there, standing proud, stoic, self-sufficient.

We spent one summer not on Cape Cod but in Newfoundland. My stepmother was from tiny West Bay Centre, and I later wrote a story about her family called "The Spirited Poor." We stayed in a white cottage on the Grand Codroy, a wide, curving blue river. It was too cold for swimming and we had no boat to take out on the river, so the entire summer it seemed to flow apart from us, a boundary of experience. I was fourteen and the fishing there filled me with despair. Early in the morning, inching my way out on a log as far as I could, I cast toward the middle of the river. The direction was right, but the distance far too vast. I caught only slimy eels, which my stepmother cut up and fried for lunch. She enjoyed them though the sections inexplicably moved on the cookie sheet after they'd been baked. The rest of us ate pickles and bread.

It broke my heart to read what a famous fishing river I was living on. At night I dreamed up ways to reach the deeper water. Could I make a raft? I begged my father please, if he cared about what kind of summer I was having, to find somewhere to rent a boat. Early in the morning, several times that summer, I saw salmon jumping far out there, the silver arcs of their bodies dreamlike in the middle of the river.

I imagined I could separate my fears into levels. The first was the actually seen, the actually experienced. I remembered being alone in a small boat, fishing on Middleground between Martha's Vineyard and the Cape. Over the long sandbar the water is as shallow as six feet. I was motoring slowly toward an oily slick on the surface. Coming closer, I could see menhaden were jumping and the bluefish were still feeding, the water tinted dark with blood, the smell sharp, but sweet at the same time, like watermelon.

I wanted to cut the motor uptide from the slick and drift down toward it, making casts to the edges. I stood as I started the drift, holding the tiller high, pushing it hard right to swing the boat left. When I looked down, over the side of the boat, I thought for a moment the shark was a shadow. It made a swell before its blunt wide head, while in back of the boat I saw its tail bending the water. I swayed toward it, then gripped the tiller hard. For a long instant I saw its dark blue-gray body beyond both ends of the boat. Then it glided on, the surface of the water wavering behind it.

Losing control. I associated that sort of fear, struggling against a known force, with times in a borrowed boat as well. Motoring through the harbor alone, through the Hole where rip currents converged, I had a sickening feeling at times, steering in one direction, toward an opening in the rocks, while the boat was sliding sideways on the current. I had the throttle open full and still I was sliding, sliding away.

The last level of fear, the unseen. I sensed it at twilight and in the dark. I would stop fishing. I would be shivering, though the wind might be warm, and I would sit on the pier, hands gripping the sharply defined corners, the block of stone dropping straight down to the water, or I would lie down in the wind and force myself to listen.

I tried to imagine warnings in the wind, saw black tunnels of death, but they looked like sewer pipes. Ridiculous.

Why was I terrified? I listened as the wind grew shrill over the dark water. Half-words, syllables I couldn't quite grasp.

Was it my own body growing, did I fear myself? Was it the entire world of encounters and accidents I would need to negotiate, soon?

Helping my mother load the yellow Chevrolet, years ago. Suitcases not even shut properly, sleeves dangling. No house behind, no apartment ahead. Where are we going?

Syllables opening in the wind, going on, another beginning. I lay there listening, at twilight when the water turned opaque, reflecting the sky, and long into the night while the wind gusted and waves ran against the wall beneath me.

Cousins

ere is a scene. Two sisters are fishing together in a flat-bottomed boat on an olive green lake. They sit slumped like men, facing in opposite directions, drinking coffee out of a metal-sided thermos, smoking intently. Without their lipstick they look strangely weary, and passive, like pale replicas of their real selves. They both have a touch of morning sickness but neither is admitting it. Instead, they watch their bobbers and argue about worms versus minnows.

My cousin and I are floating in separate, saline oceans. I'm the size of a cocktail shrimp and she's the size of a man's thumb. My mother is the one on the left, wearing baggy gabardine trousers and a man's shirt. My cousin's mother is wearing blue jeans, cuffed at the bottom, and a cotton blouse printed with wild cowboys roping steers. Their voices carry, as usual, but at this point we can't hear them.

It is five A.M. A duck stands up, shakes out its feathers and peers above the still grass at the edge of the water. The skin of the lake twitches suddenly and a fish springs loose into the air, drops back down with a flat splash. Ripples move across the surface like radio waves. The sun hoists itself up and gets busy, laying a sparkling rug across the water, burning the beads of dew off the reeds, baking the tops of our mothers' heads. One puts on sunglasses and the other a plaid fishing cap with a wide brim.

In the cold dark underwater, a long fish with a tattered tail discovers something interesting. He circles once and then has his breakfast before becoming theirs. As he breaks from the water to the air he twists hard, sending out a cold spray, sparks of green light. My aunt reels him in, triumphant, and grins at her sister, big teeth in a friendly mouth.

"Why you dirty rotten so-and-so," my mother says admiringly.

It is nine o'clock on Saturday night, the sky is black and glittering with pinholes, old trees are bent down over the highway. In the dark field behind, the corn gathers its strength, grows an inch in the silence, then stops to rest. Next to the highway, screened by vegetation, a deer with muscular ears and glamorous eyes stands waiting to spring out from the wings into the next moving spotlight. The asphalt sighs in anticipation.

The car is a late-model Camaro, black on black with a T-roof and a tape deck that pelts out anguish, Fleetwood Mac. My cousin looks just like me except she has coarse hair and the jawline of an angel. She's driving and I'm shotgun, talking to her profile. The story I'm recounting to her is full of what I said back to people when they said things to me. She can sing and listen at the same time, so she does that, nodding and grimacing when necessary.

She interrupts me once. "What's my hair doing?"

"Lying down. I'll tell you if it tries anything." Her hair is short but so dense it has a tendency to stay wherever the wind pushes it. When she wakes up in the morning her head is like a landscape, with cliffs and valleys, spectacular pinnacles.

"Okay, go ahead," she says. I finish my story before my favorite song comes on so I can devote myself to it.

We sing along to a tune about a woman who rings like a bell through the night. Neither of us knows what that means, but we're in favor of it. We want to ring like bells, we want our hair to act right, we want to go out with guys who wear boots with turned-up toes and worn-down heels. We're out in the country, on my cousin's turf. My car is stalled in the city somewhere on four low tires, a blue-and-rust Volkswagen with the door coat-hangered shut. Her car is this streamlined, dark-eyed Camaro with its back end hiked up like a skirt. We are hurtling through the night, as they say, on our way to a bar where the guys own speedboats, snow-mobiles, whatever else is current. I sing full-throttle: *She is like a cat in the dark and then she is the darkness, she rules her life like a fine skylark and then da-da-da-da-da*. I turn the rearview mirror around, check to see what's happening with the face.

Nothing good. But there you have it. It's yours at least, and your hair isn't liable to thrust itself upward into stray pointing fingers. It doesn't sound like corn husks when you brush it.

My cousin, beautiful in the dashboard light, glances over at me. She has a first name but I've always called her Wendell. She pushes it up to eighty and the song ends, a less wonderful one comes on. We're coming to the spot on the highway where the giant trees dangle their wrists over the ground. In the crotch of an elm, during daylight hours, a gnarled car is visible, wedged among the branches.

Up ahead, the cornfields are dark and rustling. The deer shifts nervously behind the curtain of weeds, waiting for its cue. The car in the tree's crotch is a warning to fast drivers, careening kids. Hidden beneath the driver's seat, way up in the branches, is a silver pocketwatch with a broken face. It had been someone's great-grandfather's, handed down and handed down, until it reached the boy who drove his car into the side of a tree. Below the drifting branches, the ground is black and loamy, moving with bugs. In the silence, stalks of corn stretch their thin, thready feet and gather in the moisture. The pocketwatch is stopped at precisely 11:47, as was the boy. Fleetwood Mac rolls around the bend and the deer springs full-blown out of the brocade trees. In the white pool of headlights, in front of a swerving audience, it does a short, stark, modern dance, and exits to the right. We recover and slow it down, shaking.

"He could have wrecked my whole front end," Wendell says. This is the farm kid mentality. Her idea of a gorgeous deer is one that hangs upside down on the wall of the shed, a rib cage, a pair of antlers, a gamey hunk of dinner. She feels the same way about cows and pigs.

We're in the sticks. Way out here things are measured in shitloads, and every third guy you meet is named Junior. I've decided I don't even like this bar we're going to, that howling three-man band and the bathroom with no stalls, just stools. Now I'm slumped and surly, an old pose for me. That deer had legs like canes, feet like Dixie cups.

Wendell pats my knee, grinning. "Settle down," she says. "It didn't *hit* us. We're safe." She likes excitement as long as her car doesn't get hurt. I light a cigarette, begin dirtying up her ashtray, and mess with the tape until our favorite song comes on again. We're back up to eighty on the narrow highway, daring the ignorant to take a step onto the asphalt. This is Illinois, a land of lumbering raccoons, snake-tailed possums, and flat-out running bunnies, all trying to cross the road. The interior of the car smells like leather and evergreen trees, the moon peers through the roof, and Wendell drives with one finger.

"Hey, how's my hair?" she asks suddenly. Her eyes are clear brown, her cheekbones are high and delicate, brushed with pink, her lips aren't too big or too little. She's wearing my shirt. A clump of hair has pushed itself forward in the excitement. It looks like a small, startled hand rising from the back of her head.

I make an okay sign, thumb and forefinger. The music is deafening.

Back in the cluster of trees, the deer moves into position again and the willows run their fingers along the ground. The corn whispers encouragement to itself. In the bar up ahead waitresses slam sloe gin fizzes down on wet tables and men point pool cues at each other in the early stages of drunkenness. The singer in the three-man band whispers *test* into the microphone and rolls his eyes at the feedback. The sound guy jumps up from a table full of ladies and heads over to turn knobs.

We crunch over the parking lot gravel and wait for our song to finish. *Dreams unwind, love's a state of mind.* The bar is low and windowless, with patched siding and a kicked-in door, the lot is full of muscle cars and pickups. A man and a woman burst through the door and stand negotiating who will drive. He's got the keys but she looks fiercer. In the blinking neon our faces are malarial and buttery. As the song winds down, the drama in front of us ends. He throws the keys at her as hard as he can but she jumps nimbly out of the way and picks them up with a handful of gravel, begins pelting his back as he weaves into the darkness.

Wendell turns to me with a grin, a question on her lips. Before she can ask I reach over and press her excited hair back down.

Their house has a face on it, two windows with the shades half-down, a brown slot of a door and a glaring mouthful of railing with a few pickets missing. Pink geraniums grow like earrings on either side of the porch. It's August and the grass is golden and spiky against our ankles, the geraniums smell like dust. A row of hollyhocks stands out by the road, the flowers are upside down ladies, red, maroon, and dried-up brown. An exploded raccoon is abuzz over on the far side of the highway and crows are dropping down from time to time to sort among the pieces. On either side of the house, fields fall away, rolling and baking in the heat.

The sisters are sitting on the stoop shelling peas, talking over top of one another. My mother says mayonnaise goes bad in two hours in the hot sun and my aunt says bullshit. They've just driven out to the fields and left the lunches for the hired men. They argue energetically about this, until the rooster walks up and my aunt carries her bowl in the house to finish the discussion through the screen door. She and the rooster hate each other.

"He thinks you're a chicken," my mother explains. "You have to show him you won't put up with it." She picks up a stick, threatens the rooster with it and he backs off, pretends to peck the yard. My aunt comes back out.

The front of her head is in curlers, the brush kind that hurt, and she keeps testing her hair to see if it's done. She has on a smock with big pockets and pedal pushers. Her feet are bare, one reason why the rooster is scaring her so much. My mother doesn't wear curlers because her hair is short, but she has two clips crisscrossed on either side of her head making spit curls in front of her ears. Every time a car drives by she reaches up automatically, ready to yank them out. She has on bermuda shorts and a wide-bottomed plaid blouse with a bow at the neck. They are both pregnant again.

We're going to be in a parade at four o'clock, Wendell and I, riding bikes without training wheels, our dolls in the baskets. We asked to have the training wheels put back on for the parade but they said no. Our older sisters are upstairs somewhere, dumping perfume on one another and trying on bracelets. They'll be in the parade, too, walking behind us and throwing their batons in the air, trying to drop them on our heads.

Wendell jumps at the rooster suddenly and he rushes us, we go off screaming in different directions while he stands there furious, shifting from one scaly foot to another, slim and tall with greasy black feathers and a yellow ruff like a collie. He can make the dirty feathers around his neck stand up and fall back down whenever he gets mad, just like flexing a muscle. Even his wives give him a wide berth, rolling their seedy eyes and murmuring. They get no rest. I haven't yet connected the chickens walking around out here with what we had for lunch, chopped up and mixed with mayonnaise.

The mothers give up and go in the house to smoke cigarettes at the kitchen table and yell at us through the windows. Wendell and I work on decorating our bikes and complaining about no training wheels.

"What about if there's a *corner*?" I say.

"I know," says Wendell. "Or if there's *dog* poop?" I don't know exactly how this relates but I shudder anyway. We shake our heads and try twisting the crepe paper into the spokes the way our mothers showed us but it doesn't work. We end up with gnarled messes and flounce into the house to discipline our dolls.

Here is the parade. Boys in cowboy getups with cap guns and rubber spurs, hats that hang around their necks from shoestrings. The girls squint against the sun and press their stiff dresses down. This is the year of the cancan slip so we all have on good underpants without holes. Some kids have their ponies there, ornery things with rolling eyes and bared teeth, all decorated up. Two older boys with painted-on mustaches beat wildly on drums until they are stopped. Mothers spit on Kleenexes and go at the boys' faces while fathers stand around comparing what their watches say to what the sun is doing.

Two little girls wear matching dresses made from a big linen table-cloth, a white background with blue and red fruit clusters. One has a bushy stand of hair and the other a smooth pixie. Both have large bows, one crunched into the mass and the other practically taped on. The scalloped collars on their dresses are made from the border of the tablecloth, bright red with tiny blue grapes, little green stems. There are sashes tied in perfect bows and popbead bracelets. Our shoes don't match.

The dolls rode over to the parade in the trunk of the car so we wouldn't wreck their outfits. They have the ability to drink water and pee it back out but they're dry now, our mothers put a stop to that. They have on dresses to match ours, with tiny scalloped collars and ribbon sashes. We set them carefully in our bike baskets with their skirts in full view. Mine's hair is messed up on one side where I put hair spray on it once. Wendell's has a chewed-up hand and nobody knows how it got that way. We stand next to our crepe-papered bikes in the sunlight, waiting for them to tell us what to do.

Our sisters have been forbidden to throw their batons until the parade starts and so they twirl them around and pretend to hurl them up in the air, give a little hop, and pretend to catch them again. They are wearing perfume and fingernail polish with their cowboy boots and shorts. They don't like us and we don't like them.

My mother tells me to stand up straight and Wendell's mother tells her to push her hair back down. The baton twirlers get a last minute talking-to with threats. The parade moves out ragged and wobbly, someone immediately starts crying, a pony wanders out of line and looks for some grass to chew. The main street is crowded with bystanders and parked automobiles. It is never clear what this parade is for except to dress the children up and show them off, get the men to come in from the fields for awhile.

As the parade pulls itself slowly down the street, the mothers stand with wry, proud faces and folded arms while fathers stand smoking, lifting the one finger farmer's salute as their sons go by. Wendell and I steer carefully and watch our mothers as they move along the sidewalk, following. Tall, lanky frames and watermelon stomachs, the gray eyes and beautiful hands of the Epperson side of the family. Our dolls are behaving perfectly, staring straight ahead, slumped forward in their baskets. My sash has come untied and Wendell's underpants are showing. We don't care, they won't bother fixing us now, we're in the parade and they have to stay on the sidewalk.

The street is brilliant in the sun, and the children move in slow motion, dresses, cowboy hats, tap shoes, the long yellow teeth of the mean ponies.

At the count of four, one of our sisters loses control, throws her baton high in the air and stops, one hand out to catch it when it comes back down.

For a long, gleaming moment it hangs there, a silver hyphen against the hot sky. Over the hectic heads of the children, the smooth blue-and-white blur of crepe-papered spokes and handlebar streamers, above the squinting smiles and upturned eyes, a silver baton rises miraculously, lingers for a moment against the sun, and then drops back down, into the waiting hand.

Back at the bar, someone has hold of me and I'm on the dance floor. Wendell's standing just inside the door. I'm going backwards swiftly in a fast two-step, there's an arm slung across my shoulder. It's good old Ted, trying to make a girl feel welcome. The bar is as dark as a pocket and my eyes haven't adjusted yet. Ted runs me into a couple of people and I tell him his arm weighs a ton. He grins but doesn't move it. He has long legs and a drinking problem. Two ex-wives follow him everywhere, stirring up trouble.

When the song finally ends, I untangle from Ted and look for Wendell. She's got us a table back by the wall, beneath the bored head of a deer. As I pass the bar several guys in turn swivel their stools around and catch me. Blue-jeaned legs are parted, I'm pulled in, pressed against a chest, clamped. Hello, hello. I bum a cigarette from the first one and blow smoke in the face of the second when his hand crawls like a bull snake up the back of my shirt. Even way out here I'm known for being not that easy to get along with.

Wendell takes her feet off my chair and pushes a rum and Pepsi my way. She tries to tell me something over the din.

"What?" I holler back and turn my ear to her.

"I *said*, Your *bud*dy's here," she yells into my hair. I pull back and look at her. She jerks a thumb upward to the passive, suspended face of the deer. Someone has stuck a cigarette butt in one of its nostrils. I show her my middle finger and she sits back again, satisfied. Side by side at the spindly table, we drink our drinks for awhile and watch the dancers go around.

Ida's out there, going to town, seventy-five if she's a day, with dyed black hair and tall, permanently arched eyebrows. From nine to midnight, even when it's just the jukebox, she takes herself around the dance floor – fox-trot, swing shuffle, two-step. She comes here every Saturday night to dance by herself while her grandson drinks Mountain Dew and plays pool in the back room. Her tennis shoes look like they're disconnected from the rest of her body. Every once in awhile she presses one hand against her waist and closes her eyes for an instant, keeping time with her shoulders, all part of some interior dancing-drama, some memory of Pete and her, before they got old, before she up and got widowed. Apparently, they were quite a deal on the dance floor. Nobody ever bumps into her out there, even the drunkest of the drunk make a space for those shoes and that head of hair. She's dancing with a memory, putting all the rest of us to shame. Here comes our darling Nick.

Everyone's in love with him, blond hair in a ponytail and wire-rims, drives a muddy jeep. Too bad he's related to us. He sets us up with two more drinks, takes a joint out of his shirt pocket, puts it in my cigarette pack and lays a big kiss on Wendell, flat on the lips. Right as he leaves, he zooms in on me unexpectedly. I give him one hand to shake and put the other one over my mouth. Wendell takes a drink and leans over.

"Gross," she shouts into my ear. I nod. Cousin-cooties.

"I'm telling Aunt Bernie," I shout back. Aunt Bernie is his mom.

We've been sitting too long. Wendell carries her drink, I light a cigarette, and we move out into the revelers and lose each other. The rum is a warm, dark curtain in my chest. I suddenly look better than I have in weeks, I can feel geraniums blooming in my cheeks, my mouth is genuinely smiling for once, my hair, fresh from the ironing board, falls like a smooth plank down my back. It's Saturday night and I'm three rum and Pepsis to the wind. I love this bar, the floor is a velvet trampoline, a mirrored ball revolves above the dance floor, stars move across faces and hands, everyone encountered is a close personal friend. I'm in line for the bathroom, chatting with strangers.

"I like your shirt." This from the woman behind me, she may be trying to negotiate her way up the line.

"Thanks," I tell her back. She's pretty. "I like yours, too."

"Your cousin's really drunk," she says, rolling her eyes. I guess she knows me. She means Nick, not Wendell. Women are always striking up conversations about Nick.

"I know," is what I tell her. I smile when I say it and shrug, trying to indicate that she can come to family dinners with Nick as far as I'm concerned. We lapse back into silence until the door bursts open and three women come out, reeking of reefer and perfume.

I look at the woman who struck up the conversation with me. We raise our eyebrows.

"Nice perfume," she says, wrinkling her nose.

"Nice reefer," I say. I let her come in while I go and she checks her makeup and examines her teeth in the mirror. I wait for her, too, bending over at the waist, shaking the hair out, and then flipping it back. It makes it fluffier for a few minutes before it settles back into the plank again. The bending and flipping sends the room careening for a moment, I'm in a centrifugal tube, then it halts. She wants to know who Nick's going out with.

"His dog, I think," I tell her. I'm politely not noticing her peeing. "He's got the nicest golden retriever you ever saw." I love that dog, it refuses to hunt, just walks along and stirs up ducks and pheasants, watches with surprise when they go flapping off. "That's one thing about Nick. His dog's nice." I don't think Nick ever shoots anything anyway, he just looks good in the boots and the vest.

Actually, I think cousin Nick's going out with everyone, but I don't tell her that. She looks hopeful and sparkly and she's not nearly as drunk as me. I give her a swimmy smile on the way out and we part company forever.

The band rolls into a slow one, with a creaky metallic guitar hook and a lone warbling voice. Someone asks me to dance and we stroll around the floor, amid the stars and the elbows. I close my eyes for a moment and it's night inside my head, there are strange arms moving me around, this way and that, feet bumping into mine. The steel guitar comes over top of it all, climbing and dropping, locating everyone's sadness and yanking on it. In the shuffling crowd the dark curtain of rum parts for an instant and reveals nothing. I open my eyes and look up at my partner. He's leading away, a grinning stranger, his hand strolls down and finds my back pocket, warms itself. Christ almighty.

Ida swims through and past, eyes blank as nickels, disembodied feet, arms like floating strings. One song ends and a new one starts up, I shake my head at my partner and he backs off with a sullen shrug. Apparently he likes this song because he begins fast-dancing by himself, looking hopefully around at the other dancers, trying to rope a stray.

This is Wendell's favorite song, *She's a good-hearted wo-man, in love with a two-timing man.* Here she is, ready to dance. I move with her back into the lumbering crowd on the dance floor, and we carve out a little spot in front of the band. *She loves him in spite of his wicked ways she don't understand.* The bar has gone friendly again while I wasn't looking, the faces of the other dancers are pink with exertion and alcohol, Nick's dancing with the bathroom girl, Ted's twirling an ex-wife, the singer in the band knocks the spit out of his harmonica and attaches it to his neck again. Look at Wendell's face. She's twenty-one and single, her hair has a story to tell. In the small sticky space in front of the band we twirl a few times, knuckles and lifted elbows, under-and-over, until I get stomped on. We're singing now, recklessly, it's almost closing time and we girls are getting prettier by the moment. *Through teardrops and laughter we pass through this world hand in hand.* Of course, both Wendell and I would like to be good-hearted women but we're from the Epperson clan and just don't have the temperament for it.

The sisters are making deviled eggs. They have on dark blue dresses with aprons and are walking around in nyloned feet. No one can find the red stuff that gets sprinkled on top of the eggs. They're tearing the cupboards apart right now, swearing to each other and shaking their heads. We all know enough to stay out of the kitchen.

We're at my grandma's house in our best dresses with towels pinned to the collars. Our older sisters are walking around with theatrical, mournful faces, bossing us like crazy, in loud disgusted whispers. They have their pockets loaded with Kleenex in preparation for making a scene. We're all going to our grandfather's funeral in fifteen minutes, as soon as the paprika gets found.

Wendell and I only get to go because we promised to act decent. No more running and sliding on the funeral home rug. Someone has *died*, and there's a time and a place for everything. We'll both get spanked in front of everyone and put in chairs if we're not careful. And if we can't keep our gum in our mouths then we don't need it: both pieces are deposited in a held-out Kleenex on the ride over. Wendell and I are in disgrace from our behavior last night at the visitation.

"It wasn't our fault he moved," Wendell had explained, right before being swatted in the funeral home foyer. Our grandfather had looked like a big, dead doll in a satin dollbed. We couldn't stop staring, and then suddenly, simultaneously, got spooked and ran out of the room, squealing and holding on to one another. We stayed in the foyer for the rest of the night, greeting people and taking turns sliding the rug across the glossy floor. We were a mess by the end of the evening.

Our dads have to sit in a special row of men. They're going to carry the casket to the graveyard. We file past them without looking and the music gets louder. The casket sits like an open suitcase up front. After we sit in our wooden folding chairs all we can see is a nose and some glasses. That's our grandpa up there, he won't be hollering at us ever again for chewing on the collars of our dresses, or for throwing hangers out the upstairs window. He won't be calling us giggleboxes anymore. He doesn't even know we're all sitting here, listening to the music and the whispers. He is in our hearts now, which makes us feel uncomfortable. Wendell and I were separated as a precautionary measure, I can just see the tips of her black shoes. They have bows on them and mine have buckles. She is swinging hers a little bit so I start to swing mine a little bit too. This is how you get into trouble, so I quit after a minute and so does she.

Pretty soon the music stops and my mother starts crying into her Kleenex. My aunt's chin turns into a walnut, and then she's crying too. Their dad is dead. Wendell puts her shoe on the back of the chair in front of her and slides it slowly down until it's resting on the floor again. I do the same thing. We're not being ornery, though. A lady starts singing a song and you can hear her breath. I can only see one inch of her face because she's standing in front of the dads. It's a song from Sunday school but she's singing it slower than we do and she's not making the hand motions. I do the hand motions myself, very small, barely moving, while she sings.

Wendell's mom leans over and tells me something. She wants me to sit on her lap. She has a nickname for me that nobody else calls me. She calls me Jody and everyone else calls me Jo. She's not crying anymore, and her arms are holding me on her lap, against her good blue dress. It's too tight in the armpits but you can't tell from looking. My mom's got Wendell.

After awhile everyone starts crying, except Uncle Edgar, my grandma's brother who always spits into a coffee cup and leaves it on the table for someone else to clean up. My aunt rests her chin on my head and rearranges her Kleenex so there's a dry spot. I sit very still while the preacher talks and the mothers cry, not moving an inch, even though my arms don't have anywhere to go. Wendell keeps moving around but I don't. Actually, I don't feel very good, my stomach hurts. I'm too big to sit on a lap, my legs are stiff, and now my heart has a grandpa in it.

The fairgrounds are huge and hot, an expanse of baking bodies and an empty stage. There are guys monkeying around on the lighting scaffold, high in the air. Mostly they're fat, stoned, and intent on their tasks but Wendell's spied one that might be okay. Ponytailed and lean, he has his T-shirt off and stuck in the waistband of his jeans. I can't look at him because he's too high up, hanging off of things that don't look reliable. Wendell trains her binoculars on him, focuses, and then sets them down. "Yuck," she reports.

We will see God this afternoon – this is an Eric Clapton concert. We're sitting on one of our grandmother's worn quilts, spread out on the ground twenty feet from the stage. "Hey look," I show Wendell a scrap of fabric. It's blue and red plaid with dark green lines running through. She and I used to have short-sleeved shirts made out of that material, with embroidered pockets. On the ride over here we each took a small blue pill, a mild hallucinogen, and now Wendell has to put her face about an inch away from the quilt in order to get a sense of the scrap I'm talking about.

"It used to be seersucker," she says sadly. "And now it isn't." We think that over for a few minutes, how things change, how nothing can be counted on, and then Wendell remembers something. "My shirt had a pony on the pocket and yours had a *schnauzer*." She snickers.

For some reason that irritates me no end. I hadn't thought of that schnauzer in years, and she has to bring it up today. Thanks a whole hell of a lot. It did used to be seersucker, too, which is very strange, because now it's not. What could have happened to it? How can something go from being puckered to being unpuckered? You could see if it was the other way around, but this just doesn't make sense. My halter top keeps feeling like it's coming undone.

We put the cooler over the unsucked seersucker so we can quit thinking about it. Wendell stretches out on her back and stares at the sky. I stretch out on my stomach and stare at some grass. We are boiling hot but we don't know it, my hair is stuck to my back and Wendell's is standing straight up in a beautiful manner.

"Your hair is standing straight up in a beautiful manner," I tell her. She nods peacefully. She holds her arms up in the air and makes a C with each hand.

"I'm cupping clouds," she says. I try to pay closer attention to my grass, which is pretty short and worn-down. It looks like it's been grazed. I read somewhere once that hysterical fans used to eat the grass where The Beatles had walked.

"Do you think Eric Clapton walked on this grass?" I ask Wendell. She looks over at me and considers. She thinks for so long that I forget the question and have to remember it again.

"No," she says finally. I feel relieved.

"Well then, I'm not eating it," I tell her flatly.

"Okay," she replies. I wish she had said Okeydokey but she didn't. She said *Okay* which has an entirely different meaning.

I sit up and my halter top sags alarmingly. All I can do is hold it in place. There's nothing else to be done, I wouldn't have any idea how to retie it. Wendell is curled up in a ball next to me with her eyes shut.

"My top is falling off," I tell her. She doesn't open her eyes. I can feel sweat running down my back like ball bearings. Wendell groans.

"The clouds are cupping *me* now," she says. "Get them off." She's still got her eyes shut and is making a whimpering sound. I don't know exactly what to do because I can't see any clouds on her and my shirt is falling off. I have to think for a moment. If I had just taken one bite of grass this wouldn't have happened.

A guy on the blanket next to us tries to hand me a joint. I can't take it because I'm holding my chest. He looks at me, looks at Wendell balled up on the ground and nods knowingly. "Bummer," he proclaims.

I can't stand to have Eric Clapton see me like this. I let go of my shirt for one second and wave my arms over Wendell. My halter top miraculously stays in place. In fact, it suddenly feels too tight. "I just got the clouds off you," I inform her. She opens one eye, then the other, and sits up.

"You look cute," she tells me. She's turning pink from the afternoon sun and her hair is hectic and alive. We open beers from our cooler and start having fun.

By the time old Eric comes out, we've completely forgotten about him, so it's a pleasant surprise. We climb up on our cooler and dance around, waving our arms in the air. We're so close to the stage he is almost life-sized. This is amazing. We dance and mouth the words while Eric sings tender love songs about George Harrison's wife and plays his guitar in a godlike manner.

The sky has turned navy blue. Eric stands in a spotlight on the stage. I pick him up once, like a pencil, and write my name in the air, then put him back down so he can play his guitar again. My halter top stays stationary while I dance around inside it naked. *Darling,* we sing to Eric, *you look won-der-ful tonight.* The air is full of the gyrations of six thousand people. My cousin is covered with clouds again but she doesn't seem to notice. Although it's still five months until Christmas, tiny lights wink on and off in her hair.

The tablecloth is covered with pie crumbs and empty coffee cups, a space has been cleared for the cribbage board and ashtrays. The sisters are smoking, staring at their cards, and talking about relatives. Neither of them can believe that Bernice is putting indoor-outdoor carpeting in her kitchen.

"You can't tell her a thing," my mother says. She lays down a card and moves her red peg ahead on the board.

"Shit," my aunt says softly. She stares at her cards. One of the husbands comes in for more pie. "What do I do here?" she asks him. He looks at her hand for a moment and then walks around the table to look at my mother's hand. He points to a card which she removes and lays down. "Try that on for size," she tells my mother.

The back door flies open and two daughters enter. There is a hullabaloo. Barbie's little sister, Skipper, was sitting on the fence and accidentally fell off and got stepped on by a pig. "She's wrecked," Wendell reports. "We had to get her out with a stick." I show them the stick and Wendell shows them Skipper.

"Stay away from the pigs," my aunt says. She's looking at her cards.

"We *were* staying away from the pigs," I answer, holding up the muddy stick as evidence. "Tell them to stay away from *us*, why don't you?" My mother looks up. "Well," I say to her.

"You might find out *well*, if you're not careful," she tells me.

Wendell takes a whiff of Skipper, who is wearing what used to be a pair of pink flowered pajamas. A small bit of satin ribbon is still visible around her neck but the rest, including her smiling face, is wet brown mud and something else. "Part of this is *poop*," Wendell hollers.

My aunt turns around finally. "Take that goddamn doll outside." She means business so we go upstairs, put Skipper in Wendell's older sister's underwear drawer, and find our Barbies.

"Mine's going to a pizza party," I say. My Barbie has a bubble haircut, red, and Wendell's has a black ponytail.

"Let's just say they're sitting home and then Ken comes over and makes them go to a nightclub," Wendell suggests. Hers doesn't have a pizza party outfit so she never wants mine to get to wear one either.

"Mine's going to sing at the nightclub then," I warn her.

"Well, mine doesn't care," Wendell offers generously. She's eyeballing a white fur coat hanging prominently in my carrying case. Her Barbie walks over to mine. "Can I wear your fur tonight?" she asks in a falsetto.

"If I can wear your bola," my Barbie replies.

"It's boa, stupid," Wendell tells me. She digs out a pink feathered scrap, puts it in her Barbie's hand, and makes her Barbie throw it at mine.

"Let's say it's really hot out and they don't know Ken is coming over and they're just sitting around naked for awhile," I suggest.

"Because they can't decide what to wear," Wendell clarifies, "all their clothes are in the dryer." She wads up all the outfits lying around and throws them under the bed.

"Oh god, it's so hot," my Barbie tells hers. "I'm just going to sit at the kitchen table for awhile." Naked, she sits down in a cardboard chair at a cardboard table. Her hair is a smooth auburn circle, her eyes are covered with small black awnings, her legs stick straight out like broomsticks.

Black-haired, ponytailed Barbie stands on tiptoe at the cardboard sink. "I'm making us some pink squirrels," she announces. "But we better not get drunk, because Ken might come over."

Both Barbies do get drunk, and Ken does come over. He arrives in an ill-fitting suit and the heat in the Barbie-house is so overwhelming that he has to remove it almost immediately.

"Hey baby," Ken says to no one in particular. The Barbies sit motionless and naked in their cardboard kitchen, waiting for orders. This is where Dirty Barbies gets murky – we aren't sure what's supposed to happen next. Whatever happens, it's Ken's fault, that's all we know.

The Barbies get tired and go lie down on their canopied bed. Ken follows them in and leans at a forty-degree angle against their cardboard dresser. He's trying to tell them he's tired, too.

"You're going to prison, buddy," Wendell finally says, exasperated. She heaves him under her bed and we get our Barbies up and dress them.

"Ken better not try anything like *that* again," ponytailed Barbie says. She's wearing a blue brocade evening gown with the white fur coat, and one cracked high heel shoe.

"He thinks he's funny but he's not," my Barbie replies ominously. "He's in jail and *we're* the only ones who can bail him out." She's got on a yellow satin and net dress with a big rip up the back, and the boa is wrapped tightly around her neck. By the time they get Ken out of jail and into his tuxedo, the whole evening is shot. The judge has to be bribed with a giant nickel that ponytailed Barbie holds in her outstretched hand.

"Crap," Wendell says when they holler at us from downstairs. I pack up my carrying case, drag it down the steps and out to the car. I keep sitting down the whole way because I'm tired.

"Get moving," my mother tells me. My aunt calls me Jody and gives me a little whack on the behind, but she doesn't mean anything by it. I climb in beside my sister and roll down the window.

"Whaaa," Wendell says to me. This is the sound her Betsy-Wetsy makes when it gets swatted for peeing.

The car pulls out onto the highway and turns toward town. I left my Barbie's pizza party outfit under Wendell's pillow so she could use it until next time. I imagine she'll find it right after she gets yelled at for Skipper in the underwear drawer. Too bad, I miss it already. Red tights and a striped corduroy shirt with tassels that hang down. It goes better with a bubblecut than a ponytail, really. I should never have left it.

Another August, this time it's early evening. We're crammed into Uncle Ed's yellow Caddie, driven by Little Eddie, our cousin. I have on a low-backed, peach-colored dress with spaghetti straps and a giant, itching wrist corsage made of greenery and tipped carnations. Wendell is wearing an ivory wedding gown with a scoop neck and a hundred buttons down the back. It's the dress our grandmother married our grandfather in and it makes Wendell look like an angel. There are guys present – my boyfriend, a sweet, quiet type named Jon, and Wendell's brand new husband, Mitch, a mild-mannered, blue-eyed farmer who is gazing at the cornfields streaking by.

Cousin Eddie is in control at this point, possibly a big mistake. One misplaced elbow and all the windows go down at once, causing hot air to whirl around inside the Caddie, stirring up everyone's hair and causing a commotion. "Okay, okay," Eddie says in a rattled voice. He pushes another button and all the windows go back up, the commotion stops, the air conditioning comes back into play.

Wendell has a wreath of baby's breath perched on top of her head like a crown of thorns. A slight crevice has appeared in the front of her hair, the baby's breath has lifted with the landscape and sits balanced on two distinct formations. The back is untouched. She wrestles herself over to the rearview mirror and gets a glimpse.

"Oh my god, it's the Red Sea," she says. "You parted my *hair*, Eddie."

There is an audible combing noise inside the car for a moment as she tries to impose some discipline on it. Eddie looks at her in the rearview mirror. He's got Uncle Ed's five o'clock shadow and Aunt Velma's tiny teeth, he's wearing a powder blue short-sleeved shirt and a flowery necktie, fashionably wide. "We can borrow you a rake at one of these farmhouses," he says, braking. The Caddie, dumb and obedient as a Clydesdale, slows down, makes a left and then a right, pulls onto a dirt track leading into a cornfield. Eddie gets his wedding present from under the seat, lights it, and passes it back. We pile out into the evening and stand, smoking, next to the car.

The sky is way up there, a lavender dome. There's a gorgeous glow of radiation in the spot the sun just vacated, a pale pink burst of pollution that matches my dress. The corn is waxy and dark green and goes on forever. We're standing in a postcard.

"This is my big day," Wendell mentions. The crown of thorns is resting peacefully, swifts are swooping back and forth, way up there, drinking bugs out of the sky. We're trying to keep the hems of our dresses from dragging in the dirt.

"This corn is *ready*," Mitch says quietly, to no one in particular. The stalks are taller than us by a foot, a quiet crowd of ten million, all of them watching us get high and wreck our outfits.

"Don't lean on the car," I tell Wendell. She stands in her usual slouch, one arm wrapped around her own waist, the other bringing the joint to her lips. She squints and breathes in, breathes out. "You look like Lauren Bacall only with different hair," I say.

She considers that. "You look like Barbara Hershey only with a different face," she says kindly. We beam at one another. This is Wendell's big day.

"Hey, bats," Jon says suddenly. He's looking up into the air where the swifts are plunging around. I'm very fond of him for a moment, and then I feel a yawn coming on. A breeze has picked up and the corn is rustling, a low hiss from the crowd. We're making Wendell late to her own party.

The Caddie takes us out of the cornfield, haunch first, Eddie steers it up to the highway, sets the cruise, and we all lean back, stare out the side windows, and watch the landscape go from corn to soybeans to cows to corn. Next thing you know we're getting out again, this time at Wendell's old house, the farm.

The wedding cake is a tiered affair with peach-colored roses and two very short people standing on top. Our mothers made the mints. This is a big outdoor reception, with a striped awning and a skinned pig. The awning is over a rented dance floor, the pig is over a bed of coals. There are as many relatives as you'd want to see in one place; the men standing around the revolving pig, the women putting serving spoons in bowls of baked beans, potato salad, things made with Jell-O, things made with whipped cream, things made with bacon bits.

Two uncles are tapping the beer keg. They keep drawing up tan glasses of foam and dumping it on the ground.

"I need a beer bad," Wendell says. She touches her head. "How's the crown?"

"Firm," I tell her. We get ourselves two glasses of foam to carry around and wander over to the food tables.

"This has prunes in it, if you can believe that," an aunt tells us, uncovering a bowl full of something pink that just came from the trunk of her car. Our mothers are standing at a long table where more women are unwrapping gifts and logging them in a book. Wendell's mother is wearing a long dress, gray silk with big peach-colored roses and green leaves down the front. My mother has on a pantsuit that everyone keeps admiring. They're both wearing corsages. "Ooh," my aunt says. A box has just been opened containing an enormous macramé plant hanger, with big red beads and two feet of thick fringe.

"Holy shit," Wendell says, taking a drink of foam.

The guests eat salads and chips and pig, the sky turns pewter, deep cobalt, then black. The band strikes up; four guys, two of them relatives. They play a fast number and everyone under the age of ten gets out there to dance. The littlest kids concentrate on trying to get it exactly right, swinging their hips and whirling their arms around. After about two songs all of them are out of control and sweating, hair stuck to their heads, girls seeing who can slide the farthest on patent leather shoes, boys taking aim and shooting each other without mercy. The parents have to step in, remove a few examples and put them in chairs. One gets spanked first for calling his mother a dipshit in front of the whole crowd.

A waltz begins to play and the older couples move out onto the floor, husbands with wives, various uncles with various aunts. My own dad dances me around a few times, tells me my dress is pretty, and delivers me in front of Jon, who looks stupendously bored and not quite stoned enough. "Hey, lotta fun," he says insincerely. I make him go dance with my mom.

Wendell takes a break from talking to people and we pull up lawn chairs next to the dance floor. Her ivory dress shines in the darkness. "I keep losing my drink," she says. We share a full, warm beer that's sitting on the ground between our chairs, passing it back and forth, watching the fox-trotters.

"I wish I could do the fox-trot," I say wistfully.

She nods. "We can't do anything good," she says wearily.

"We can two-step," I answer, in our defense.

"Yeah," she says through a yawn. "But big whoop, the two-step." Two short great-aunts glide by at a smart clip and wave at us, the bride and the bridesmaid. Wendell waves back like a beauty queen on a float, I smile and twinkle my fingers. "Yee-haw," I say quietly. On the other side of the dance floor Mitch stands listening intently to one of our distant, female relatives. He winks at us when she isn't looking and we wink back hugely. "That's my first husband, Mitch," Wendell says fondly.

The night air is damp and black against my arms, like mossy sleeves. There are stars by the millions up above our heads, Wendell and I are sitting directly under Gemini, my birth sign, the oddball twins, the split personality. Part of me wants to get up and dance, the other part wants to sit with my head tipped back. All of me wants to take off my wrist corsage.

"Nice ragweed corsage," I tell Wendell. My arm itches like fire, long red hives are marching up to my elbow. I take it off and put it under my chair.

"Give it a heave," she suggests, and I do. It lands within twenty feet of our lawn chairs. A giant calico farm cat steps out from nowhere, sniffs it, then picks it up delicately and fades back into the blackness. Under the awning the air is stained yellow, the band is playing a disco song. Our mothers are in the midst of a line dance, doing their own version of the hustle, out of sync with everyone else. Their work is done, they've mingled, they've been fairly polite. Now they've got about twenty minutes of careening before they collapse in lawn chairs and ask people to wait on them. They're out there trying to kick and clap at the same time, without putting their drinks down. I decide I'd better join them.

My mother's cheeks are in bloom, from sloe gin and exertion, her lipstick has worn off but her corsage is still going strong, a flower the size of a punch bowl. She tries for the relaxed shuffle-kick-pause-clap of all the other line dancers but can't do it. She sets her drink down at the edge of the dance floor where it's sure get knocked over, and comes back to the line, full-steam ahead. She starts doing the bump with Wendell's mom and another aunt. Before they can get me involved, I dance myself over to the edge of the floor and step out into the darkness.

"The moms need to be spanked and put in chairs," I tell Jon, who hands over his beer without being asked. He looks peaceful and affectionate; his hair is sticking straight up in front and there's something pink and crusty all over the front of his shirt.

"One of those kids threw a piece of cake at me," he says placidly. He's been smoking pot out in the corn with Eddie, I can tell. The band pauses between numbers and the mothers keep dancing. In the distance, two uncles stand talking, using the blue glow of a bug zapper to compare their mangled thumbnails. Up by the band, the bride is getting ready to throw the bouquet. I'm being summoned to come stand in the group of girl cousins clustered around Wendell. I walk backward until I'm past the first row of corn, Jon following amiably, pink-eyed and slaphappy. He's using a swizzle stick for a toothpick.

Inside the corn it is completely dark, the stalks stand silent, the sounds of the party are indistinct. We can hear each other breathing. There is a muffled cheering as the bouquet gets thrown, and then someone talks loud and long into the microphone, offering a toast. Jon begins nuzzling my ear and talking baby talk.

"Hey," I whisper to him.

"Mmmm?" he says.

"Have you ever seen a corn snake?"

He refuses to be intimidated. A waltz begins and we absently take up the one-two-three, one-two-three. Around us the dark stalks ripple like water, the waves of the Blue Danube wash over us. "I can show *you* a corn snake," he says softly, into my hair.

Here is a scene. Two sisters talk together in low voices, one crochets and the other picks lint carefully off a blanket. Their eyes meet infrequently but the conversation is the same as always.

"He's too young to retire," my mother says. "He'll be stuck to her like a burr, and then that's all you'll hear. How she can't stand having him underfoot." One of my uncles wants to retire from selling Amana refrigerators and spend the rest of his years doing woodworking.

"How many pig-shaped cutting boards does anybody need?" my aunt says. She holds her crocheting up to the window. "God*damn*it. I did it again." She begins unraveling the last few rows, the yarn falling into a snarl around her feet.

"Here," my mother says, holding out a hand, "give me that." She takes the ball of pale yellow yarn and slowly, patiently winds the kinked part back up. While they work, a nurse enters and reads a chart, takes a needle from a cart in the hall and injects it in the tube leading into my mother's arm. When the door snicks shut behind her, my aunt quits unraveling long enough to get a cigarette from her purse.

"They better not catch me doing this," she says, lighting up. She's using an old pop can for an ashtray. The cigarette trembles slightly in her long fingers and her eyes find the ceiling, then the floor, then the window. She adjusts the belt on her suit, a soft green knit tunic over pants, with silver buttons and a patterned scarf at the neck. She's sitting in an orange plastic chair.

My mother is wearing a dark blue negligee with a bed jacket and thick cotton socks. She takes a puff from my aunt's cigarette and exhales slowly, making professional smoke rings. "Now I'm corrupted," she says dryly.

"If any of them walked in right now, they'd have a fit," my aunt replies uneasily. She's worried about stern daughters, crabby nurses.

"Do I give a good goddamn?" my mother asks peacefully. She's staring at the ceiling. "I don't think I do." She's drifting now, floating upward, her shot is taking effect. She gets a glimpse of something and then loses it, like a fish swimming in and out of view in the darkness under water. She struggles to the surface. "I hope you get a girl," she says.

My aunt is crocheting again, the long needles moving against one another, tying knots, casting off, creating small rosettes. Wendell is ready to have a baby any day now. "Well, she's carrying it low," my aunt answers skeptically. The room is dimming, she turns her chair more toward the window. There is a long pause, with only the needles and the tedious breath, the sterile landscape of cancer country.

"That doesn't mean anything," my mother finally replies. Her father bends over the bed to kiss her, as substantial as air; he's a ghost, they won't leave her alone. She moves slowly through the fluid and brings a thought to the surface. "We carried all of ours low, and look what we got." They swim through her lake, gray-eyed sisters, thin-legged and mouthy. They fight and hold hands, trade shoes and dresses, marry beautiful tall men, and have daughters together, two dark-eyed cousins, thin-legged and mouthy. A fish splashes, a silver arc against the blue sky, its scales are like sequins. She startles awake.

"I hope you get a girl," she says again. This is all she can think to say. Her sister, in the dimness, sets down her work and comes to the bed. She bends over and pulls the blanket up, straightens it out. She can't think of what to say either. The face on the pillow is foreign to her suddenly, distant, and the weight of the long afternoon bends her in half. She leans forward wearily, and lets herself grimace.

"We got our girls we wanted so bad, didn't we?" my mother whispers to her, eyes still shut. My aunt straightens and fingers a silver button at her throat.

"Those damn brats," she comments. She presses both hands against the small of her back and shuts her eyes briefly. For an instant she sees the two original brats – wearing their droopy calico dresses, sassing their mother, carrying water up from the pump at the home place, knocking into each other. "You were always my sister," she says softly.

My mother is completely without pain now, the lake is dark, the fish move easily out of her way. Her sister swims by and makes a statement. "I know it," she answers. She tries to think of a way to express something. Sequins fall through the water, fish scales, and a baby floats past, turned upside down with a thumb corked in its mouth. The morphine is a thin vapor in her veins. She rouses herself.

"He did do a nice job on those Christmas trees," she says. My aunt nods. She's talking about the woodworking uncle now, who made Christmas trees for all the sisters to put in the middle of their dining room tables.

"I told him to make me a couple more for next year," my aunt says. "My card club went nuts over it." She lights another cigarette, hating herself for it. My mother is silent, her hands cut the water smoothly, like two long knives. The little gray-eyed girls paddle and laugh. She pushes a spray of water into her sister's face and her sister pushes one back. Their hair is shining against their heads.

In the dimness of the hospital room, my aunt smokes and thinks. She doesn't see their father next to the bed, or old Aunt Grace piddling around with the flower arrangements. She sees only the still form on the bed, the half-open mouth, the coppery wig. She yawns. Wendell's stomach is out to here, she remembers, any day now. That's one piece of good news.

My mother sleeps silently while my aunt thinks. As the invisible hands tend to her, she dives and comes up, breaks free of the water. A few feet over a fish leaps again, high in the air. Her arms move lazily back and forth, holding her up, and as she watches the fish is transformed. High above the water, it rises like a silver baton, presses itself against the blue August sky, and refuses drop back down.

Tea and Sympathy

One of the most haunting movies I remember from my adolescence is *Tea and Sympathy* (1958). The film is set in a New England boarding school whose headmaster is a loud, hearty, back-slapping, relentlessly cheery, outdoorsy type – what you might get if you crossed a football coach, a Scoutmaster, and a Marine drill sergeant. He's the American version of Rudyard Kipling. His mission is to "turn boys into men," into replicas of himself. To understand this type, one need only remember the Boy Scout Law: "A Scout is trustworthy, loyal, helpful, friendly, courteous, kind, obedient, cheerful, thrifty, brave, clean and reverent." "Brave, clean and reverent." These are the qualities of a good German shepherd dog. Such a dog would give his life for his master. Such a man is an unusually good civic leader, but not very sensitive or verbal.

The school in the movie is like Sparta. All but one of the boys has fallen into line. The outcast, played by the actor John Kerr, is a type of the artist. He is sensitive and slightly effeminate. Like Goethe's young Werther, he's the kind of boy who in the '50s in my high school we called a "longhair." "*We*" called a "longhair." "*We*?" The Lone Ranger and Tonto are surrounded by Indians. The Lone Ranger says, "Tonto, what shall we do?" The reply: "What you mean *we*?" It's the most fundamental American joke.

The boy played by Kerr was a character I could identify with all too well. He was like Stephen, my identical twin brother who, even in grade school, had been singled out as different. The gang leader was our fourth grade teacher, Mrs. Lee. A frosty-haired lady with jowls and age spots, she was married to a diminutive man named Percy. All her life, I think, she had been hankering after some ideal he-man. When President Truman fired General MacArthur, Mrs. Lee spent the morning lecturing us about what a great man MacArthur was. Truman, she whispered, might be in league with the Communists.

In the movie, the other boys torment Kerr. He's already been branded as a pansy. One of the movie's subtexts is the '50s theme of conformity, and in one of its most poignant scenes, Kerr's roommate, the most popular kid in the school, tries to show him how to walk correctly, like a man, but Kerr soon quits in exasperation. He just *can't*.

The only person in the entire school who sympathizes with him is the headmaster's wife, played by Deborah Kerr. A pale, fragile-looking redhead and an intellectual, she is downtrodden – little more than a maid for her husband. At night, she lies with her back to him, crying silently. She and Kerr are two kindred spirits trapped in a rah-rah fraternity. As she watches the misery that the boys inflict on Kerr, she wants to intervene. She tries to explain the boy to her husband. He doesn't even listen.

Meanwhile, the heckling and hazing of Kerr has gotten so intense that he's on the edge of cracking up. To save him, she "makes a man of him." In the movie's epiphany, she is touching his cheek. "Years from now," she pleads, "when you speak of this – as you will – be kind." Her voice is at once oracular and sad and we know that she doesn't care if the headmaster finds out. She will eventually leave him. She is going to save Kerr and by saving him begin to save herself.

"Years from now, when you speak of this – as you will – be kind." Decorous as the phrasing is, in 1958 it seemed revolutionary to me. Now, over thirty years later, it sounds naive. The notion that a lady could or should help a slightly effeminate boy "become a man" by initiating the boy to her own sexual mysteries is a sentimental lie. It's an interesting lie, though. It reveals, in caricature, the subtly fascistic nature of American middle-class culture in the years of "Ozzie and Harriet" and "Father Knows Best."

All of Stephen's life, and despite the best psychotherapy that money could buy, despite even several affairs with girls, Stephen was as resolutely bent on being gay as I was on being straight – anything to avoid the stigma of being even suspected of effeminacy. All through high school and even through the first year of college, I pitied him for it and, far too often, would patronize him – if not explicitly then in conversations about him with my parents and some of my friends, suggesting that we would be very kind if we all made allowances for him. Whenever the subject of Stephen came up, I suddenly felt quite moral and grown-up. It felt suddenly quite good simply to wear a Navy crewcut, to tell jokes about Amos and Andy, and the one about the "homo" in the bathtub surrounded by a flotilla of bobbing turds: Question: "What's going on?" Answer, proudly, mincing with a conspicuous Liberace lisp: "Theeth are my children." It felt better to talk and think like a swine than with sensitivity. To be a swine seemed almost honorable – the choice of a mature, adult outlook over childish self-indulgence.

From earliest childhood, Stephen had been different from me. Born fifteen minutes before me, according to our mother, Jaynet, he emerged head first. I followed him, feet first. Stephen turned out to be right-handed, I turned out to be a southpaw. Stephen never learned to throw correctly "like a man." He threw "like a girl," a distinction which would be ludicrous anywhere in the world except in America. The distinction is, of course, outrageously false. Watching the College Women's Softball Championships in Boulder, Colorado, I've seen countless women throw harder than most men can, harder than I ever could (and I used to have a decent arm). But the stereotypes run deep.

When I was teaching in a squalid boys' preparatory school in West Orange, New Jersey, the white-haired headmaster, George Douglas Hofe, convened a special assembly where two New Jersey state troopers had been invited, like Starsky and Hutch, to recruit students and talk about the nature of their profession. The year was 1966, and the Vietnam War was in full swing. The troopers held the 120 boys of Carteret School rapt. They talked breezily about the virtue of "intestinal fortitude." The younger of the two explained, "One of the first tests we give is, we hand the applicant a baseball. Can you throw this? We watch how he throws. If you can throw a baseball, you can throw a punch." The boys were awed. The troopers were confirming everything that the boys had seen on television. It was real: cops really *were* tough.

I sat silent. The only reason why I was teaching mathematics at this school was because it afforded me "occupational deferment" from the draft. As Hofe, who was pro-war, had said, presenting me a carbon copy of the letter he'd written to the local draft board, "We wouldn't want you to be cannon fodder, Holden."

Stephen had actually appeared for his physical. On the medical questionnaire, he had indicated that he was homosexual and, after a brief interview with an Army psychologist, was released.

I'm not sure when or how it was that I first decided that I should practice being as unlike Stephen as possible. Not all identical twins decide that. At Oberlin, the Loesch twins, William and Robert, two mild and generous guys, were almost as inseparable as they were indistinguishable. Both later became ministers. Their ministries are both in Massachusetts, and they are not far apart.

Stephen and I, on the other hand, competed for everything. When serving us orange juice, our mother, Jaynet, would squint at our two glasses to make sure the level of juice was exactly the same in each. If it weren't, there would be an argument. It was probably in the third or fourth grade that I began to notice that at recess Stephen and another boy, Chick Hall, preferred to hang out with the girls. Instead of playing baseball, they'd join the girls for "parties" off in the woods around the parking lot, where they would all trade candies.

Though Stephen and Chick hung out with the girls, the other boys left them alone, for they had already singled out a scapegoat – a boy named Derek Remsen. Every single recess, Ray "Cheechee" Frischconnect or Tommy Conger would suddenly exclaim, "Hey, let's git Remsen!" A pack of boys would begin to chase Derek across the parking lot. He'd let out a blood-curdling falsetto scream. That did it. They'd pile on him. I'd watch from the sidelines. I had one single thought: *anything* not to be Remsen. Years later, during the Vietnam War, I wrote a poem about it:

Why We Bombed Haiphong

When I bought bubble gum
to get new baseball cards
the B-52 was everywhere you looked.
In my high school yearbook
the B-52 was voted "Most Popular"
and "Most Likely to Succeed."

The B-52 would give you the finger
from hot cars. It laid rubber,
it spit, it went around in gangs,
it got its finger wet and sneered
about it. It beat the shit
out of fairies.

I remember it used to chase
Derek Remsen around at recess
every day. Caught, he'd scream
like a girl. Then the rest
of us pitched in and hit.

Only once did I pitch in and hit – a light, half-hearted token of a blow. A token. *Anything* not to be Remsen.

After school and on weekends, I'd play touch football and hours of a pick-up baseball game called "inners" with the other neighborhood kids. Stephen would never join us. He spent most afternoons and weekends upstairs in his room listening to the radio, daydreaming of someday being a star. Every Saturday morning, he would tune in to Martin Bloch's "Make Believe Ballroom" on wjz and tend his chart of the Top 100 Popular Songs. He kept graphs of their progress, like a fever chart. By the age of eleven, Stephen was subscribing to *Billboard* and *Variety*. When he wasn't alone upstairs, he was in the kitchen talking with Jaynet.

My family was a paradigm of the type of family which, psychologists assure us, is likely to produce homosexual sons – a family with a distant father and a frustrated, overnurturing mother – only in the case of the Holden family the full weight of Jaynet's pent-up romanticism crashed down on Stephen. Jaynet treated him to tap-dancing lessons, piano lessons, acting lessons. I was left largely alone – doubly so, because Alan could rarely be disturbed from the dining room table where, even on weekends, he worked on his mathematics and his books. I used the fathers of my boyhood pals as surrogate fathers.

The few times when Jaynet could persuade Alan to play catch with me, I discovered that Alan, like Stephen, couldn't throw a baseball. He threw "like a girl." In fact, Alan may have been, at some time in his life, bisexual. While at Harvard, his two closest friends, the late Virgil Thomson and Thomson's long-time lover, the painter Maurice Grosser, were homosexual. I recall once, when Alan was trying to prepare Stephen and me for the coming adjustment to college life, over dinner he related how, at some large outdoor orientation at Harvard, another student sat down beside him, unzipped Father's fly and put his hand inside his pants, asking carefully, "Do you mind?"

To which Alan replied, "No, I don't mind."

I wondered at the time what this story was intended to illustrate. The virtue of tolerance? Of having an open mind? I couldn't decide. It left me bewildered, thinking, "Why the hell did he do *that*?" and "Why tell *us*?"

In retrospect, I think it may have been out of a combination of arrogance and naivete. Perhaps Alan was boasting. It was the kind of incident that could easily have happened at Cambridge University among some of Bertrand Russell's circle. There was a tradition of buggery among Cambridge intellectuals. But it would have been naive of Alan to honor it, and even more naive to imagine that it would be of any help to his sons.

Perhaps Alan's story, though seemingly addressed to both of us, was really addressed to Stephen. By addressing it to both of us, Alan was trying to let Stephen know without embarrassing him by singling him out that he wouldn't hold Stephen's effeminacy against him; though this latter possibility (a charitable one) seems to me unlikely. Alan was not interested enough in us to take the time to be that considerate.

Pleasantville Road began to change. When I was in first grade, there had been three families on the road – the Garritys, the Dawsons, the Thompsons. The whole south side of Pleasantville bordering the Great Swamp was pasture. Occasionally a cow would wander out onto the road. It would graze there, blocking the view, suddenly exotic, out of place as a whale. By the time Stephen and I were in fifth grade, the pasture had been replaced by split-levels, and our side – the north side – had more families: the Kendalls, the Cissells, the Emorys, the Pardees, and the Jarvises. The Jarvis family, in retrospect, reminds me of the Glass family in J. D. Salinger's *Franny and Zooey*.

There were three children, Edwinna, Paige, and Frederick. Raven-haired and elegant, Frederick had just graduated from Yale and was working in New York for a restaurant guide. Frederick had a fair tenor voice and ambitions to sing opera. I remember our family driving into New York to watch him play Don Giovanni in a tiny opera house called The Amato Opera in Greenwich Village. Stephen and I wore matching pale blue summer suits. We were eleven years old. With our twin scrubbed faces, our twin blond crewcuts, we were the picture of innocence. One of the men lounging on a doorstep whistled at us. I had no idea what the whistling meant, but I felt foolish.

In stifling suburban New Jersey, Frederick Jarvis, like William Holden in *Picnic*, was by far the most interesting thing around. He was charming, worldly, dangerous. On sultry July afternoons, when my parents threw lawn parties for their friends, Frederick would orchestrate elaborate croquet games on our lawn. Jaynet and Alan knew that he was homosexual, but in their penchant for expecting the best of people (and usually seeing their optimism vindicated), they assumed that he would not touch the twins. And he didn't – not until Stephen was eighteen.

Years later when Stephen and I were in college, after Stephen had "come out," Jaynet told me that she had asked Frederick not to touch Stephen. Jaynet was still indignant, and her indignation surprised me. We were no longer children. As she saw it, she had let him into our house, and he had broken his word.

For me, Frederick was a godsend. He would not only play catch with me, but he would let me pitch to him as hard as I could while he announced the play-by-play: "Duke Snider stepping in. There's a ferocious slider in on the hands. Call strike." Sometimes Frederick would pitch to me. He had an arm like Stephen's, but he had mastered a sort of curve ball which actually crept sideways a little, and it was by studying Frederick's creaky curve that I came to understand that a ball would curve away from the axis of its spin. I verified this with ping-pong balls.

As Stephen and I were about to enter seventh grade in Harding Township School, my parents decided to send us to a private school. Over the previous two years my grades had declined from A's to C's. On school mornings, I had begun to hunt even the faintest headache down, any excuse not to go to school – not to make more tooth-decay posters for National Tooth Decay Week, not to learn long division for the third year in a row, not to make color wheels again or learn more about the Four Food Groups ("Our Four Friends"), or mumble the Lord's Prayer, or recite the Pledge of Allegiance to the Flag, or learn all over again about the Three Evils: Communism, Narcotics, and ("when it rears its ugly head") Sex.

The new school, Far Brook, which my parents had learned of by word of mouth, was run by a sort of contemporary Margaret Fuller. Far Brook was steeped in the philosophy of John Dewey's *Art as Experience*, a book which, in turn, harkens back to Emerson's "The American Scholar," presented originally as a lecture at Harvard. In that lecture, Emerson urged his intellectual audience to try to complement their book learning with hands-on experience in the physical world: one could learn more about sailing by trying to build a boat than one could learn from a book. In Dewey's philosophy, the term "Experience" is synonymous with empirical "Experiment," though the word "experience" has now been thoroughly corrupted and attenuated by schools of Education into the term "learning experience."

Far Brook had ducks and vegetable gardens. In many ways, it recalled Brook Farm, that noble, doomed transcendentalist experiment so exactly dissected in Hawthorne's novel *A Blithedale Romance*. The teachers at Far Brook were not the homogenized, public-school variety brainwashed by schools of Education. Eccentric, idealistic, renegade, they were constantly inventing their own curricula.

For three years, from the seventh through the ninth grade, Stephen and I thrived with other sensitive kids in a protective environment, like goldfish in an aquarium where sensitivity was honored, cooed over. The curriculum was oriented almost entirely around art, drama, and music. But there was an air of unreality about it, the knowledge that this world was but a momentary reprieve from the real world: public high school. By the time Stephen and I had to go back, I dreaded it.

We tend to forget great pain, once it is over. My first year of Morristown High School – I was a sophomore – I can't remember very well. I had no friends to speak of. In the change-over time between classes, I tried to remain invisible. Because the school had an Advanced College Preparatory track, and because Stephen and I were reasonably smart, we were together in nearly all of our classes.

Stephen made friends. He did it through the Drama Club. Passive, sullen, scared, I watched his life from a safe distance. I watched it with envy but also with disapproval. The girls in the Drama Club were beautiful and sensitive. They liked Stephen. I couldn't understand why. He didn't lust after them. The peers he hankered after were boys. Occasionally Stephen would marvel to me about the "physique" of Walt Morris, Tom Hays, Buddy Kopp. I listened with pitying interest and compassion. Both Stephen and I had been born scrawny, but Stephen had begun to lift barbells, and was acquiring shoulders. I had the shoulderless carcass of a chicken. I was the classic "125-pound weakling" who gets sand kicked in his face on the beach. I desired a handsome body, but I found Stephen's vanity about his body unmanly. In my patronizing view of Stephen, I believed that his popularity might not be in his best interest. I was sure that some of the boys in our class, like dogs smelling fear, could sense Stephen's difference and his fear of them. It was, of course, my own fear of them that I attributed to Stephen. Tom Hays, the captain of the swim team – a guy voted in the yearbook as having "nicest smile" and whose motto in the yearbook was "How's your grapes" – would occasionally coo to Stephen in falsetto: "*Ste*-phen! Steeee-vie!" My only thought at such times was, "Anything not to be Stephen." Being anonymous was worth it: it was preferable to terror. Stephen should have the good sense to try and learn to walk and throw correctly.

Stephen went to Yale, I went to Oberlin. We exchanged letters. We both had ambitions of writing and publishing poetry, but Stephen's talent for poetry was prodigal. He began sending me some of his fledgling poems. Their surface sophistication had a kind of authority that I knew immediately I could never attain.

Van Gogh beat his temples
Till his mind was clotted with magenta spectres
Till the anthem soared to supersonic pitch.

I showed it to the editor of *The Yeoman*, Oberlin's student literary magazine. He wanted to publish it.

Stephen wrote me about two of his friends in Timothy Dwight College, both from California, Tom Mankowitz and somebody named Chip. He idolized them. Then, in the middle of the fall semester, Stephen suffered what must have been a sort of nervous breakdown. He refused to leave his room. Jaynet and Alan located a psychoanalyst on Park Ave., and Stephen began seeing Zira DeFries regularly. I had almost immediately found a girlfriend, Georgia Clark. We huddled together, chain-smoking, playing bridge, talking about Existentialism, necking on fire escapes, necking in the alcoves of buildings, petting on army blankets in moonlit orchards, ceaselessly searching for any place to be alone together.

In the spring, I played on the tennis team. I was seventh. I was chain-smoking unfiltered Pall Malls and, to perfect my Left Bank, Existentialist and Spanish-Civil-War-veteran affectations, had taken to wearing a tattered army-surplus jacket. One noon, as I was sitting in the snack bar necking with Georgia, the matronly woman who tended the grill left her station and approached us, scolding us for such behavior.

I squinted up at her and suggested archly, "My don't you shut up?" I released a doughnut of smoke lazily in the direction of her face.

The following afternoon, the Dean of Men, who assisted as tennis coach, approached me: "I've had a complaint about you, Jon."

In my own, spoiled passive-aggressive way, I was going to pieces too.

Late in the spring semester, the director of a summer camp named Camp Roosevelt advertised in the classified section of the Oberlin student newspaper for somebody who could direct their tennis program. I applied for the job, and the director, Bill Lorimer, drove to Oberlin from where he lived in Shaker Heights to have a look at me. We stroked a few tennis balls to each other, and he decided that I would do.

I was pleased. I'd never had a summer job before. In previous summers, Jaynet had created jobs for Stephen and me. On my parents' seven acres, there was plenty to do: mowing lawns, mowing the fields around the house and raking up the hay, clearing brush from the woods. But it didn't feel like real work, working for one's mother. It was an admission of defeat. It made me feel like a baby. Vernon Hull, a local dairy farmer, often hired local boys to buck hay. But the guys he hired were strapping youngsters used to real labor. As I quavered before Mr. Hull, wondering if he needed any help, I was keenly aware of what a pitiable specimen I presented to him. He said that he already had enough help.

Camp Roosevelt was my first real summer job, and, preparing to leave on a Greyhound bus for the camp (it was in Perry, Ohio, on the shore of Lake Erie), I felt proud of myself, especially because Stephen didn't have a summer job. He was going to have to suffer the dishonor of staying home and working for Mother.

Lorimer had been in the Navy, and he ran his camp that way. Many of the other counselors had been in summer camps before, and a few of them were alumni of Camp Roosevelt itself. In addition to teaching tennis, I was in charge of a cabin of "younger intermediates": seven twelve- and thirteen-year-old boys. I was to sit at their table during meals, know the whereabouts of each of them during the day, devise some supervised activity during the slots when they had nothing scheduled, be in attendance during their afternoon rest period, make sure my cabin was absolutely quiet after 9:00 P.M., and, twice a week, stand sentry duty at night while the camp slept. Nearly all the campers were Jewish, from the Squirrel Hill area of Pittsburgh or from the more immediate suburb of Shaker Heights, twenty miles to the west. One of the boys, Freddie Prater, a languid, heavy boy with black curls and cherubic lips, was supposedly a genius.

The camp was perched on the banks of Lake Erie. It was like living next to the ocean, except the air stank. In the summer of 1960, Lake Erie was so polluted that it had been given up for dead. The corpses of fish washed up on the beach and rotted. It was around that time when the Cuyahoga River flowing out of Cleveland's industrial zone had earned the distinction of actually catching fire. It was like the Rhine River. All day, freighters could be glimpsed on the northern horizon, and at night, over the fitful slosh, slosh of the waves, their lights made tiny towns out in the darkness.

From my first moment at camp, in the midst of meeting parents and escorting campers to the storeroom for their bedding and supplies, I was lonely. I missed Georgia, I missed Stephen, and I missed even more the solitude which I had coveted. Such solitude was impossible at a camp. In the slivers of free time I had, like a soldier shipped overseas, I wrote and waited for letters. Stephen's life on Pleasantville Road sounded as humid and depressing as life at camp: work for Jaynet, my parents' Fourth of July party with its great annual croquet game where everybody, getting steadily more red-faced from Alan's tall mint juleps, broke up into teams of two partners, the Kendalls, the Andersons, the Landers, Mrs. Singer, Paige Jarvis and, seeking respite from the stinking streets of New York City, Frederick.

At camp, I had some success making up bedtime stories, and because of them my seven younger intermediates looked forward to lights out. But a situation came up which I wasn't sure how to handle. One of the boys, Jimmy Kushner, began kissing some of the other boys, especially Freddie Prater. The boys giggled about it, and Kushner liked the attention it brought him. One afternoon, during quiet time, as some of the boys were roughhousing, Kushner straddled Freddie Prater and began kissing him on the mouth. The other boys giggled. Alan Liffman, a jackal of a kid who, if the food being served was something he particularly liked and he was particularly hungry, would actually make a production of spitting on the meat to discourage the other boys from eating it, announced: "Hey, look! Kushner's a homo!"

It became a sort of feeding frenzy.

"Hey, Kushie-tushie! Lookit Tushie!"

I did nothing to stop them, reasoning that Kushner would have to learn for himself how to behave.

Midway in the summer was Visiting Day for parents. Several of the fathers, as we parted, edged me aside and, glancing around surreptitiously, pressed a twenty-dollar bill into my hand. "Here's a little cigar money. Keep an eye on my boy." We weren't supposed to accept tips; but to decline them was out of the question.

Late in the afternoon, I found myself confronted by Mr. and Mrs. Kushner and Jimmy and Mr. Lorimer. Jimmy had been crying.

The Kushners were livid with indignation. "What's been going on here!" Mrs. Kushner demanded.

I explained that I had decided that the best way to put a stop to Jimmy's behavior was to let him see for himself what others thought of it.

Lorimer turned to the Kushners. "That may be the way they do things at Oberlin," he explained, "but it's not the way we do things here."

I didn't know what he meant, until the Kushners left. They were taking Jimmy home.

Lorimer turned to me and shook his head sadly. "That may be the way they do things at Oberlin," he repeated, "but why didn't you just give him a good smack?"

I had no answer. Things like the Good Old-Fashioned Spanking, the Swift Kick in the Butt were like the expression "To Make a Man of Him." They were part of a rhetoric so old-fashioned and sentimental it was quaint. I remembered the ending of Kipling's poem, "If":

If you can fill the unforgiving minute
With sixty seconds worth of distance run

Yours is the Earth and everything that's in it,
And – which is more – you'll be a Man, my son!

An appropriate line of advertising for a nineteenth-century English boarding school that required many semesters of Latin—the kind of place where stern, snowy-haired preceptors disciplined boys with a cane. It was a world I remembered only at graduations, where older men clustered in academic robes and cap and gown, where patriarchy was visible, where for a moment as the organ rolled one could almost believe in "standards" and in the Old World.

Recessional.

Son I call him –
such a serious word
it sobers me to say it –
as if I'd dropped
into his arms a weight
he could not let go –
the whole, drab encyclopedia
of *conduct, duty* –
words so obsolete
simply to utter them
would make the afternoon
slow as Latin.
I do not know
myself why, though our fathers
have passed from this world,
I would want one,
why, still, at the graduation
recessional, when the armies
in the chapel organ roll
and the grand old chords
unfurl their scrolls
of dusty laws, I feel
that weight gather
like Rudyard Kipling, brow
thunderous,

and even though I don't
believe in it
I know the urge
to look up to that tall
weather, a coward,
and hear my own small voice
call *Father*.

The last day of camp we spent lugging equipment back to the storerooms. My friend Paul Raupack, an all-state swimmer from Buffalo who had directed the swimming program at camp, said he wanted to show me Buffalo nightlife. We drove to Buffalo and began barhopping with his buddies. Around midnight, I began to feel sick and told him to party on, it was okay, I'd wait in the car. On my way to the car, the parking lot began to rotate me like a Ferris wheel, and for the first time in my life I puked from booze. I hated puking, yet it seemed somehow like a significant milestone in my life. Life in the real world.

The next morning, I decided to surprise my parents. Instead of submitting to the drudgery of a Greyhound bus an the way back to New Jersey, I would use some of my new-earned money and fly back. I would make a glamorous, unannounced arrival. I sipped a Pall Mall like Laurence Harvey in the movie *Room at the Top*, imagining my return. Earthy, wry and hungry as Simone Signoret, Georgia would be waiting for my phone call. I would release a contemplative smoke ring and remark to her about the exigencies of the real world.

The flight back, on a Lockheed Electra, was a mere fifty-eight minutes. It began with spectacular cumulus clouds in the late morning, a corny winter wonderland of snowballs, snowmen and, off to the northwest, snow forts, entire fortresses with battlements. Then they were becoming jaundiced, fading, and we had dropped into haze and humidity, the hopeless light of New Jersey.

Jaynet was surprised when I called to ask her to pick me up. In 1960, though the actual distance from Newark Airport to Pleasantville Road was about twenty miles, the nearest Interstate highway was the New York Thruway. From Pleasantville to Newark Airport took nearly an hour.

Stephen was waiting for me upstairs in his room. I barged up the stairs, a returning veteran bringing Stephen news of the real world. He closed the door hurriedly. He seemed to be brimming with some urgent news of his own. He was aglow with it.

"I'm in love with Frederick!"

His news moved me almost to tears. Suddenly I knew many things I hadn't known that I knew. I said simply and from my heart:

"Oh, that's *wonderful!*" Then we hugged.

Casa: A Partial Remembrance of a Puerto Rican Childhood

At three or four o'clock in the afternoon, the hour of *café con leche*, the women of my family gathered in Mamá's living room to speak of important things and retell familiar stories meant to be overheard by us young girls, their daughters. In Mamá's house (everyone called my grandmother Mamá) was a large parlor built by my grandfather to his wife's exact specifications so that it was always cool, facing away from the sun. The doorway was on the side of the house so no one could walk directly into her living room. First they had to take a little stroll through and around her beautiful garden where prize-winning orchids grew in the trunk of an ancient tree she had hollowed out for that purpose. This room was furnished with several mahogany rocking chairs, acquired at the births of her children, and one intricately carved rocker that had passed down to Mamá at the death of her own mother.

It was on these rockers that my mother, her sisters, and my grandmother sat on these afternoons of my childhood to tell their stories, teaching each other, and my cousin and me, what it was like to be a woman, more specifically, a Puerto Rican woman. They talked about life on the island, and life in *Los Nueva Yores*, their way of referring to the U.S. from New York City to California: the other place, not home, all the same. They told real life stories, though, as I later learned, always embellishing them with a little or a lot of dramatic detail. And they told *cuentos*, the morality and cautionary tales told by the women in our family for generations: stories that became a part of my subconscious as I grew up in two worlds, the tropical island and the cold city, and that would later surface in my dreams and in my poetry.

One of these tales was about the woman who was left at the altar. Mamá liked to tell that one with histrionic intensity. I remember the rise and fall of her voice, the sighs, and her constantly gesturing hands, like two birds swooping through her words. This particular story usually would come up in a conversation as a result of someone mentioning a forthcoming engagement or wedding. The first time I remember hearing it, I was sitting on the floor at Mamá's feet, pretending to read a comic book. I may have been eleven or twelve years old, at that difficult age when a girl was no longer a child who could be ordered to leave the room if the women wanted freedom to take their talk into forbidden zones, nor really old enough to be considered a part of their conclave. I could only sit quietly, pretending to be in another world, while absorbing it all in a sort of unspoken agreement of my status as silent auditor. On this day, Mamá had taken my long, tangled mane of hair into her ever busy hands. Without looking down at me and with no interruption of her flow of words, she began braiding my hair, working at it with the quickness and determination that characterized all her actions. My mother was watching us impassively from her rocker across the room. On her lips played a little ironic smile. I would never sit still for *her* ministrations, but even then, I instinctively knew that she did not possess Mamá's matriarchal power to command and keep everyone's attention. This was never more evident than in the spell she cast when telling a story.

"It is not like it used to be when I was a girl," Mamá announced. "Then, a man could leave a girl standing at the church altar with a bouquet of fresh flowers in her hands and disappear off the face of the earth. No way to track him down if he was from another town. He could be a married man, with maybe even two or three families all over the island. There was no way to know. And there were men who did this. Hombres with the devil in their flesh who would come to a pueblo, like this one, take a job at one of the haciendas, never meaning to stay, only to have a good time and to seduce the women."

The whole time she was speaking Mamá would be weaving my hair into a flat plait that required pulling apart the two sections of hair with little jerks that made my eyes water; but knowing how grandmother detested whining and *boba* (sissy) tears, as she called them, I just sat up as straight and stiff as I did at La Escuela San Jose, where the nuns enforced good posture with a flexible plastic ruler they bounced off of slumped shoulders and heads. As Mamá's story progressed, I noticed how my young aunt Laura lowered her eyes, refusing to meet Mamá's meaningful gaze. Laura was seventeen, in her last year of high school, and already engaged to a boy from another town who had staked his claim with a tiny diamond ring, then left for Los Nueva Yores to make his fortune. They were planning to get married in a year. Mamá had expressed serious doubts that the wedding would ever take place. In Mamá's eyes, a man set free without a legal contract was a man lost. She believed that marriage was not something men desired, but simply the price they had to pay for the privilege of children and, of course, for what no decent (synonymous with "smart") woman would give away for free.

"María La Loca was only seventeen when *it* happened to her." I listened closely at the mention of this name. María was a town character, a fat middle-aged woman who lived with her old mother on the outskirts of town. She was to be seen around the pueblo delivering the meat pies the two women made for a living. The most peculiar thing about María, in my eyes, was that she walked and moved like a little girl though she had the thick body and wrinkled face of an old woman. She would swing her hips in an exaggerated, clownish way, and sometimes even hop and skip up to someone's house. She spoke to no one. Even if you asked her a question, she would just look at you and smile, showing her yellow teeth. But I had heard that if you got close enough, you could hear her humming a tune without words. The lads yelled out nasty things at her, calling her *La Loca*, and the men who hung out at the bodega playing dominoes sometimes whistled mockingly as she passed by with her funny, outlandish walk. But María seemed impervious to it all, carrying her basket of *pasteles* like a grotesque Little Red Riding Hood through the forest.

María La Loca interested me, as did all the eccentrics and crazies of our pueblo. Their weirdness was a measuring stick I used in my serious quest for a definition of normal. As a Navy brat shuttling between New Jersey and the pueblo, I was constantly made to feel like an oddball by my peers, who made fun of my two-way accent: a Spanish accent when I spoke English, and when I spoke Spanish I was told that I sounded like a *Gringa*. Being the outsider had already turned my brother and me into cultural chameleons. We developed early on the ability to blend into a crowd, to sit and read quietly in a fifth story apartment building for days and days when it was too bitterly cold to play outside, or, set free, to run wild in Mamá's realm, where she took charge of our lives, releasing Mother for a while from the intense fear for our safety that our father's absences instilled in her. In order to keep us from harm when Father was away, Mother kept us under strict surveillance. She even walked us to and from Public School No. 11, which we attended during the months we lived in Paterson, New Jersey, our home base in the states. Mamá freed all three of us like pigeons from a cage. I saw her as my liberator and my model. Her stories were parables from which to glean the *Truth*.

"María La Loca was once a beautiful girl. Everyone thought she would marry the Méndez boy." As everyone knew, Rogelio Méndez was the richest man in town. "But," Mamá continued, knitting my hair with the same intensity she was putting into her story, "this *macho* made a fool out of her and ruined her life." She paused for the effect of her use of the word "macho," which at that time had not yet become a popular epithet for an unliberated man. This word had for us the crude and comical connotation of "male of the species," stud; a *macho* was what you put in a pen to increase your stock.

I peeked over my comic book at my mother. She too was under Mamá's spell, smiling conspiratorially at this little swipe at men. She was safe from Mamá's contempt in this area. Married at an early age, an unspotted lamb, she had been accepted by a good family of strict Spaniards whose name was old and respected, though their fortune had been lost long before my birth. In a rocker Papá had painted sky blue sat Mamá's oldest child, Aunt Nena. Mother of three children, stepmother of two more, she was a quiet woman who liked books but had married an ignorant and abusive widower whose main interest in life was accumulating wealth. He too was in the mainland working on his dream of returning home rich and triumphant to buy the *finca* of his dreams. She was waiting for him to send for her. She would leave her children with Mamá for several years while the two of them slaved away in factories. He would one day be a rich man, and she a sadder woman. Even now her life-light was dimming. She spoke little, an aberration in Mamá's house, and she read avidly, as if storing up spiritual food for the long winters that awaited her in Los Nueva Yores without her family. But even Aunt Nena came alive to Mamá's words, rocking gently, her hands over a thick book in her lap.

Her daughter, my cousin Sara, played jacks by herself on the tile porch outside the room where we sat. She was a year older than I. We shared a bed and all our family's secrets. Collaborators in search of answers, Sara and I discussed everything we heard the women say, trying to fit it all together like a puzzle that, once assembled, would reveal life's mysteries to us. Though she and I still enjoyed taking part in boys' games – chase, volleyball and even *vaqueros*, the island version of cowboys and Indians involving cap-gun battles and violent shoot-outs under the mango tree in Mamá's backyard – we loved best the quiet hours in the afternoon when the men were still at work, and the boys had gone to play serious baseball at the park. Then Mamá's house belonged only to us women. The aroma of coffee perking in the kitchen, the mesmerizing creaks and groans of the rockers, and the women telling their lives in *cuentos* are forever woven into the fabric of my imagination, braided like my hair that day I felt my grandmother's hands teaching me about strength, her voice convincing me of the power of storytelling.

That day Mamá told how the beautiful María had fallen prey to a man whose name was never the same in subsequent versions of the story; it was Juan one time, José, Rafael, Diego, another. We understood that neither the name nor any of the *facts* were important, only that a woman had allowed love to defeat her. Mamá put each of us in María's place by describing her wedding dress in loving detail: how she looked like a princess in her lace as she waited at the altar. Then, as Mamá approached the tragic denouement of her story, I was distracted by the sound of my Aunt Laura's violent rocking. She seemed on the verge of tears. She knew the fable was intended for her. That week she was going to have her wedding gown fitted, though no firm date had been set for the marriage. Mamá ignored Laura's obvious discomfort, digging out a ribbon from the sewing basket she kept by her rocker while describing María's long illness, "a fever that would not break for days." She spoke of a mother's despair: "that woman climbed the church steps on her knees every morning, wore only black as a *promesa* to the Holy Virgin in exchange for her daughter's health." By the time María returned from her honeymoon with death, she was ravished, no longer young or sane. "As you can see, she is almost as old as her mother already," Mamá lamented while tying the ribbon to the ends of my hair, pulling it back with such force that I just knew I would never be able to close my eyes completely again.

"That María is getting crazier every day." Mamá's voice would take a lighter tone now, expressing satisfaction, either for the perfection of my braid, or for a story well told – it was hard to tell. "You know that tune María is always humming?" Carried away by her enthusiasm, I tried to nod, but Mamá still had me pinned between her knees.

"Well, that's the wedding march." Surprising us all, Mamá sang out, "Da, da, dara . . . da, da, dara." Then lifting me off the floor by my skinny shoulders, she would lead me around the room in an impromptu waltz – another session ending with the laughter of women, all of us caught up in the infectious joke of our lives.

Jinx

E ven now, I can't think of Slippery Rock without a little revulsion. For years I hated the entire state of Pennsylvania simply because it contained Slippery Rock. Later, I decided I liked the eastern half of the state because Philadelphia was a mitigating factor.

We had moved to Slippery Rock after my father's death and my mother's return to school to earn a Master's degree. This was her first teaching job: Slippery Rock State Teacher's College. One sometimes heard the unlikely name of Slippery Rock on the tail end of sports reports across the country – partly because Slippery Rock had a good football team and partly because newscasters liked to say Slippery Rock.

Slippery Rock is located about seventy miles north of Pittsburgh, and supposedly its name derived from an unlikely incident in which a settler, chased by Indians, led them across the creek, where they all slipped on the stones in the river, save the wily settler, who knew his way around. "Watch out for the slippery rocks," he yelled back at them. If Slippery Rock had a tourist industry, one might produce large quantities of coffee mugs depicting such a hilarious scene. Or not.

In 1969 Slippery Rock had about three thousand residents and perhaps as many students. The nearest big town was Grove City; it had an ice cream parlor – that's what made it big to me. Slippery Rock had one main street, one restaurant, a newsstand, a town drunk who doubled as the town artist, and freshmen at the college wore beanies around campus, to make them feel silly, I suppose. We lived in an apartment complex, and my friends consisted of neighborhood kids who doubled as classmates. The neighborhood kids wanted to know right off where I was from, where I was born, and I told them New York City. They had heard of New York City, but Slippery Rock was their world, and in a strange reversal of THE NATURAL LAWS OF THE UNIVERSE they started calling me a hick.

"No, you're the hicks," I insisted.

My main friends were a red-haired kid named Joe, a tall kid named

Dick, and a blond kid named Steve. Their families: The Smiths, The Stones, and The Minks, did not believe in wasting syllables on either first names or surnames. Steve Mink spat all the time – all the time, even indoors – Steve never had much spit in him as a consequence; he never allowed moisture to accumulate, but I remember him spitting once on our carpet. "Don't do that in here," my mom told Steve. "That's disgusting."

"I do it at home," Steve said.

"You're not at home," she told him.

We used to go to Steve's house down the road to play football. Steve had a go-cart and a grandmother who beheaded chickens while we played football, like she was part of some kind of surreal and evil cheerleading squad. I was generally the quarterback because I was too skinny to actually tackle anyone, but pretty much fun for the other guys to tackle. I played without shoes and was rarely tackled because I was so terrified that I did all kinds of amazing maneuvers to avoid any body contact whatsoever – leaping over my opponents as they lunged for me, zigzagging and whirling with the grace of a pro. But I soon tired of this play figuring the odds would eventually get me, and I retreated after school each day to my room, where I tried to memorize Hamlet's soliloquy – I'm not sure why I chose this – while below my window my contemptuous friends yelled up at me, demanding that I play football or they'd beat me up.

"Whether 'tis nobler in the mind to suffer the slings and arrows of outrageous fortune," I replied.

At that time, I wanted to be an actor – who doesn't? – and I thought that memorizing Shakespeare would lift me out of Slippery Rock. It didn't, and I suffered my share of slings and arrows at the hands of my friends. One night, on my way home from Boy Scouts, Dick, Steve, and Joey ambushed me near our apartment complex: for refusing to play football anymore, for being a hick, a Jew, a Boy Scout (they hated Boy Scouts, too). Joey and Steve grabbed me and held me against a wall while gangly Dick started beating me, but with an improbable object, a gigantic inflated inner tube. It *kind of* hurt, but not much. It surprised me more than anything, and it was awkward for him. I think it wore him out before he could hurt me. "Goddamn hick," he kept yelling, until finally I broke free. Joey called me a kike as I fled. He had previously served notice that he could no longer play with me – his parents had told him I had killed Christ.

"No, you killed Christ," I told him. These kids had everything backwards, so I figured they had that wrong, too.

My revenge came later that fall when I scored the only copy within the county of The Archies hit single, "Sugar, Sugar." I bought it in Grove City for less than a dollar and taunted Dick with it, who was desperate for the single. He offered to buy it from me, but I wouldn't sell. Finally, he offered me $25 for it. I didn't ask where he got the money and I didn't care. But who knows. Maybe it's worth $25 again by now, if Dick still owns the record. I suppose he still lives in Slippery Rock and does things backwards. Maybe he owns the booming tourist concession, selling those mugs that read, "Watch out for the Slippery Rocks," to all those hicks from New York blowing through town.

I hated Slippery Rock because in 1969, to an eleven-year-old boy from an oddball intellectual family, it was a hateful place.

I know I'm being mean to the past and present citizens (denizens?) of Slippery Rock, that I'm being unfair, that I'm being petty in condemning them with such a broad brush. I tell you, I would not mind if God broke off Slippery Rock like an icicle from a roof and tossed it over his shoulder. I know it's irrational, but when you're eleven years old and in despair, you carry a part of that despair for the rest of your life. There's a sharpness to life at eleven that later you're inured to. And you cast around for blame even when you know that the source of your hatred, fear, and sadness is not, in all likelihood, solely where you live.

Maybe it has to do with the death of my father four years before, but not even that completely.

Maybe it has to do with the death of my friend Tommy Alfazy, earlier that year. Tommy was my best friend from Long Beach, New York, where I spent all my summers at my grandmother's beach house. Tommy and another friend, Vince, had been building a fort in the sand on the beach. They dug a hole, piled boards on it, and covered it with more sand. They had asked me if I wanted to do it with them, and I said no, that I thought it was stupid, but they went ahead and did it anyway, and the boards and sand collapsed on Tommy and smothered him. I was in Slippery Rock when I heard the news, and maybe this is in part why I still hate Slippery Rock. The town is death to me, broiling skies and coal veins underneath. I started forming a theory after Tommy's death that I was some kind of jinx, and that people I loved died, especially when I was away from them and couldn't be there to help. Three years earlier I had been sent to a friend's house when my father suffered his heart attack. I had been away from home when I learned the news. The same was true of Tommy's death – I was stunned when I heard that Tommy, only ten years old, had died. It didn't seem possible. My father's death was possible, but a ten-year-old's death was something I had never been prepared for.

At eleven, death was so real to me that I tried to kill myself. Maybe I shouldn't have been reading *Hamlet*. One afternoon I went to the bathroom cupboard and swallowed as many aspirin as I could before my throat swelled up and I could swallow no more. If I'd been older, I suppose I would have used something more powerful than aspirin, but even aspirin in large quantities can seriously fool with your metabolism. The intent to kill myself was there. Attention wasn't what I sought. After that, I went to sleep and didn't wake up until the next morning when it was time for school. I must have slept for fourteen or fifteen hours, and I'm not sure why my mother didn't try to waken me, or if she did, why she didn't realize that I was more unconscious than asleep.

When I awoke, I felt slightly ashamed of myself, and really wasn't sure why I'd done this – I just felt lonely. The only person I ever told was a boy named Donald who stood in front of me in the lunch line the next day at school.

"You know what I did last night," I said as we slid our trays along. "I swallowed about seventeen aspirin."

He turned and gave me a skeptical look. "Why'd you do that?"

"I don't know," I said.

"You could have died," he said. "That's pretty stupid."

I agreed and felt chastised, but at least he said something that wasn't backwards, that I could understand. I didn't feel like telling my mother. My mother wouldn't have understood. She would have overreacted. But this kid Donald reacted just right, with just the right amount of disapproval. My mother set no limits for my older brother and sister and me when we were kids, and we were often told by relatives that we were spoiled and unruly – all true – but my mother had her hands full after my father died, simply trying to make a living for us. I hardly remember seeing my mother during those days in Slippery Rock. Or my brother and sister.

My sister Nola had graduated from Ohio University on the same day in 1968 as my mother received her Master's. Nola, who was Phi Beta Kappa, went off to Brandeis for a Ph.D. in Philosophy. This was my brother Jonathan's freshman year at O.U. He was sixteen, following in the family tradition of attending college without graduating from high school. My father had attended Amherst at fourteen. My mother started college at sixteen, and Nola had started at seventeen. In fact, I'm the only high school graduate in my immediate family – a strange intellectual joke, a reversal of the normal meaning of such a statement – there's something slightly embarrassing that the only thing my family had to overcome in its education was boredom.

Most of my memories of that time are of me alone, watching TV in the basement or sitting up in my room, memorizing *Hamlet*. I guess, in such a vacuum, I needed to create my own limits – and that, perhaps, is what the aspirin was about. I had successfully negotiated a limit.

I invited Donald home that day and we listened to my recording of the musical soundtrack from *Hair*. We sat on my mother's couch and sang along. "This is the dawning of the Age of Aquarius." Donald liked to sing and he liked to talk about books, both activities I was used to. Donald and I became best friends, *only* friend for me, and we went sledding together or stayed indoors and sang songs from *Hair*. He lived on Elm Street, and I asked my mother what an elm looked like. She said it was a kind of tree, and I asked what kind of tree, and she said she couldn't really explain – most of them were dead anyway. That seemed appropriate for Slippery Rock. I don't remember any of the other street names in Slippery Rock, not even the street on which we lived, only a street named after a diseased tree. I still take nightmare journeys up the hill to our apartment complex sometimes. In my dreams, Slippery Rock is built on frosty terraces with slippery roads and rickety stores that look like the faded wooden structures on the surface of coal mines. Of course, Slippery Rock looks nothing like this, but my dreams build the town into a rockpile of metaphor.

I developed all kinds of compulsions in Slippery Rock. When I ran up the stairs, I had to take them two at a time. On the way down, I skipped the third stair because three was evil, I decided, and if I stepped on the third stair something bad would happen. When returning a snack to the cupboard I had to return it to the exact spot where I had found it. The rules kept changing, appearing in my head like flash cards a moment before the necessary action had to be taken.

Place your spoon on the right side of your bowl. Leave one green Lucky Charms marshmallow floating alone in the milk.

When I think back to that boy I was, I'm almost worried for him, amazed that he ever made it out of Slippery Rock alive, that he survived into adulthood. Now I see what I was trying to do at the time, how I was trying to give my life some order, but back then I could only await the next commands in this mental boot camp in which I existed.

My grandmother was living at the time in Hollywood, Florida, with my Uncle Joe and my Aunt Rose, and after I started getting D's in school, someone suggested (whether my grandmother or my mother, I'm not sure) that I might go down to Florida and finish the school year there. I was ready. The week before we left, there were two hijackings of planes bound for Florida to Cuba. I didn't mind the danger. Even Cuba seemed preferable. I understood the hijackers. I understood why someone might want to risk jail to leave a place they hated living in, why death might be preferable. I didn't understand the politics of it. To me, this was a simple case of needing to get away from where you lived, desperation.

My mother and I went down to Florida together over the winter break and stayed the first few days with a woman in Miami named Marjorie, whom my mother had known in college. Marjorie was the editor-in-chief and restaurant critic for *The Miami Star* – the paper's stationery proclaimed it as "One of America's Most Interesting Newspapers." Certainly, Marjorie was one of America's most interesting people, at least to me. In a letter to my mother not long after my father died, Marjorie complained nonstop: about her asthma, a growth that might be cancerous, and a "daughter who will not even take me to the hospital when my ankle is broken." She claimed to write every one of her restaurant columns in five minutes: "In spite of the 'flighty' way of composing, I've gotten compliments on some of my columns . . ." Marjorie fascinated me. She told me that none of the restaurateurs knew her identity, and that they were always trying to find out. She ate out every night. She had a pool, and a mini sauna in her bedroom – the sauna looked like something out of "Get Smart," a chamber that you sat in with your head poking out.

We went to a restaurant one night where Marjorie ordered frogs' legs for me. As we ate she told my mother and me a story.

"In this very restaurant, I saw a man die. He was eating some fish and he swallowed a bone."

"My God," my mother said.

"And you know what, no one helped him. There were doctors in the restaurant, four of them, and not one of them helped the poor man. They were all afraid of being sued. I mentioned that in my review, but it's still a fine place to eat."

I think I've remembered that scene for so long because I was so horrified. We sat at a corner table and I could see the entire restaurant. The restaurant was large and airy and low-lit. We sat by the porch, and I could see waiters carrying their trays, and men and women, a few children sitting at tables, laughing and talking – I focused on one man, a little large, a little red in the face, and imagined him falling out of his chair, coughing, grasping his hands around his throat.

Maybe I hadn't escaped Slippery Rock, merely taken a detour.

The next day Marjorie drove us around on the freeway. I was sitting in the back seat and Marjorie and my mother were chatting up front. Marjorie drove a Mustang, about sixty-five miles an hour, and as she roared up the road I noticed what seemed like a hundred cars heading toward us. I screamed, "Marjorie, look," and for a moment we all looked at the cars in a line four lanes wide heading straight for us – none of us quite sure what was wrong with this picture.

"Those fools!" Marjorie yelled and swerved her car onto the median, between two palms, and made her own entrance ramp onto the right side of the freeway.

I was the first one of us to develop the Hong Kong flu. Until my mother took my temperature, I wasn't quite sure what was wrong with me, why I felt so lightheaded. I had attributed this feeling to spending the night with Marjorie's grandson – he was an avid Elvis fan, the first I ever met, and, like all REAL ELVIS fans I've met since, he left me vaguely unsettled. All night long I had to hear Elvis songs, and not even early Elvis, but late Elvis. Not *too* late. Not puffy, sweaty jumpsuit Elvis, but Comeback Elvis. Suspicious-Minded Elvis. Kentucky Rained-on Elvis. Spanish Harlem Elvis. My theory is that people don't really care about his music anymore – they just can't stop saying Elvis. Elvis, like Slippery Rock, is fun to say.

Slippery Rock Demolishes Elvis, 140 to zip.

What *I* liked was worse, far worse, of course. "Sugar, Sugar" by The Archies, who didn't even exist – at least Elvis once walked the earth, or so it has been told. "Spinning Wheel" by Blood, Sweat, and Tears. I had watched Barbara Feldman from "Get Smart," on whom I had a terrific crush, do a knock-off of "Spinning Wheel" on the Ed Sullivan Show.

"Watch all your troubles by the riverside / catch a painted pony let the spinning wheel ride," she sang while caressing a painted pony on a carousel.

To a literal-minded eleven-year-old, it seemed like the perfect staging for the song.

Now it's funny, but it wasn't funny at the time. And The Archies weren't all that funny either. Not even Elvis was funny. Now all that stuff is dead, no matter how much people want to resurrect it, even Elvis. It's so dead it's laughable.

We didn't stay long with Marjorie after that. Marjorie and my mother came down with the flu, too, and though Marjorie begged us to stay to take care of her, we couldn't. We couldn't even take care of ourselves. We had to move to my grandmother's place so that she could help nurse us back to health. I hope someone took pity on poor Marjorie and helped her, if not her daughter who wouldn't take her to the hospital for a broken ankle, then some other more merciful relative or friend. I've probably never met a person more terrified of death than Marjorie, though comically unmindful of it at the same time. We never saw her again, and as far as I know, she and my mother never communicated after that disastrous stay.

The next two weeks I spent in bed at my grandmother's place with the Hong Kong flu, a fever that broke at 104. My mother had it too, and she was in the bed next to mine. While my grandmother waited on us, we read to each other and played games. My mother introduced me to a play by the French writer, Jean Giradoux, "The Madwoman of Chaillot," about an elderly woman in Paris who, together with her destitute and powerless friends of the street, trap a group of ruthless oil magnates and developers in the sewers of the city because they want to drill for oil under Paris.

Strangely, being sick with the Hong Kong flu, on the brink of death and dementia, is one of my fondest memories of childhood. Sure, what leaps to mind are the obvious Freudian reasons – my mother all to myself – in the next bed ha ha! – and while I won't deny these possibilities, I also simply have to say that the reason those two weeks were enjoyable was because they were so enjoyable. I liked things of the mind, still do, and this was the first time I could relax and do what I enjoyed doing in a long while. Not that I disliked playing football – though I did, intensely. Not that other kids weren't more normal than me – spitting on the carpet, beating people with inner tubes, going gaga over Elvis.

I was allowed for two weeks to be sick, abnormal. And so, I did things that I wasn't supposed to do as a kid. I read and memorized a part in a play. I read poetry aloud. I played a poetry game called "Exquisite Corpse." Appropriate for a boy transfixed by and obsessed with death.

I'm always suspicious of people who say they had a normal childhood. What happens to those people? I think maybe they're in a restaurant one day and they see someone choking on a fishbone, and they don't know what to do. They have no frame of reference. They write an unfavorable review. They're afraid of a lawsuit. They're tempted by the frogs' legs.

I know I'm being unfair to those people who live idyllic lives. I admit it. No, they're the ones who save the person's life. I'm the one who watches, glad it wasn't me this time. I'm the one who has no frame of reference, no experience with safety. That blue pallor looks almost normal to me. I'm the one who orders the frogs' legs.

After my mother and I recovered from the Hong Kong flu, she returned to Slippery Rock and I was left to spend the rest of the school year with my grandmother Ida, my great Uncle Joe, and my Aunt Rose. Actually, I wasn't related to either Joe or Rose, though I considered them my aunt and uncle. Joe had been married to Ida's sister, my great Aunt Frances, and after Frances died, Joe married Rose, a Hungarian Jew who had survived the death camps. It was impossible not to like Rose, who had the cheeriest personality of anyone I've ever met, bar none, despite the fact that she lost her entire family in the Holocaust, with the exception of her son, whom she didn't know had survived until thirteen years after the war when she ran into him by accident on the streets of Tel Aviv. Rose had owned a newsstand in Manhattan in front of a restaurant frequented by the Gabor sisters, and Rose was always telling us about her Gabor encounters – she liked them both immensely. She looked like a slightly older, zaftig version of the Gabor sisters, with dyed blonde hair, what they might have looked like if they had owned a newsstand in midtown Manhattan and sat on a stool all day, and been through death camps and had blue tattoos on their wrists.

Rose was one of those people, chiefly women of an older generation who, once they've identified a favorite food of a favored grandchild, niece, or nephew, will forever make it for that child whenever she or he visits. With Rose and me, it was apple strudel. My grandmother Ida was a lovely person, and had the same idea, but with her the signals somehow got crossed, and she thought my favorite food was meatloaf – which I have nothing against, but it's not what I'd order for a last meal.

Joe was completely the opposite of Rose, a dour man who always looked concerned or worried. Joe was built like Barney Rubble, with white scrub-brush hair and a white mustache. He had been a signalman in the Navy in World War I and had a ship sunk from under him. He and my Aunt Frances had met and married in the thirties, and had run a little soda fountain in Jamaica, Queens. Frances was always considered the great beauty of my grandmother's family, but when I knew her, she was old and pretty dotty, having suffered a stroke. At seven, I liked talking to her because she was so funny, inadvertently so, but I didn't know any better, and couldn't understand why the adults looked so unhappy when she said something funny. One night Joe fell asleep at the wheel of his car and hit a utility pole – and Frances was killed. To most of the family, her death was a relief. Sad, but a relief. No one, of course, ever talked about Frances or her death after she died. I learned about her death on a train ride – my grandmother told me, and said I shouldn't say anything to Joe because it would make him sad. This is one thing I learned about death at a young age, that after someone died, you were never supposed to mention them again. If it had been the other way around, Frances would have talked. She would have babbled happily about Joe, maybe thinking he was still alive, because of her *condition*, because she didn't know any better.

For four months I lived with Joe, Rose, and Ida in their retirement community in Hollywood, and I loved it. By any yardstick other than a conventional one, I was essentially an elderly person. I ate Meals on Wheels, nightly played a Hungarian version of canasta called Kalooki with my relatives, and played shuffleboard with Joe every day – we had a shuffleboard court right outside the door! I really liked being old. Age, I decided, is wasted on the elderly. None of my relatives seemed aware how much better it was to be old than young. They even complained about it.

And I enjoyed the school I attended. Classes were held in open-air metal huts. The walls would drop away when the weather was good, which was almost every day. I went from D's in Slippery Rock to A's in all my subjects. This was a little idyll for me – shuffleboard at home instead of football, and the entire school went bowling on Fridays right after the Spelling Bee, which I always won. The only sore spot in this happy time was one boy named Frank Parker, who I disliked for one reason or another. So I put a curse on him. I took a piece of notebook paper and drew two swords crossed like the Wilkinson swords, and I made up a name for an honorary society, The Silver Sword Society. In between the swords, I wrote the initials of this secret society. Underneath this picture, I made up my curse:

A curse upon Frank Parker. Something bad will happen to him.
So sayeth Robin Hemley, President of the Silver Sword Society™

After I wrote the curse, I put it in my desk, but it must have fallen out when I removed one of my books because Frank Parker found it on the floor.

"Did you write this?" he asked me, rubbing the top of his head. I expected him to get into a fight with me, but he didn't look angry. He told me that he was reading the curse as he stepped out the door, and a tile fell off the roof and knocked him in the head.

"Really?" I was quite pleased with myself.

"Take the curse off, okay?" he asked.

"Sure, okay," I said. I made Frank stand completely still and I advised him that an invisible sword was sticking through his gut. Carefully and elaborately, showing much strain, I tugged the sword from Frank's belly.

In the way of the kid world, Frank and I became good friends after that. I could afford to be generous. I had some control. I could direct some of the bad things that seemed to follow me, could make them stick in some-one else's gut if I wanted.

That day, contented, I went back to the retirement village, ate some Meals on Wheels chow and watched my favorite TV show, *Dark Shadows*, about a good but still deadly vampire named Barnabas Collins, who was always traveling back and forth in time trying to save the world. I identi-fied with Barnabas, still do. But he scared me and he scared himself, like I scare myself sometimes. Barnabas was always fighting one monster or another, when he wasn't fighting himself and his own tendencies toward self-destruction. This week, it was something called The Leviathan. The worst thing about The Leviathan was that no one had yet seen it, but you could sure hear the damn thing. Its breathing was labored and intense and hollow, and it made splashy footprint sounds as it walked. It lived in water and always left puddles of it, like so much pee, wherever it went. That's how you could tell The Leviathan had been around – that and the fact that whenever you saw that puddle of water, you knew that The Leviathan had snatched another victim. But you never saw it, and you never saw its victims, and that's what killed me. It was, by far, the scariest monster around.

I had to turn the TV off. I couldn't watch anymore, and I never watched *Dark Shadows* again after that week.

One day a letter arrived in the mail from an Assistant Counsel to the Attorney General of the United States. I had written to President Nixon because of an incident I had seen on the TV news one evening when Joe and Ida and Rose were watching in the living room.

Dear President Nixon,
You don't know me, but I am a concerned boy. Tonight on the news I saw some people throwing rocks at little kids on a bus going to school in Arkansas. How can you let this happen? Children should be safe when they go to school. Please do something about it right now! I am eleven.
Sincerely,
Robin Hemley
P.S. – I am a boy, not a girl even though my name is Robin. Boys in England are called Robin, even though I am not from England that is my name.

The scene on TV had shown several orange school buses being pelted with rocks by angry parents – some of them were trying to tip the buses over. The picture was shot from a little distance from the bus, but you could clearly make out children on the buses, and you could hear them screaming as the windows shattered and the metal was dented. The scene transfixed me. I couldn't understand how adults could throw rocks at little children. Wasn't childhood dangerous enough? Kids terrorized one another just fine – they didn't need any help from adults. I didn't know a thing about busing or integration, and only a little about the civil rights movement, but I knew a lot about children feeling unsafe, feeling that death was right around the corner.

The letter I received back from the government was addressed to Master Robin Hemley, which I didn't understand until my grandmother explained that this was a term of respect used when addressing boys.

March 2, 1970
Dear Master Hemley,
President Nixon has asked me to respond to your letter of concern in regards to the incident in Fayetteville on January 21 of this year. The President shares your concern. However, appropriate action was taken by the state of Arkansas, and so it does not seem fitting at this time for the federal government to intervene.
Sincerely,
Harold W. Varina
Assistant Counsel to the Attorney General

Ida read this letter aloud to Rose and Joe that afternoon, and I was treated like a hero. Rose didn't understand English perfectly and was convinced that the President had signed the letter himself, and that Harold W. Varina was indeed the President. Ida wanted to frame the letter, and even Joe seemed happy – the beginning, he said, of a distinguished life in politics for me. I was happy for all the attention, but not really satisfied by the letter. The man who answered my letter had not, after all, answered my question. How could this happen? I wasn't only asking for a solution or an excuse. I wanted a reason.

My grandmother and I went to Miami Beach a couple of weeks before I was to return to Slippery Rock. She said that we had to go to a hotel where Cousin Ruth was dying of Lou Gehrig's Disease. I didn't even know who Cousin Ruth was, and visiting someone who was dying did not seem to me a suitable activity for young or old alike. The less said about death, the better, and watching someone die seemed like an embarrassing activity, akin to watching them on the toilet.

"What am I supposed to say to her?" I asked my grandmother. I wasn't going to tell her I was sorry she was dying. When my father had died, someone had told my brother Jonathan that they were sorry, and he'd said, "What are you sorry for? You didn't kill him." And that's the attitude I adopted afterwards. That seemed properly embattled and hostile. I imagined Ruth would say the same thing if I told her I was sorry. "What are you sorry for, kid? I don't even know you." And then I'd be humiliated and would plunge a silver sword in her for revenge.

"You don't have to say anything," my grandmother told me. "There will be a lot of people there, and Ruth can't speak anymore. Just say hello and smile. Everyone loves your smile."

"Should I tell her I'm sorry she's dying?"

"That's not polite," my grandmother said. "Don't mention it. Pretend to be happy to see her."

To seal my approval, my grandmother offered me a death bribe. I was familiar with death bribes – to make death more palatable, you were given something that you wanted. When my father died, a friend of our family took me downtown and said I could have any toy I wanted. She seemed dismayed when I couldn't think of anything, so I pointed to a model car in a drugstore window. The car was wrapped up for me and my mother's friend seemed relieved. I tried to put the car together, but gave up halfway through the project. Wheels on a chassis, that's all it ended up as, nothing at all like the perfect picture of a Camaro on the box.

My grandmother's death bribe was a banana split, the largest, she claimed, that could be found anywhere, big enough for two people. And, as an added bonus, the soda shop where the banana splits could be had was located on the bottom floor of Cousin Ruth's hotel. Ida and I sat at the counter with a giant boat of whipped cream, bananas, ice cream, and syrup, fortifying ourselves with dollops of sugar before we met dying Ruth. Ida kept asking me if it tasted good, and I kept having to reassure her that this was indeed the best banana split I'd ever eaten. We gorged ourselves and then went up to Ruth's room.

Though other people milled around the room, it was the dying person who immediately captured my attention. She sat in a recliner, her legs propped up, covered up to her neck with a loose, colorful blanket. And then I looked away, forcing myself not to stare. The windows of the room were open and people were quiet. My Aunt Carrie was there, and my Uncle Morty, and a few other people I didn't recognize. A friend of the family named Anne Deutsch sat on the bed near Ruth. Anne was not simply a friend of our family, but a kind of camp follower, a fanatical devotee. She was the same age as my great aunts and uncles, in her sixties at the time, and wherever they or my grandmother went, she went too.

She was always around. I can hardly remember an occasion when she wasn't there. I didn't mind her. She was a very sweet woman, sweeter than many of my relatives by a long shot, but I was not happy to see her because of a falling out of sorts we'd had the previous summer. We were walking to the store near my grandmother's beach house when she asked me if I'd start calling her Aunt Anne.

"You're not my aunt," I said.

"I know," she said, "But I'd like it if that's what you'd call me from now on."

"I don't want to," I said. No one in my family liked to be called Aunt or Uncle. I once tried it out on my Uncle Allan and Aunt Rene and they told me to stop immediately.

"How about this, Robin," she said. "If you call me Aunt Anne, I'll treat you like one of my own, and you know what that means?"

"What?"

"Presents."

This whole conversation made me uncomfortable, and the more she pressed me the less I was inclined to call her Aunt, or even Anne.

"Just say it," she said. "Just say Aunt Anne."

"No."

"I mean it, Robin. I'm only going to make this offer once."

But I hadn't relented. Now I saw her on the bed looking forlorn and I felt sorry for her. I approached and she gave me a little hug and peck on the cheek and I said, "Hello, Aunt Anne." She smiled faintly at me.

Weeks later, my grandmother reported to me that this gesture of mine hadn't gone unnoticed or unappreciated – I was surprised that Anne's request was known by the entire family. I never called her Aunt Anne again. Soon she had a grandchild anyway, and I was left in the dust.

Next, I approached Ruth. I had to face her sooner or later. I remembered Ruth vaguely now. She had a nice face and a gentle smile. I had already been told that she couldn't talk, but that didn't seem necessary. She looked at me and I didn't feel so frightened of her, though I could see she was weak and dying. We didn't touch, but I smiled back and made a gesture that I hoped no one else noticed. I grabbed the scabbard of a sword and pulled it from her body, gently, almost imperceptibly. To the uninitiated, it might have looked like a half-hug, pulled away from at the last moment.

I didn't want to return to Slippery Rock, and made every attempt to avoid going home, but my mother missed me too much, and in April she came down to Hollywood. I missed her, too, but not enough to want to return. I was having a great time as an old timer. And my shuffleboard game was getting really good – I even started winning at Kalooki.

There used to be a picture of me walking around a fountain in Miami wearing sunglasses, a Naugahyde vest, a Nehru shirt, and a sun medallion as big as my face. A destructive dog of mine chewed it up several years ago, but that's just as well. It's an embarrassing picture, not simply because the styles are so laughable now. Of course, we laugh at whatever isn't current, whether music or fashion. And why not? We all want to be young, or most of us anyway.

The photo was embarrassing because it was so fake. This was my impression of a young person, not the real thing. I was an actor, and I was sure that I was going to be discovered as I walked around that fountain. I knew that someone important must be watching, someone who'd recognize I had the exact look they wanted.

I was so sure, just as I was sure that this time the plane would be hijacked and my mother and I would begin a brand new life in Havana.

The first night back in Slippery Rock my mother told me she had something important to tell me. We were halfway through dinner.

"Your friend, Donald," she said. Then she said something I couldn't hear, but I pretended to hear it, pretended it made perfect sense.

"Oh," I said and kept on eating.

But my mother wasn't finished. "I'm sorry I have to tell you this, Robin. Did you hear me?"

"Yes."

"I know you were close."

I kept eating.

"No one is really sure what happened. It happened during the winter. Apparently, Donald and his younger brother . . ."

"You mean Fred?"

"I don't know which one."

"He only has one."

My mother was looking at me and then she looked at her plate. "They were down near Slippery Rock Creek. A man started chasing them or something, no one's really sure, and Donald fell through the ice. His brother . . ."

"Fred?"

"Yes, Fred. His brother saw the whole thing happen and he hasn't spoken a word since."

Then my mother told me an alternate version of Donald's death, that they had been climbing trees, a branch had broken, and Donald had fallen through the ice. I didn't need to hear an alternate version. However he died, however he came to be there, the results were the same. He'd fallen through the ice, and unable to find his way out again, had drowned. I understood that. I nodded. I understood that. They shouldn't have been out there on the ice alone. I understood that. But it didn't sound like Donald. It didn't sound like something he'd do. He was so cautious. He never got in trouble. He thought death was stupid.

I understood his brother's inability to speak, to shed light on the true story. I understood that, in the face of death, no words were necessary, no words were appropriate, no words could suffice or describe. The less said the better.

We finished dinner in silence and then my mother went to the living room couch and started sorting through her mail. I stood up slowly from the table, turned around, and ran to her. I collapsed in her lap and cried. "I wasn't home again," I said, sobbing. She stroked my head, not sure what I meant, what being home had to do with anything. If I had been there, I thought, this might not have happened. Somehow my being there could have saved him. There was no comforting me and never could be.

Donald was the only one I cried for. I didn't cry for my father. I tried. I knew I was supposed to, but I couldn't. I didn't cry for my friend Tommy, smothered earlier that year in the sand fort he'd built – though I remember his face much more clearly than Donald and knew him longer. But Donald, who I barely knew, who had shown me the kindness of disapproval, who told me it was stupid to die, he was the one I couldn't stop crying for. Even now, nearly thirty years later, the grief smothers me like so much sand, like ice I can't find my way out of. Donald's death convinced me once and for all that I was, indeed, a jinx, that whoever I loved would die – and I haven't seen anything to convince me otherwise – except that now I know we're all jinxes.

When I think of Slippery Rock now, the picture I invariably see is a storm rolling in from the vantage point of the kitchen of our apartment – I see hills with skeletal trees. I don't know why it's this image, unremarkable and bland, not even fixed in a specific moment of memory that stays with me so deeply, that seems to embody all my terror and angst over the place – except that what terrifies me most about life are exactly those moments that are unremarkable and bland, that are erasable. Loss of memory terrifies me. Loss of identity terrifies me.

The world is supposed to make sense, that's what childhood is about, what at least we pretend it's about. That's when we give our children all the explanations for why things work and how they work, or if we can't, we stay silent and, by our silence, ask them to try to figure it out. We try to keep them away from things they won't understand, things we can't understand, pictures on the news, atrocities, the deaths of parents, of young friends, of siblings. We give them explanations, but still they crawl into our bed at night and tell us they're afraid, they've had a nightmare, even the young ones who have survived relatively unharmed so far, our children who we wish we could protect forever, whose childhoods we want to be an idyll.

We don't even need to know what their nightmares are about. Nightmares are all the same. You're being chased – that's all you need to know. Or you're in an unfamiliar place. Or a familiar place with stores that look like coal mines, streets that are slippery, frosted terraced hills, a drum-kettle sky and winter in the air.

I know what it's like to wake up in terror, alone, unable to catch a breath. I still wake up hating myself many nights. For unspecified reasons, for many reasons that don't even always make sense. This is Slippery Rock's legacy. This is where I still live.

Something That Will Last

When my cousin Sue recognized her mother's dreams in my novel, *Things Invisible to See*, she was surprised and pleased. "That dream of my mother's – the one where she goes to heaven and back," said Sue. "It's nice. But did you ever hear about the time she woke up and saw twelve angels standing around her bed with candles in their hands? Come over for a visit, and I'll tell you that story."

The night of my mother's funeral, I heard bits and pieces of that story. Sue and her husband Ben had driven from Grosse Pointe to my mother's house in Ann Arbor. The house was full of cousins and second cousins, in-laws and grandchildren, who had flown in from Washington, New York, Montana, Texas, Pennsylvania. English is peculiarly deficient in words for family relationships. Sue's husband, Ben, for example. Was he my cousin? My cousin-in-law? Did it matter? He was family. I let it go at that.

In the morning we committed my mother's body to the earth, and in the evening we returned to my mother's house and reminded ourselves that she was happiest when the family was gathered in this place, enjoying each other's company. It was June, the beginning of hot weather in Ann Arbor, and all the windows and doors stood open. We sat around the coffee table in the living room and played *Ubi Sunt?*, a board game involving maps and a knowledge of geography. Where is the capital of Brazil? Where is the capital of Nigeria? The last time I saw Ben alive he was shouting "Ubi sunt" and pointing to Paris on a map that looked much too colorful to be taken seriously. I had forgotten the capital cities of all except a handful of countries, but I hadn't forgotten François Villon's poem, "The Ballad of Dead Ladies," with its famous refrain:

Where is Echo, seen by no man,
Only heard on river and mere,

She whose beauty was more than human?
But where are the snows of yesteryear?

If Villon were alive today, he might have used a different metaphor to show our mortality: Where are the voices telling good news and bad to the message machines so many of us have added to our telephones? *Ubi sunt?*

Erased.

I have been suspicious of these devices ever since my husband and I stayed in the apartment of a friend whose answering machine, he assured us, required no special attention. For days the machine was silent, sullen, and suspiciously well-behaved. On our last night in the apartment, it woke us at two in the morning in response to a call and shouted all the messages it had been storing up for a week, filling the dark with a cacophony of voices: a schizophrenic confessing to two groggy and astonished listeners.

Nevertheless, after years of railing against such devices, Eric and I broke down and bought one. We set it up, turned it on, and forgot about it, until early the next morning it woke us with the voice of my niece, calling from Ann Arbor.

"Hello. This is Margaret. Sue called to say that Ben was killed by a sniper last night on his way home from a business meeting."

I sprang out of bed, lunged for the phone, missed it, and called her back. Sue had asked Margaret to call other members of the family and tell them about Ben's death.

"His picture was on Channel 2 news," said Margaret. "I videotaped it."

Many calls later, I was able to piece the story together. Ben was driving home from a meeting at the Detroit Yacht Club. The car was new, a Cadillac. Did Ben especially admire Cadillacs? Probably not. There is an understanding among those who work in the auto manufacturing business: if you have the account, you drive the car. Ben had the Cadillac account and drove, therefore, a midnight blue Cadillac with red upholstery and a telephone. He took the river road, through Bayview. He might have chosen a safer route but the river road was the fastest, and he was eager to be home. I imagine he sped up as he entered the deserted block with its empty Chrysler plant and its lonely stretch of asphalt. Not far ahead lay the green lawns of Grosse Pointe and the mansions that looked out on the trim yachts bobbing over the white-capped waves. St. Paul's also faced the water; Ben and Sue went to early Mass there on Sundays.

When Ben spied a tree limb blocking the middle of the street, he did not climb out of the car to drag it aside. Ben was born and raised in Detroit, and he knew about the homemade roadblocks car thieves set for the unwary. Climb out of your car to move it, and chances are you'll never see that car again. Ben sped up and tried to swerve around it. Did he see the man jump out of the dark and fire point blank the bullet that ripped the door of the car, passed through one lung, and entered his heart? Ben's last act on earth was to pick up the telephone and call his son.

These were the bare facts. But for anyone with imagination – we all have imagination in these circumstances – it's ourselves we see in that car, and the bare facts are only the beginning. The facts of Ben's death haunted me all day, as if my own fate were stalking me, just out of sight. Our ancestors spoke of fate as three goddesses. The first chooses your life, the second spins the thread, the third cuts it. When I think of fate, I don't see three goddesses. I see a writer, who dreams up my story, writes it, and one day will finish it.

Life as story. Crazy? Perhaps. But what are our lives if not stories? The realist who first told the Grimm's fairy tale "Godfather Death" ends the story with the main character's life-as-story, the better to wring our hearts.

"Death . . . walked up to the physician with long strides and said: 'All is over with you, and now the lot falls on you,' and seized him so firmly with his ice-cold hand, that he could not resist, and led him into a cave below the earth. There he saw how thousands and thousands of candles were burning in countless rows, some large, some medium-sized, others small. 'See,' said Death, 'these are the lights of men's lives. The large ones belong to children, the medium-sized ones to married people in their prime, the little ones belong to old people; but children and young folks likewise have often only a tiny candle.' 'Show me the light of my life,' said the physician, and he thought it would still be very tall. Death pointed to a little end which was just threatening to go out, and said, 'Behold, it is there.' 'Ah, dear godfather,' said the horrified physician, 'Light a new one for me . . .' Death behaved as if he were going to fulfill his wish, and took hold of a tall candle; but . . . purposely made a mistake in fixing it, and the little piece fell down and was extinguished. Immediately the physician fell on the ground, and now he himself was in the hands of Death." (*The Complete Grimm's Fairy Tales*, introd. by Padraic Colum, commentary by Joseph Campbell, New York: Pantheon, 1972, pp. 211–12.)

It is surely no accident that some of our finest writers have been doctors or students of medicine: Chekhov, Rabelais, and Keats, Sommerset Maugham and William Carlos Williams, Walker Percy and Robert Coles. What Dr. John Stone, a poet and teacher at the Emory School of Medicine, has to say about literature and the training of doctors is good medicine for any writer:

"Literature, indeed, can have a kind of laboratory function. In other words, the medical ear must be properly trained to hear stories – a medical history, after all, is a short story. In this sense, a person's life can be thought of as a series of stories, coalescing over time to form the most idiosyncratic novel ever written. The good doctor must learn to listen for the real message in these stories of his patients, to read them, as Robert Frost used to say, 'with a listening ear.'" ("Listening to the Patient," *Literary Cavalcade*, February 1990, p. 27.)

Writers too are listeners, both to the stories people tell them and the stories they tell themselves. As writers, what are we listening for that helps us shape our material? Let me go back to the story of Ben's death.

Neither the television nor my niece could give me enough facts to put the whole story together. Eric suggested I call Sue herself. Is there any among us who is not tongue-tied when confronted with someone who has suffered a terrible loss? Grief has no special syntax or vocabulary. To bend ordinary language to your own subtle purposes – it's like trying to mend a wedding dress with an ice pick.

Nevertheless, I called my cousin, and she came to the phone.

"It's on the front page," she said. " 'Wealthy Grosse Pointe executive killed.' Wealthy – ha! People keep coming by with food. You can't imagine how much food we have in this house."

In a calm voice she informed me that Ben's wake would be on Saturday ("No viewing, just people dropping by"), the Rosary on Sunday, the funeral Mass on Monday, and the burial on Tuesday.

"Ben went out the front door and he never came back," she said. "Channel 2 has set up cameras in our front yard. We had to pull the drapes. I never liked those drapes when we moved into this house. But I'm awfully glad for them now."

And she burst into tears.

Earlier I mentioned the bare facts of the story. But of course to a writer no facts are bare. In the depths of sorrow and the heights of danger, we may find ourselves both weeping and watching ourselves weep. The English novelist, Arnold Bennett, once boasted that the death scene of one of his characters could not be improved upon, "because I took infinite pains over it. All the time my father was dying, I was at the bedside making copious notes." (*The Literary Life and Other Curiosities*, by Robert Hendrickson, New York: Viking, 1981, p. 28.) Of course we find this appalling. But who among us does not take copious notes in his head even while we are giving ourselves over to grief and fear?

Let me tell you a story. When I was a student at Stanford, I too met violence at the hands of a stranger. I was biking home from the library at night through the palm grove that surrounds the campus, when a man leaped out from the trees and knocked me to the ground. His intention, I discovered later in court, was to kill me first and rape me later. He put his hands around my neck, tightened them, and waited for me to die. Neither of us knew that over our struggle the light on my bicycle was shining into the tops of the palm trees like a wayward star.

At this point the story sounds like the script for a bad TV series. The captain and the quarterback of the Stanford football team were returning from a movie and spied a mysterious beam cutting through the foliage over their heads. So it came to pass that I found myself in the police station with the two football players who had saved me and the policeman who was writing up the report. The policeman said,

"Were you raped?"

"No," I said.

"Step into the other room and examine yourself to make sure," he said.

I stared at him in bewilderment.

"But why? There's absolutely no question about this."

The policeman sighed and put down his pen.

"It's part of the procedure. There has to be an examination," he said. "I can't leave it blank on the form."

There was no dissuading him, so I stepped into the back room of the police barracks. Suddenly the writer part of me took over. I'd never been in a police barracks, and who knew when I might want to write a story requiring just such a scene? I glanced at the desk, the notices on the wall, the calendar, the bookshelves. Instead of books they held bowling trophies, a flock of small golden men perched on marble blocks who leaned forward in unison, hands extended, each hand sending a golden ball down an invisible alley.

These are the bare facts. But bare facts are not stories. Stories are facts as they happen to people, and I could not write the story of what happened to me in the palm grove until I'd found the voice to tell it, the voice of someone who was like me and yet not like me at all. We speak of finding the right voice for a story or novel. The characters, the scenes, the events gather in our heads like the cast of a play on opening night. But the voice is the director, without whom the performers may wait for years on the dark stage before the curtain rises. I do not think we find these voices, I think they find us, sometimes only after we have lived with the characters for years and even abandoned them.

It took ten years for the voice that could tell that story to find me. And what the voice gave me was not a short story but a poem, "Clearing the Air."

It's been ten years since you tried to kill me.
Biking home one night, I saw only your legs
stepping behind a tree, then you fell on my throat
like a cat. My books crashed the birds out of sleep.
We rolled in the leaves like lovers. My eyes popped
like Christmas lights, veins snapped, your teeth wore

my blood, your fingers left bars on my neck.
I can't remember your name,
and I saw your face only in court.
You sat in a box, docile as old shoes.
And I, who had never felt any man's weight,
sometimes felt yours for nights afterwards.

Well, I'm ready to forgive
and I don't want to forget.
Sometimes I tell myself we met
differently, on a train. You give me
a Batman comic and show me your passport.
I have nothing but my report card,

but I offer my mother's fudge for the grapes
rotting the one paper bag you carry.
In my tale you are younger and loved.
Outside you live in a thousand faces
and so do your judges, napping in parks,
rushing to fires, folded like bats on the truck,

mad and nude in a white Rolls
pinching dollars and leather behinds.

Burned from a tree by your betters, you take
to the streets and hang in the dark like a star,
making me see your side, waking me
with the blows and the weight of it.

To understand all is to forgive, says Flaubert. He might have added that such understanding takes time. Only to a few people does it come naturally, and I am not one of them. To William Carlos Williams it came naturally, if we are to believe Ezra Pound. "Where I see scoundrels and vandals," writes Pound, "Dr. Williams sees a spectacle or an ineluctable process of nature." ("Dr. Williams' Position," *The Dial*, 85, November, 1928, p. 398.)

What did I see when I heard the news of Ben's death? Scoundrels and vandals. Certainly nothing so objective as a process of nature.

When I arrived at my cousin's house, the living room was so full of friends laughing and chatting that I felt as if I were at a New Year's Eve party. All afternoon the flowers kept coming; baskets ascended the steps leading to the second floor like a procession of debutantes waiting to be photographed. A large colored photograph of Ben stood on the piano. Safe in his gold frame, Ben seemed to be watching us, making sure the glasses were filled and the guests were happy. On shelves and coffee tables, the model trains he loved seemed to have stopped in their tracks. In the kitchen, a headline caught my eye: SLAIN DRIVER AN AVID SAILOR, TAUGHT SPORT TO THE YOUNG. Someone had left the clipping from the *Detroit Free Press* on the counter:

"Half a block from the blue waters of Lake St. Clair where he loved to sail and taught many others, family and friends gathered in shock Friday at the home of Benjamin Gravel, who was killed in an apparently random shooting on a Detroit street.

"Gravel was returning to his home in Grosse Pointe Farms from a meeting at the Bayview Yacht Club around 10 P.M. Thursday when he was shot in the chest as he drove through a construction zone on Conner, just south of Jefferson.

"Police said the shot was fired from outside the car, on Gravel's left side.

"Gravel died about an hour later at St. John's Hospital in Detroit."

At the end of the article, a single sentence jumped out at me:

"Gravel was asked to serve as a judge in the America's Cup race in 1987 but had to decline the offer because he could not leave his job as a manufacturer's representative in the auto industry."

Ben a judge in the America's Cup race? I hadn't known that. Reading the article and the obituary, I felt as if I were meeting Ben for the first time. And I thought of a much earlier meeting with Ben, not my first but nearly so, the summer I graduated from college. My graduation present from my parents was a trip to Europe. Ben was in the army, stationed in Germany, and he and Sue were not yet married. Sue asked me to look him up.

We met in a beer hall, in Heidelberg. Most of the other customers were older men. Ben and I sat down at a long table opposite one of them, who introduced himself as a veteran of the Second World War. Hundreds of questions flooded my mind, and I didn't dare ask any of them: *What did you know? What did you do and to whom did you do it?* I could not rid myself of the thought that if Ben had been born a few generations earlier, the man sitting before me might have killed him at Dunkirk or Ardennes. But now the young soldier and the old one were smiling at each other like the best of friends. I scanned Ben's face. Where I saw a scoundrel, he saw a human being, part of the ineluctable process of nature that has nothing to do with history or politics. At that moment I learned something about traveling light and how little baggage we really need to get where we're going.

Tourists learn this more easily than writers.

The writer as outside observer and the writer as inside participant are like two sisters destined to fight with each other from the moment they are born. Let us imagine Miss Experience and Miss Gatherer have just entered the door of my cousin's house, a place they have often visited on more cheerful occasions. Miss Experience says, "What a lovely room! You've redecorated it!" Miss Gatherer says, "How much did you pay for this sofa? Where did you get it? Is your dress real silk?"

My cousin announces that Father Murphy has arrived to say the Rosary, and everyone sits down. Father Murphy begins by praising Ben the sailor and Ben the family man, proud of his son, whose photograph he carried in his wallet. The guests who have brought rosaries take them out of pockets and purses. Miss Experience has chosen a seat on a sofa near the back of the room. When Father Murphy begins to pray, she folds her hands. All around her tumble the words, one after another, like wings brushing her ears.

Miss Gatherer has found a seat in front, close to the priest; she doesn't want to miss a thing. Since she is a Protestant, she must work harder to remember the words as she listens for the images and metaphors that will help her shape the story she wants to tell. Indeed, she is already composing the story, editing, selecting what is useful to her. She cannot take notes – even she has some sense of propriety – but she makes a mental note of everything in the room. Family pictures on the piano. Model trains on the coffee table. Baskets of flowers on the stairs. To fix the priest's eulogy in her mind, she memorizes key words that will recall the main points: Boat. Wallet.

Later, when the sisters compare their impressions, Miss Gatherer is dismayed to discover that she can remember the key words but not what they point to. She can list nearly everything in the living room, but she knows she could have done this at any other time. Since her list does not include feelings, it tells her nothing of what made this day different from all other days. She feels as if someone had reached into a long-hidden tomb and handed her an exquisite tapestry that crumbled to dust when she held it to the light. Time, which preserved it, also destroyed it.

And what does Miss Experience recall of the afternoon? Why, every-thing. She is astonished that her sister remembers so little. She, too, noted the room and its contents, for it takes a long time to say the Rosary, and even those for whom piety is a calling do not attend to every word. What was she doing during her lapses? She was daydreaming, wool-gathering. Her gaze rested on the bowl of pink tulips on the coffee table, and her mind roamed back to the last time she saw that table, at Christ-mas. On it Sue had arranged the Nativity scene Ben had sent her from Germany. The stable, the star, the angels, the wise men, the shepherds, Mary, the baby – all the principals were present except Joseph. Miss Experience remembered asking what had happened to Joseph.

"I loaned him out to our next door neighbor when she was trying to sell her house," Sue replied. "If you bury a statue of St. Joseph on the property, a house will sell right away. The market is awful around here, but she sold her house in a week."

The downside of this arrangement, she added, was that Joseph's mortal part, being papier mâché, had rotted away, leaving nothing behind but his head. Well-meaning friends had brought her replacements, and she soon had half a dozen Josephs, plaster, wood, and plastic: a polygamy of hus-bands for Mary.

"But I gave them all away," she said. "None of them belonged to Mary like the one she'd lost."

Hail Mary; Miss Experience's mind returns to the present moment and to Father Murphy. Back and forth between past and present she moves, like a seamstress stitching, reinforcing, reworking the tapestry of these events, binding them to each other by many different threads. Her sub-ject is not the funeral but the human condition. Miss Gatherer's approach is rather like that of an inexperienced doctor, or a first-year resident, who lets himself become bogged down in circumstantial details. What Dr. Robert Coles says he learned from his teachers in medical school applies to writers as well as doctors.

"I slowly began to realize that we doctors had become diggers, trying hard to follow treasure maps in hopes of discovering gold. . . . If we didn't know, we knew what it was that we wanted to know and *would* know, once we'd made our discovery . . .

"Dr. Ludwig urged us to let the story itself be our discovery. . . . He urged me to be a good listener in the special way a story requires: note the manner of presentation; the development of plot, character; the addition of new dramatic sequences; the emphasis accorded to one figure or another."

And from William Carlos Williams: "Their story, yours, mine – it's what we all carry with us on this trip we take, and we owe it to each other to respect our stories and learn from them." (*The Call of Stories*, Boston: Houghton Mifflin, 1989, pp. 22–23, 30.)

The difference between Miss Gatherer and Miss Experience is the difference between a handful of details and a real story. The details alone are like shells picked up at the beach. What looks so luminous in the water turns parched and chalky on the land. Details for a writer are parched when we isolate them from our feelings, luminous when we preserve them in the medium of memory. Nobody describes the difficulty of keeping our past intact better than Proust. "It is a labour in vain to attempt to recapture it: all the efforts of our intellect must prove futile. The past is hidden somewhere . . . beyond the reach of intellect. . . . Will it ultimately reach the clear surface of my consciousness, this memory, this old, dead moment . . . out of the very depths of my being?" (*Swann's Way*, pp. 47–48, 50.)

What has happened here? The process of gathering has shifted from the surface to the depths, the well from which all stories come. And though we are not concerned with the healing power of stories, I think what doctors and therapists have said about the way stories heal children also describes the way stories happen to writers. Through non-directed play, says one storyteller-therapist, the children find their stories. "From week to week, if you just let the stories come out, you can listen to them and see an unfolding. . . ." (Elizabeth Radecki, quoted in "The Home of Healing," by Mary Weaver, *Storytelling Magazine*, summer, 1989, p. 20).

Whole, resonant – isn't that what all writers want their stories to be? Don't we all want to rise from our desks with the feeling that we have written, not out of what we know, but more than we know? Isn't one of the objections to minimalism in fiction simply this: that the writer has gathered from the surface and not from the depths?

Let me tell you a story.

The first funeral I ever attended was that of my grandmother, who died when I was a sophomore in college. I'd never seen a dead person before, except in the movies. At the funeral parlor, I peered into the coffin and tried to connect the body lying in front of me with the woman who had lived with us, on and off, and given us both joy and suffering. Quite unconsciously, my hand snaked out and touched my grandmother's face.

When I stepped back from the coffin, I nearly bumped into my father. My father was a man of great feeling. He was also a scientist whose vocation has trained him to gather facts.

"What did it feel like?" he asked.

He was not asking, what did you feel like in the presence of this woman, but what did her flesh feel like? Of all the people in the room, he knew I alone could both understand the question and answer it, because writers and scientists share the curse of detachment in the midst of emotion. And writers must know the look and feel of the visible world of the flesh if they are to describe the invisible world of the spirit.

Several months ago I was browsing in a bookshop and a curious title caught my eye: *How to Capture Live Authors and Bring Them to Your Schools*. The owner of the bookshop assured me it was a very good book, and though I did not read it, I have no reason to doubt her. The purpose of bringing authors and their readers together, she told me, is to encourage students to write. I hope very much there will be a sequel called *How to Capture Dead Authors* since there are many writers I would hate to see excluded from schools because the fine print at the bottom of the lease on life we are born with says it is not renewable.

Of that group, who would I hope to capture? I'd go after the anonymous tellers of folktales, because I know of no other literature that can teach writers so much about shaping narrative. Let me tell you how I invited a particular story to visit me and what Ben's death taught me about making that story my own. The story is one I am sure you know, "Beauty and the Beast," not to be confused with the TV series of the same name. It's the story of a rich merchant with three daughters, the youngest of whom is called Beauty. The story begins when his ships are lost at sea, and the family, suddenly impoverished, is forced to move into the country. When word reaches the merchant that one of his ships has been found, he returns to the city, but not before asking his daughters what presents he should bring for them. The oldest two beg for gold and jewels.

Beauty, not wishing to burden her father with an expensive request, asks for a rose. On his way home, a storm drives him into the woods, which was no doubt as lovely and dangerous as the palm grove mentioned earlier, in which I escaped danger of a different kind. To the merchant's relief, the mysterious mansion where he takes shelter appears to be empty. A good dinner, a new suit of clothes, a soft bed – every comfort is offered him by invisible servants. But the woods are lovely, dark, and deep, and it's no surprise to the listener when the merchant picks a rose from the garden for Beauty and a beast rushes out and growls, "Your daughter or your life." It's one of the oldest themes in literature: the beautiful young girl who learns to love a beast, thereby breaking the spell and restoring him to human form.

Once upon a time an editor called and told me that one of the illustrators she worked with, Barry Moser, had long been fascinated by the story and wanted to illustrate it. Would I retell it for him?

I said no. Why retell what has been told beautifully in the first place? The editor pointed out that there is no single correct version of "Beauty and the Beast." Many older versions exist and she sent me some to look at. I read them with curiosity and admiration. They were different from each other, yet true in the way that fairy tales have always been true: they hold up a mirror to our deepest wishes and fears.

Still I said no and explained to her that I was already hard at work on another story. A story? It felt more like a fish that kept slipping away from me. Every time I picked it up, I found scenes that didn't belong for all sorts of reasons. Here was a scene I'd added because a friend had told me a funny anecdote and I wanted to include it, the way as a child I once put olives into my ice cream because I loved olives and thought the ice cream could only be improved by so delicious an addition. Well, it wasn't. And here was an opening scene I'd written to give information I thought the reader should have as early as possible. The opening pages creaked under the weight of both the scene and my reasons for writing it, neither of which had anything to do with the real story. Finding the real story is hearing the voice of the story itself and following it. Suddenly I thought how pleasant it would be to write a narrative in which I didn't have to discover the story. So I agreed to write yet another version of "Beauty and the Beast."

The beast and his magic mansion in the forest – that's what most of us love about the tale, isn't it? We can hardly wait for Beauty to leave her father and sisters behind, so we can enter the kingdom of the Beast. But what does the Beast look like? The traditional storytellers tell us only that he was frightful. Sitting in our living room, I discussed this problem with the one person who had to know the answer: Barry Moser. Was the Beast an animal? A human, badly deformed? Our one-eyed cat walked round and round us, eavesdropping, now and then pausing to give Barry an odd look.

When I started working with the original story, I felt as if I'd mounted a wise horse who knew exactly where to go and the best way of getting there. And why shouldn't he know? He's been making the trip for years, and the road is as fresh as it was when once upon a time the first teller of that tale laid it down. Why not give the old story a new time and place? I thought, New York at the turn of the century. I had the plot, the characters, the time, the place. This would be smooth sailing. Very soon I discovered the error of my ways.

Here is the opening of a traditional version of "Beauty and the Beast":

"There was once a very rich merchant, who had three daughters; being a man of sense, he spared no cost for their education, but gave them all kinds of masters. His daughters were extremely handsome, especially the youngest; when she was little everybody admired her, and called her 'the little Beauty' so that, as she grew up, she still went by the name of Beauty, which made her sisters very jealous. The two eldest had a great deal of pride, because they were rich. . . . They went out every day upon parties of pleasure, balls, plays, concerts, etc. and laughed at their youngest sister, because she spent the greater part of her time in reading good books."

Trying to retell this was a humbling experience. That expensive education, for example. Did the daughters of the wealthy go to boarding school or did they have governesses? What and how were they taught? And those parties of pleasure mentioned so casually in the third sentence – what did it feel like to be a guest at one at the turn of the century in New York? And what does it feel like to be *rich*?

To find out, I turned to the biographies of people who had firsthand knowledge: J. P. Morgan, Cornelius Vanderbilt, Andrew Carnegie, John Jacob Astor. I skimmed and scanned, looking for the singular detail or observation that would make my own story believable. And the more I read, the more I heard my own memories waking and muttering: Remember that party your cousin Sue took you to in Grosse Pointe when you were fifteen? Remember the receiving line, the young girls descending the staircase, the young men leaning in the doorways? Remember the white gloves you wore? You wondered what the other girls would say if they knew your daddy was not a stockbroker and not an auto manufacturer but a college professor. You wondered what the young men would say if you told them you wanted to be a writer.

Four months after embarking on this project, I had enough courage to write the first paragraph of "Beauty and the Beast":

"Long ago, when the century was still young, a rich merchant lived with his three daughters in a splendid townhouse in New York. The house looked out on Central Park on Fifth Avenue at Fifty-ninth, and the merchant had filled the house with treasures from his travels, tapestries and candelabra, chests and cameos, marble angels and bronze beasts. In the evening, when lights blazed in every window, men in white waist-coats and women a-glitter with jewels were ushered into the dining room where a long dinner table covered with gold damask and gold china and the finest crystal awaited them. Behind every highbacked chair stood a footman. And beyond the French doors lay the greenhouses and gardens. The merchant favored orchids and roses."

The traditional stories do not say exactly where the merchant took his family after he lost his money, but I could not get off so easily. It seemed likely they would head north, to one of the little towns along the Hudson. But which town? The countryside around Saugerties is different from the country around Highland, and the countryside around Rhinebeck is different from both of them. Nevertheless, I felt on sure ground, for I know something about small towns along the Hudson and something about living in the country and quite a lot of about the business of keeping a garden, washing clothes, cleaning house, and cooking dinner.

But when I started to write this part of the story, I found out all over again how much you have to know in order to write a single line. What would Beauty see and hear and smell in the country at the turn of the century? Of course there were no supermarkets, no refrigerators, no lap top computers, no message machines, no Federal Express, and no free-ways. There was also no traffic and no parking problems. Beauty would have traveled to the nearest town by horse, and she could have recognized far more birds and wildflowers than I can. In winter, without central heating and insulation and down jackets, she would have felt the cold more keenly than most of us. Along the river she would have seen men chopping huge blocks of ice and carrying them away to underground storage rooms where they would stay until they were called for in warm weather. Beauty would have kept the family provisions in a root cellar under the kitchen floor, she would have hauled water from a well, washed in the creek, and cooked the meals on a wood-burning stove. When Beauty sets off across the frozen fields to meet the Beast, she is leaving behind a life filled with passages of great sweetness and chapters of great hardship. Life in the magic mansion hidden along the Hudson was surely a glorious change, in spite of its ugly owner.

The magic mansion presented a new problem. What did it look like, feel like, both inside and out? This is the moment you can either throw up your hands or invoke that patron saint of writers, Saint Chance. Her creed is simple: What you need ye shall find. But you will never find her if you don't believe in her power, the power of things beyond your control to help you. One of her most devoted followers was James Joyce, who said, "Chance furnishes me what I need. I am like a man who stumbles along; my foot strikes something, I bend over and it is exactly what I want." (Brenda Maddox, "Joyce, Nora and the Word Known to All Men," *New York Times Book Review*, May 15, 1988, p. 1.) While he was writing *Love in the Time of Cholera*, García Márquez relied on Saint Chance as well. To an interviewer he confessed that at the end of the day "when the sun started going down I would go out on the street to look for places where my characters would go, to talk to people and pick up language and atmosphere. So the next morning I would have fresh material I had brought from the streets." (*New York Times Book Review*, April 10, 1988, p. 48.) When you are deeply immersed in your story, chance can become a magnetic field that draws you to the very people and places you need to finish it. Whatever passes through that field – conversations, books, movies, letters, dreams – it all belongs to the story itself.

What Saint Chance sent me was a historic site, a mansion called Wilderstein, fifteen miles up the Hudson River from where I live. The ninety-seven-year-old woman who resided in it was born and raised there, the last surviving member of her clan. Like the merchant, her father had lost his money during a depression. Unlike the merchant, he did not lose his land. The moment I spied the house, dark, looming, with turrets and weather vanes rising over the surrounding trees, I said to myself, "What a perfect mansion for the beast!" There was a bronze dragon coiled around the newel post, which threw a sinuous shadow on the Tiffany windows over the landing. The andirons in the fireplace looked as if they might bark or howl at a stranger: they had the shape of gryphons with glass eyes that glowed when a fire was lit. There was gold damask wallpaper in the living room and a coat of arms in the dining room window. Soon I found myself calling this mansion the Beast's house.

When I sat down to write the scene in which Beauty enters the Beast's house, Miss Gatherer whispered, "This will be easy. Since the Beast's house is a real place, you have only to take notes on it and describe it." So

I did exactly as Miss Gatherer instructed me, and the writing went badly. The scene was cluttered, the language dull. What started by inspiring me ended by fettering me. And finally I understood what Miss Experience was trying to tell me all along: the Beast's house in the story was magic, and magic has nothing to do with real estate. The gift of the mysterious mansion was not a real gift until I let it go. For a writer, knowing what to save is tricky business. Ben had taught me that years before, when I met him in the beer hall in Heidelberg. Travel light. Trust your own imagination. It takes very little baggage to get where you're going.

At Ben's burial service, how little he took with him: his grandfather's prayer book, placed on his coffin by his mother, and a handful of pink tulips tossed into the grave by those of us who would remember him till our own stories were ended. *Ubi sunt?* We turned to go back to the cars. It was a sunny day, a windy day in February. Ben's mother said, "I saw three crows by my window last week. I think they were an omen." A friend of Ben's whom I did not know touched my arm and said, "Will you put all this into a story?"

His question came, I think, not from curiosity but from the hope that somebody could gather up the pieces of Ben's death and make something new. Something that will last.

Translating Translation:
Finding the Beginning

L inguists, by using electrodes on the vocal cords, have been able to demonstrate that English has tenser vowels than, for example, Spanish. The body itself speaks a language differently, so that moving from one language to another is more than translating words. It's getting the body ready as well. It's getting the heart ready along with the mind.

I've been intrigued by this information. It addresses the physicality of language in a way that perhaps surprises us. In this sense, we forget that words aren't simply what they mean – they are also physical acts.

I often talk about the duality of language using the metaphor of binoculars, how by using two lenses one might see something better, closer, with more detail. The apparatus, the binoculars, are of course physically clumsy – as is the learning of two languages, and all the signage and so on that this entails – they're clumsy, but once put to the eyes a new world in that moment opens up to us. And it's not a new world at all – it's the same world, but simply better seen, and therefore better understood.

When I was three or four, my parents bought a new house in what would later become a small suburb of Nogales, Arizona, on the border of Mexico, some four miles outside town. My father was born in Mexico, on the border of Guatemala, and my mother was born in England. I had languages.

As we kept driving out to watch the house being built, my mother got to make a number of choices regarding details, among which was the color of various rooms.

My mother, when asked what color she wanted the kitchen, said to the workers who were all Mexican, and who spoke very little English, *límon*. She said it both because she wanted the kitchen to be yellow and because she wanted to start learning Spanish. The workers nodded yes. But when we came back the next day, the kitchen was painted bright green, like a small jungle. Mexican *limones*, my mother found out, are small and green, that color exactly, no mistake.

So that's the color that wall stayed for the next eight years. She said it was a reminder to us all that there was a great deal to learn in the world. You might laugh at first, but after eight years you start to think about it.

And she was right. It was a perfect, small example of that other way to see things, and for eight years the kitchen for us was, perhaps in a very large way, an even better place than school.

Let me tell another story. Several years ago, a man, who only spoke Spanish, was arrested for illegally crossing the border from Mexico into the United States at Douglas, Arizona. He was put in a cell, but it was late in the day, the shift was changing, and the jailer forgot to tell the next shift that someone was back there. It's apparently a small jail, and nobody thought to look since no one heard anything. The man was left there from a Thursday to a Saturday, when a janitor found him.

But why didn't you say something, he was asked. Yet this very question underscores exactly the lack of understanding between the man and his jailers. The man, who was not a criminal, simply did what he was supposed to do. He had manners.

But manners don't always mean good manners.

We try to do what people want, but they have to know what they're asking for. That search for understanding is often itself a search for, and an act of, translation as well.

Several years ago I was doing an Artists in the Schools residency at the high school in Eloy, Arizona. Two memorable events occurred. The first was among a group of gifted students: a fire alarm rang, but nobody got up. We were having such a good time, nobody seemed willing to stop. One student said, "It's probably fake anyway. Couldn't we just send someone out to check?"

That was nice, but something else occurred on the same day, a Thursday. I was also working with a group of – what to call them, what were they called? Non-gifted students? In this class, there was an attentive group of four or five students in front, but in back and to the sides students were in various states of engagement, the most active of which was a poker game.

The students were Mexican and Chicano, mostly, migrant worker children, and those not being entirely attentive comprised mostly *cholos*. *Cholos* are what Pachucos used to be. The young men, in particular, have a uniform: chino pants, black belt, thick, black shoes, two T-shirts – a regular one over a thin-strapped one – and a hair net.

The hair net by itself is interesting, and to an outsider perhaps effeminate. But there were many reasons for a hair net. These boys' older brothers often worked, for example, in fast-food restaurants, and had to wear nets. And a net, it was a show of attitude – you took your net off when the important things happened. School was not that.

In working with these students, I was also faced with a substitute teacher, who had no ideas on how to control the class and who was very glad that I was the one standing up in front.

The week went its own way, with me talking and reading, the students in front responding, and the others playing cards and throwing pencils. But I know this classroom, and that was the thing. I also understood what happened next.

On this Thursday of the week, one of the boys in back got up, starting walking his walk to the front, ostensibly to sharpen a pencil, but he kind of hung around me at the desk. I was done for the day, and everyone was working, or supposed to be working, on a writing assignment.

"Hey, *ese*," he said to me, with a small pointing of the right hand.

"Hey," I said.

He nodded his head. "You really like this poetry shit," he asked.

"Yes," I said.

And then he followed with the very best thing I could have hoped for. "So, how many fights you had?"

In that moment I knew exactly what he was asking me. He was trying to understand, to make some bridge, to make some sense for himself. It was a moment I won't forget. Whatever I answered doesn't finally matter. He had already found some kind of answer in his question.

He was looking for an equation, for something to understand. And he said it in the best way he could.

Language is more than what we say – it's also how we say it, and whether or not we even understand what we are saying. Language is manners, then, well-said or not; language is the attempt to understand as much as the understanding itself. It is the how as much as the what, form as much as content, intent as much as words.

These are the lateral muscles and physical directions of language that translation often fails to use. I had to be able to hear what this young man was asking me, whether or not I was prepared. It was another vocabulary altogether, yet filled with familiar words.

But maybe that's all right. Maybe that's exactly what keeps a computer or a book from doing the job. Maybe that's what keeps us human, and engaged, and necessary.

How many fights have I had? he asked.

Just one, I said, like you.

Washing My Hands of the Ink

F ive years ago, while visiting us for Thanksgiving, my mother had a stroke. Though she had had a rare form of cancer for some time and had been receiving chemotherapy, I was somehow utterly un-prepared for seeing her lying unmoving and unspeaking on a hospital bed. She was not expected to recover. For six or seven days, then, I sat beside her, alternately crying, talking to her – really a form of talking to myself – reading, and – this still feels like a confession – writing the following poem in my head:

Duet for One Voice

1.
I sit at your side
watching the tides of consciousness
move in and out, watching
the nurses, their caps
like so many white gulls circling
the bed. The window
grows slowly dark,
and light again,
and dark. The clock
tells the same old stories.
Last week you said, now
you'll have to learn
to sew for yourself.
If the thread is boredom,
the needle is grief.
I sit here learning.

2.
In place of spring
I offer this branch
of forsythia
whose yellow blossoms
I have forced.
You force a smile
in thanks. Outside
it is still cold;
who knows how long
the cold will last?
But underground,
their banners still furled,
whole armies of flowers wait.

3.
I am waiting for you to die,
even as I try to coax you
back to life
with custards and soup
and colored pills I shake
from the bottle like dice,
though their magic
went out of the world
with my surgeon father,
the last magician.
I am waiting
for you to be again
what you always were,
for you to be there whole
for me to run to with this new grief –
your death – the hair grown back
on your skull the way it used to be,
your widow's peak the one sure landmark
on the map of my childhood,
those years when I believed
that medicine and love and being good
could save us all.

4.
We escape from our mothers
again and again, young
Houdinis, playing the usual matinees.
First comes escape down
the birth canal, our newly carved faces
leading the way like figureheads
on ancient slaveships,
our small hands rowing for life.
Later escape into silence, escape
behind slammed doors,
the flight into marriage.
I thought I was finally old enough
to sit with you, sharing a book.
But when I look up
from the page, you
have escaped from me.

(published in *A Fraction of Darkness*,
W. W. Norton & Company)

My mother unexpectedly recovered from her stroke, though never fully. She returned home, regained all of her speech and most of the movement she had lost on her left side.

Meanwhile, I couldn't decide what to do with my poem. Should I publish it in some small magazine where nobody in my family would be likely to see it? Could I include it in the new book I was about to put together? If anyone who didn't know us well happened to read the poem, he or she would probably think that my mother had died. Did that matter? I am prone to magical thinking and I think I feared that if my mother seemed to die in a poem, this could somehow make her die in real life. What was bothering me most of course was what my mother would think and feel if she read the poem, which she was sure to do if I published it in a book.

I wrote a poem called "Ethics" a number of years ago in which a high school class is asked to decide whether, in the case of a fire in a museum, one should save an old woman or a Rembrandt painting. The student I was, or pretended to be for the sake of the poem, impudently answered "why not let the woman decide herself?" Much less impudently and with many misgivings, I did just that. I told my mother that I had written a poem about her called "Duet for One Voice" when I thought she was dying, and that if she had any problems with it or with my publishing it, of course I wouldn't. My mother asked to see the poem, and I showed it to her. "That's lovely," she said, as she was wont to say of all my poems, good and bad and indifferent, "of course you must publish it." And so I did. In time my book came out, my mother phoned as she always phoned, to congratulate me on it. But there was something in her voice. . . .

"What's the matter?" I asked, "don't you like the book . . . ?" "Nothing's the matter, of course I like the book." And then she said, "But the poem you wrote about me made me feel terrible." "Mother," I protested, "you said you liked the poem." "No, not that poem, the other one, the one about my remission, about how I'm fooling myself if I think I'm OK." And for several minutes, I didn't have any idea of what she was talking about.

Here is the poem called "Remission," that was printed on the page immediately preceding "Duet for One Voice."

Remission

It seems you must grow
into your death slowly,
as if it were a pair of new shoes
waiting on the closet floor,
smelling of the animal
it came from, but still too big
too stiff for you to wear.
Meanwhile you dance barefoot
your shaky dance of pretence,
and we dance with you,
the pulses in our own wrists
ticking away.
In this small truce
the body waits,
having waged war on itself
for years. You say
the water tastes of flowers.
You steal on tiptoe
past the closet door.

(*A Fraction of Darkness*,
W. W. Norton & Company)

I had written that poem several years before about a friend in remission from cancer who had subsequently died, and so wedded was it in
my mind to that particular friend that it never occurred to me that my
mother, also in remission from cancer, might think it was about her.
Besides, it was really a poem about how all of us are dying.

What did this mean? I asked myself. Had I simply been careless?
Perhaps. Should I screen all my poems, worrying about who might be
hurt by what? Or was I too careful, worrying about "Duet for One Voice"
when clearly the effect of particular poems on particular people is often, if
not usually, unpredictable? And wasn't it all just fiction anyway?

My mother did die, just a few years later, and I wrote a whole series of
poems about her death. I wrote them compulsively, the way some people
eat compulsively or drink or gamble compulsively, and I still seem to be
writing them. I published a group of these poems in my book *The Imper-
fect Paradise*, under the heading "The Descent." And when I look through
that book and see them there together, I always feel uncomfortable, as if I
had no right to make poems, to try and make art, out of her death, my
grief. Though she's no longer around to be hurt, I still hear her talking to
me with that undefinable "something" in her voice, and I think about
Stephen Dunn's wonderful and ultimately redeeming poem "The Routine Things Around The House," which begins: "When mother died / I
thought: now I'll have a death poem. / That was unforgivable / yet I've
since forgiven myself / as sons are able to do / who've been loved by their
mothers." (And let me add here, in the matter of guilt, daughters are
usually different.)

Sometimes I replay in my head a radio interview I heard with a well-
known critic who was talking about a book he had just written about the
lives of his parents. His mother had died before he started the book and
his father had been very sick and in a nursing home. Before the manuscript was finished the father died too, and this is what that writer said to
the interviewer about the timing of his father's death: "It's macabre to
say so but there was a certain rightness to that. It enabled me to end the
book properly." Listening, I felt as if I had been delivered a body blow, and
clearly the writer too was shocked by his own words and immediately
started to backpedal, to modify them. I felt sorry for him. But somehow I
also felt implicated in the callousness of his statement, felt that all writers
somehow were so implicated (though of course, as I said at the beginning,
it is a critic I am talking about).

What are legitimate subjects for a writer anyway, and are her own
griefs or those of other people among them? "How did your grief / enter

my poem?" I once wrote in verse after a friend lost a child to leukemia. "Now it is an unwieldy package / between us – you balanced it better alone. / Your son's cells / close down / one by one, / like lights going out / in a small town / after dark. / Writing of it / I must wash and wash my hands / of the ink."

Nearly all writers use the material of their own lives in their work, but are there boundaries beyond which we should not go, and are those boundaries different for each of us?

The nonfiction writer Janet Malcolm, in her book *The Journalist and the Murderer*, includes this controversial statement: "Every journalist who is not too stupid or too full of himself to notice what is going on knows that what he does is morally indefensible. He is a kind of confidence man, preying on people's vanity, ignorance, or loneliness, gaining their trust and betraying them without remorse. . . . Journalists justify their treachery in various ways according to their temperaments. The more pompous talk about freedom of speech and 'the public's right to know'; the least talented talk about Art . . ."

This is a different, though related issue, and perhaps in my ignorance I feel as if it is a less complicated one. I think it is relatively easy, or at least a lot easier, to set up the parameters for honest portrayals of real people who are being interviewed for an article or a nonfiction book. But how about fiction?

George Kennan, in his memoirs, writes, "Personally, I would have liked to have been – I suppose more than anything I was – a novelist. But I could never muster the brutality to picture in fiction people whom I knew would be identified, who might recognize themselves."

Alfred Kazin once remarked that the world for Sylvia Plath existed only for her to write about, and I don't think he meant this as a compliment. Plath's most recent biographer, Ann Stevenson, a poet herself, attacks her subject for, among other things, writing the famous "Daddy" poem that Stevenson maintains was "factually" unfair to Otto Plath (who wasn't literally a Nazi) and, again, for writing "Medusa," which is the name of the jellyfish Aurela, Plath's mother's name, and which ends: "Off, off eely tentacle! There is nothing between us." (Let me add that I'm trying to look at all this dispassionately, as a writer, but as the mother of a writer that "eely tentacle" makes me nervous.) Stevenson sums up her feelings on the matter this way: "It is possible, of course, that in some strange way Sylvia couldn't imagine the targets of such poems as being harmed or hurt by them or that she thought the confessional mode commanded understanding on a different level from mere real life relationships, but if this was her view it was clearly mistaken: such poems have caused enormous pain to the innocent victims of her pen." Unfortunately, Plath isn't around to defend herself. John Updike, on the other hand, who is very much around, said on the TV program "Bookmark," when attacked for writing about real people, that a writer too worried about doing harm will be a less good, less eloquent writer.

I have always peopled my poems with characters named Stephen, Peter, and Rachel, names that happen to belong to my own children, and I have never worried about it very much. In one of my poems, "Marks," my poem husband gives me an incomplete for my ironing and a B-plus in bed, and when asked about this my real husband is apt to reply, in what he considers self-defense, that he doesn't believe in grade inflation. I've learned not to read that particular poem aloud at readings if he is in the audience. But poetry is made up, I tell myself, and my family usually takes my inventions with pretty good grace. Embarrassment is one thing, however, and real pain something else. There is clearly some kind of line that should not be crossed, but where that line is drawn has to be a very personal decision, one that will probably change over and over again, one that clearly I am still struggling to draw for myself. And writers do come to some peculiar rationalizations about all this. I heard the novelist Susannah Moore interviewed about her book *My Old Sweetheart* when it was about to be made into a movie. She said she had had no guilt about writing about deaths in her family in her novel, but to profit financially, as she would do with this movie, worried her. (Profiting financially, however, is one thing most poets do not have to worry about.)

I've thought a lot about what is or isn't permissible for me to put in my poems, and usually my reaction to being told by others what I should not do is to immediately do it. For instance, I once saw an ad in *Coda* in which the magazine *Response* asked for submissions of poems on Jewish subjects. The following stipulation was included, however, which I used as the epigraph to the poem I quickly sat down and wrote and named "Response."

"a ban on the following subject matter: the Holocaust, grandparents, Friday night candle lighting . . . Jerusalem at dusk."

It is not dusk
in Jerusalem
it is simply morning

and the grandparents have disappeared
into the Holocaust
taking their sabbath candles with them.

Light your poems, hurry.
Already the sun is leaning
towards the west
though the grandparents and candles
have long since burned down
to stubs.

(*PM/AM*, W. W. Norton & Company)

I rarely read "Response" at poetry readings because when I do the audience occasionally laughs at the beginning of the poem and then feels embarrassed about having done so when one of the subjects of the poem turns out to be the Holocaust. It feels wrong to even inadvertently embarrass an audience. And of course I too share that discomfort and more, for on some level I feel that I have no right to use the Holocaust as a subject when only my most distant relatives, people I knew only in photographs, died in it. I bring this up because the subject of the Holocaust is possibly the emblematic example of what I am struggling with here. When I feel compelled to write about it, because it is a subject that haunts me, I usually do so obliquely, as in my poem "Grudnow" when I speak of my grandfather's family as having died "of history."

Cynthia Ozick wrote a powerful story called *The Shawl*, which takes place in a concentration camp. After the story appeared in *The New Yorker*, she received an angry letter from a camp survivor pointing out that she had mistakenly portrayed the camp guards as wearing helmets. Ozick thought about changing that detail when it was time to put the story in a book, but chose not to. "The art was made," she said, "and I didn't want to unweave it. This is one of the reasons for my bad conscience. I have made art out of suffering, and that is a concept I hate. And I know that I couldn't have done otherwise."

And yet it obviously seems all right for those who actually were in the Holocaust to write about it. Does the fact that when Dan Pagis, for example, writes Holocaust poems, they are "true" make them more legitimate as poems because they really happened and to him? I'm not sure about the answer to this.

I have read several articles attacking Carolyn Forche's book *The Country Between Us* on the grounds that Carolyn was only briefly in El Salvador and didn't have the right to use that material as if it were her own. In fact Ira Sadoff, in a generally compelling essay in *The American Poetry Review*, calls her "a tourist to other people's suffering," though in this case he is complaining of a failure of her imagination rather than counting the days in her itinerary of Central America. I happen to disagree with Ira on this point. I think they are strong, legitimate poems, with both literary and political value. And yet I remember how disturbed I was when I read Yehuda Amichai's poem "Tourists," which begins:

> Visits of condolence is all we get from them.
> They squat at the Holocaust Memorial,
> They put on grave faces at the Wailing Wall
> And they laugh behind heavy curtains
> In their hotels.

Nobody wants to be such a tourist, even metaphorically. Yet perhaps it is something we must risk. For don't we need poetry to be our witness, our way of remembering what must not be forgotten? And don't we also need poetry to memorialize our losses as the whole range of elegies from earliest history has always done? How much of poetry is about loss! Yehuda Amichai, in his more usual, generous mode, this time at the Folger Shakespeare Library, told the story of an old woman on a train wailing "oy, oy, I'm so thirsty, I'm so thirsty . . ." A young man, trying to read, goes all the way through the train to the dining car and brings her back a drink of water, hoping to shut her up. And now she wails, "oy, oy I was so thirsty I was so thirsty . . ." This, said Amichai, is what poetry is all about. And he added: "I believe in the healing power of poetry for myself and then for my readers. . . . Every poem is a lullaby: 'The world is going to pieces, but sleep, child, sleep.' If nothing else the rhythm of the poem will lull you, no matter how painful the words." Then Amichai compared a poem to a vaccination, as if the wars he had gone through and written about could help others by giving them these wars in small, survivable doses, like cow vaccine. "The language of pain," he added, "is more exact than the language of well-being." Or as Samuel Johnson put it, "The only end of writing is to enable the readers better to enjoy life or better to endure it."

I want to talk, then, about poetry as consolation, consolation both for the reader and for the writer. On the simplest level is the recognition, when we read about the suffering of others, that we are not the only ones in pain. For a moment, at least, the loneliness of loss can be dispelled. Of the letters I get from readers, the largest number are about poems like "The Five Stages of Grief" or "The Death of a Parent" which, they tell me, helped them with their own grief.

Writing is also healing for the writer, and this is one of the things I am trying to get to, the reason that I, we, so compulsively write again and again of our griefs, as if we can rid ourselves of them, as if they will flow out of our fingers onto the page, through the intermediary of the pen or the keyboard, and we will be done with them, at least until the next poem. This is what Anne Sexton meant when she called the muse "that good nurse"; what the dancer Judith Jamison was talking about when she incorporated the still recent death of her mother into the choreography of her new dance, saying: "If there's anything tugging at your life, you use it."

In a conference on poetry therapy, the poet Myra Sklarew compared the healing work of poetry to dream work, and in an abstract of her paper described it this way: "Poetry as a means of sustaining psychological exploration, making complex structures in language while keeping open for examination issues of conflict, grief, etc. Poetry as an effort against closure." She uses as illustration Roland Flint's poem "Skin," which he wrote soon after the death of his young son, and which is ostensibly about the making of wine.

Skin

If the wood is good grain,
And the carpenter, the fit, the caulking,
The cask will be good
And if the grapes are good
The wood and the wine
Will improve each other,
In the dark long days of aging.

The separate tastes of earth
Will taste again and change again each other,
Until, like membrane, somehow

In and between the wood and wine
There will be no separation,
Wood from dark from wine.

When this goes on, anything can happen.
Go back, go back to mystery.
Now I am grateful to my small poem
For teaching me this again:
That my God is still the moment
Where the wood is no longer itself,
Where the wine is no longer, only, itself.

(*And Morning*, Dryad Press)

And here is what Myra Sklarew had to say about that poem: "In the poem 'Skin,' by Roland Flint . . . you will see what came into the hands of a workshop group many years ago. The author brought the poem to be reviewed by the group, written just following the death of his young son . . . hit by a car driven by an elderly man going slowly down a dead-end street one spring afternoon. The author of the poem had no idea the poem had anything to do with his son and his son's death. As we read the poem, I remember feeling the power of the grief contained in it, the power of the son on his journey into death and beyond. As long as these events were disguised from him. It is my contention that had the father been able to read correctly what it was he was actually writing about, he would not have been able to continue the exploration the poem was able to make – that somehow the meaning held in abeyance, permitted the psyche to travel along on its journey, asking questions, following the child through his days and nights in the earth. And the father, through the course of this poem, makes a kind of benediction finally, blessing even the process by which his son is returned to the earth, sanctifying this gradual return, blessing transformation itself, the eucharistic offering brought to bear. I use this example to say the following: It is my sense that the making of a poem is an act against closure, against psychological closure. That in the course of making the poem, judgement, interpretation, even the satisfying act of integration are held off . . . Often, it is not until years later, when a current work will suddenly provide sufficient illumination to reveal the earlier meaning . . . So this beautiful powerful poem of Roland Flint's through which he was able to work toward a resolution and acceptance of his small son's death." As Andrei Sinyavsky writes in *A Voice from the Chorus*, "The hardiest of all man's creations, art, turns even death, its enemy, into an ally."

In one of his last essays Terrence Des Pres wrote: "At times like these, perhaps because there's nothing else, poetry becomes the one thing needful. Or maybe it's because in moments that seem ultimate, nothing else is good enough, shared enough, of a precision equal to our joy or suffering. What's wanted to celebrate a marriage or a birth, what we ask to get us through pain, what we need by the side of the grave isn't solemn claims nor silence either, but rather the simple saying of right words . . . 'As essential as bread' is what Milosz says, and I think yes, the gain in strength and nourishment is real."

All of this I believe. And yet every time I write another poem about my mother's death I know a small discomfort will tug at me, and in this discomfort I also believe.

Lying for the Sake of Making Poems

I once knew a husband and wife, both aspiring poets. He had a young son from a prior marriage whose face was badly scarred. One evening, the stepmother showed me a poem in which she described her husband's first wife cutting the child in a drunken rage. Horrified, I asked, "Did that really happen?" and she answered, "No, it was an innocent accident. I just thought my version would make a better poem."

How could somebody write something like that, I wondered, just to "make a better poem?" The child's natural mother was libeled, and who knows what damage might be done to the child to have this distorted version of history on the record? Did we really *need* that poem, that lie? Has it become acceptable for a poet to exploit the misfortune of another in this way, and by so doing quite possibly gather something for herself, some credit for taking on the difficulties of bringing up a "damaged" child?

I've changed the details to protect the identity of these people because I don't believe this poet intended any malice toward the natural mother, nor was she looking for sympathy for herself. She simply hadn't thought through all the implications. She was young, just starting out as a writer, and, most important, from her reading of contemporary poets she'd gotten the idea it was acceptable to fabricate something to make a better poem.

Perhaps I am hopelessly old-fashioned. Perhaps I should accept the possibility that what the poet says happened really didn't happen at all, but I'm going to have to make a painful adjustment in the way I read poetry and honor poets. I grew up believing a lyric poet was a person who wrote down his or her observations, taken from life. I have always trusted the "I" of Walt Whitman as he dresses the wounds of fallen soldiers; I trust Mary Oliver to tell me what birds she saw as she walked through a marsh; I trust Stanley Kunitz when he describes two snakes entwined in a tree. When "I" says something happened, I believe it happened, and if something awful has happened to "I," I feel for the poet.

There are, of course, conventional poems that use the "I" in a very general manner: "I love you because . . ." In those poems, the "I" customarily suppresses specific autobiographical detail and defers to the subject, love in this instance. Shakespeare's first-person sonnets would fall into this category. And there are those poems that clearly are flights of fancy, as in "I leap the mountain in a single stride." I leave such poems out of this examination.

Nor do I include "persona" poems that are identified as fabrications by their context. The poet Ai comes to mind. When her persona poems are set side by side in one of her books, it is evident that these "I" speakers cannot be the poet, for no one writer could have had the wide variety of experience the poems present. But when her poems appear one by one in magazines, the distinction may not be so clear. I would feel more comfortable with persona poems if each poem would in some way advise me that the experience presented may not be the poet's own.

I am most concerned about poems in which "autobiographical" information is presented in such a way as to affect the reader's feelings *about the poet*. In such poems, the speaker, calling himself or herself "I" (and without forewarning the reader in any way), builds a poem around what *appears* to be autobiographical information, but that is untrue. A childless man writes with great skill and tenderness about a schoolyard experience with his small son, engendering sympathy in the audience. Another poet writes with touching sadness about the suicide of a brother, and we pity her until we chance to learn from some other source that she has no brother. Hundreds of readers may be moved by these fabrications, moved to pity the poet, moved to praise his or her courage and candor.

Poets defending this kind of poem sometimes take the position that they are writing "dramatic" poems, thus sidestepping the ethical questions. Just the same, I prefer that the poet prepare me. If a poem is framed in such a way as to inform its reader at its onset that the situation presented is a fictional dramatic monologue, that seems to me to be honest and forthright. If a poet named Melissa writes a poem entitled, "Rebecca Speaks to the Elders," we know this to be a "persona" or "dramatic" poem. We'd all agree the bishop in "The Bishop Orders his Tomb at St. Praxed's" cannot be confused with Robert Browning. Or if a poem is contained in quotation marks, we know that someone other than the poet is speaking. There are all kinds of ways to prepare a reader for a dramatic poem, and I think poets are obliged to do so.

I was recently asked to review a collection of poems, some of which were good examples of the kind of deception I am concerned about. I know a good deal about this particular poet's life, and I knew that the "autobiographical" information was fabricated. When I expressed my concerns about this issue to an acquaintance she said, "I don't have a problem with that. I've written a poem in which I talk about my disabled son, and I've never had a disabled son." She continued, "People sometimes come up to me and say that they are sorry for me, and I have to tell them that I made it all up." She went on to say that, curiously, those readers seem taken aback. Clearly, those readers have been cheated and deceived, and they have a right to be taken aback.

Weldon Kees seems to have been tinkering with this issue more than fifty years ago. His short poem, "To My Daughter," begins by speaking of "my daughter" and continues to do so, convincingly, until the last two lines, in which he confesses that he has no daughter after all, and doesn't want one either. For most of the poem, Kees' imagination tries on the idea of having a daughter. Then he rejects the idea because of all the possible heartache that might come of it. We believe him all the way through, then he pulls the rug out from under us. But since he makes his confession within the poem, we do not feel deceived.

Why are some of our poets recreating their lives? Can it be that they are merely trying to make their material more exciting? Is the country so in need of new "confessional" poems that it is necessary to construct them around events that never happened? Is this phenomenon caused by the "publish or perish" pressure on writers who are affiliated with universities, or is it indicative of some bigger ethical or moral problem?

The poet and critic Jonathan Holden has said, in a letter, ". . . much of the problem stems from the general blurring of genres in this postmodern ambience, such that the distinction between History and Fiction is no longer as clear cut as we had thought (hoped) it was." No doubt that's true. But though poets may have bought into postmodern theory, have their *readers* been prepared for this?

Since we know there are ways of writing about fictional situations – the dramatic poem, for example – the fact that some poets are not identifying their work as "dramatic" suggests that in fact they are up to no good. I credit my friend, the poet Bob King, with coming up with a pretty good test as to where the line should be drawn: does the poet get some extraliterary credit or sympathy from the lie? If the answer is no, the invented detail, the lie, is not bad.

All lyric poets, of course, alter details to some degree. On the other hand, I once knew a poet who carried fealty to the truth to an extreme. He wrote a poem about a cleaning woman he and his wife had once employed and for whom they had suffered painful indignities. When he showed it to me in manuscript he'd included a line: "The cans of pop I bought her." I said, "If you'd change that 'cans' to 'bottles,' you'd have a more interesting sound to that line," and he said, "But I can't do that; they were *cans*."

It seems acceptable to me to change a pop can to a pop bottle, but I would have felt deceived if I'd learned the poet had fabricated the story of his family's suffering at the hands of this woman. It is despicable to exploit the trust a reader has in the truth of lyric poetry in order to gather undeserved sympathy to one's self. Why do we permit this kind of behavior in poetry when we would shrink from it in any other social situation?

Where the West Begins

I n the winter of 1926, just before New Year's, a Studebaker touring car, with nine passengers and a northerly side of side curtains, left Kansas City for Los Angeles. Three weeks later I was wondering if we would ever get to Albuquerque. What with one thing or another, usually cars, over the next fifty years I continued to wonder if I would ever get to Albuquerque – but here I am.

Cars – beginning with that Studebaker – have played an extravagant role in my life and fiction. Many years ago, crossing the Texas panhandle on my way to Mexico, I was startled to see, low on the horizon, a hole in the sky through which I saw into daylight, like a window in space. Through it I saw clouds passing, huge figures grappling. Nor did anything weaken or diminish this impression. Some miles and minutes later I was able to clarify that the window in space was the giant screen of a drive-in movie, displaying the mountains and sky of the cineramic western landscape. Not then, but after considerable brooding, I realized that I had seen through the hole into the mythic world where the west begins, the great good place of our now diminishing expectations.

Periodically, or so I imagine, the members of the Western Literature Association have to pause and reflect as to what it is that constitutes a *western* writer. Is it a place on the map, or in the book? Is the writer born to it, or does he adopt it? That man of Concord, Henry David Thoreau, touched on the complexity of this matter, when he remarked how, on going for a walk, he usually found himself pointing toward the west. Something in his nature seemed drawn to it. He responded like the needle of a compass. This is surely an American predilection, and received official recognition and sanction in Horace Greeley's slogan, "Go west, young man, go west!" In the early stages of our culture this impulse may have distinguished between the seafarers and the landlubbers.

The west began at the top of the next westerly ridge, and then proceeded by a series of receding frontiers that skillfully commingled advancement and flight. The historian gives his attention to advancement, but the energies released in flight are often the most dramatic. In the pioneer's soul some confusion may persist in the matter of polarities. When we "take off for somewhere," when we "bolt" with someone, are we fleeing or progressing? It often proves to be a point of Proustian refinement. Thoreau anticipated this dilemma when he withdrew from Concord to Walden. Was that one small or giant step forward, or one of many crablike movements sideward or backward? When Neil Armstrong said, "One small step for a man, one giant leap for mankind," the direction in which it was taken remains a debatable point.

As the frontier moved westward the concept of the west began its series of transformations. Midwest, Southwest, Northwest, Far West, and that pillar of cloud on the horizon that indicates an outpost known as the Wild West. Terms that were once explicitly geographic slowly dissolve into metaphors. My remarks on this large subject are those of a fiction writer, not a scholar. I know neither where the west begins, or it ends, but I consider myself a western writer through the nature and pursuit of my expectations, periodically recycled as part of their restoration.

In my own boyhood on the plains, or so I have the impression, the west experienced one of its many mutations. The town of Central City, in Nebraska's Platte Valley, had originally been called Lone Tree – a reasonably accurate description – but as the trees were planted and the town thrived, it was felt, and rightly, that a Lone Tree was no way to attract settlers of the female sex. This original tree, a giant cottonwood, marked that point along the California trail where the Overland stage, and the Pony Express, made one of their stops. No mention of tree, stage or horse penetrated the atoll of my boyhood. Less than twenty years ago, on another westward passage, I learned of all this on the occasion of the County Centennial Celebration. Who am I to argue with what is sworn to in a book?

In 1917, a year the end of the world was locally predicted, twelve Union Pacific railroad trains stopped in Central City daily, providing old and young with an abundance of drama. I lived just north of the tracks, where the earth trembled with each eastbound, downgrade freight train, and I was never free of the admonition that each time I crossed the tracks one of them would surely hit me. The handsome railroad station, with four Doric columns that are now preserved in the city park, had been erected with a larger town in mind. The station agent at the time was my father, a man who wore sateen dusters to protect his shirtsleeves, but who knew of nothing that would protect his lips from the purple stain of his indelible pencils, and the bitter tang of his kiss. I was not encouraged to bother him at his work, but from a block down the tracks, in the dusk of evening, I could see the luminous green of his eye visor like that of the semaphore down the tracks from the station. The tracks themselves dissolved to a shimmering blur in both directions, but in the early morning, if I looked to the west, I could see the sun reflected on the roof of the grain elevator in Chapman. That was an exact ten miles: a unit of measure I still prefer to the metric system.

The first summer I was old enough to roller skate, a short stretch of concrete paving was put into the street just behind the railroad station. What shift in continental gravity dictated that when this strip of paving lengthened it would leave town headed east, not west? I reflected this same shift of allegiance in my preference, on the station's platform, for the wide diner windows of eastbound trains when they stopped for water. It may be hard to recall that the ultimate in elegance was once to dine on a train. From the platform I observed the white-jacketed porter pour water into gleaming glasses. I caught glimpses of strange faces. I did not seem to care where these travelers were from: what captivated me was where they were going. On the wall map in the station lobby I had seen the railroad lines converge on Chicago. I did not see, or care, where they went beyond it. My feelings were those of Windy MacPherson's son, Sam, who had recently shipped east out of Caxton, Iowa, the lure of the big town having replaced the attraction of the wide open spaces. A clue to this metamorphosis can be found on the covers of the Sears & Roebuck, or the Montgomery Ward, mail-order catalogues. In my mind's eye I see one that is ideal for my purpose, encouraging me to fill in the missing details. A steamer is drawn up to a pier where cranes unload huge cartons on to waiting trucks and freight cars: one half of a drawbridge rises on a polluted sky through which I dimly see the towers of Zenith: clouds of smoke, of many colors, clot the sky as if the city is burning, but I deeply inhale these fumes as the pure oxygen of longing. Smoke and steel, Sandburg's city of merchants and hog butchers, had displaced the sod buster as the emblem of the future.

A further mutation, enjoying its first nationwide premier, was the emergence of the wild west as a Hollywood production we describe as *The Western*. Many trails crossed at the turn of the century, but the mingling of history, geography, and that new novelty, the moving picture, would result in changes more revolutionary than the invention of the pistol. Tom Mix, William S. Hart, Hoot Gibson, Harry Carey, among others, restored to common experience the mythic figure of the man on horse-back who appears to be part of the macho male's unconscious longing.

I quote from *The Western,* by George Fenin & William Everson:

On August 29th, 1900, a few minutes after 8 P.M., train no. 3 of the Union Pacific Railroad Co., after having passed the station at Tipton, Wyoming, began to slow down as it approached Table Rock. Four men emerged from the darkness, forced the conductor to uncouple the passenger cars while the express and mail cars were pulled a mile distant and subsequently robbed. The thieves were some of the wild bunch boys: Butch Cassidy, Deaf Charlie Hanks, Bill Carver and Harvey Logan . . . to which we might recently add the Sundance Kid.

Just three years later Edwin S. Porter filmed *The Great Train Robbery,* and with the glorification of the western outlaw, the west began its meta-morphosis from a place to a state of mind. What is the current state of that mind? Great Western Savings, of California, recently released a news bulletin. The "Great Tradition" of John Wayne's TV commercials, for Great Western Savings, will not, like so much, pass into nothingness, but be continued – for a suitable fee – by John Huston, Glenn Ford, Maureen O'Hara, and others.

The difficulties we now encounter, in all phases of our lives, to make sensible, verifiable distinctions between fictions, facts, and commercials, may prove to be insurmountable. Increasingly, on the mind's grid, the ineluctable modality of the TV commercial – the window through which we look more than any other – may prove to be the more ponderable, the more indelible, reality.

In 1918, my father's horizons expanding, he rode to Omaha on his rail-road pass, but returned in a gas buggy he had left the train to buy in Columbus, then driven the forty miles to Central City in second gear rather than risk the complications of shifting. I see that car, the lights flickering, panting and vibrating in the yard at the side of the house, where my father sat gripping the wheel as he waited for me to come and look at it. The woman who cared for me, sensibly, would not allow me out of the house.

I also remember my astonishment, more than thirty years later, of learning that my father and mother, on their honeymoon, had gone to San Francisco on his railroad pass, from where he had wired his bank for another $50. Very briefly, that is, the call of romance had taken prece-dence over the call of commerce.

My window in space, at the end of the first World War, opened to the east. We go to Omaha, then to Chicago, where we live within sight of the trees in Lincoln Park, but I often meet my father, who once more works for the railroad, in the big lobby of the station on La Salle street. There we would sit on the hardwood benches watching the throngs of people who were going places. The litany of the train callers filled the great hall. I was subject to the spell cast by these place names since I had long studied them on the sides of freight cars. Chicago, Burlington & Quincy; Atchison, Topeka & Santa Fe; Baltimore & Ohio; Chicago & Northwestern; the Missouri Pacific; the Great Northern, etc.

Attentive to this chanting, the travelers milling about us, we often lifted our eyes to the mural-size posters advertising the far places we might go to. The Garden of the Gods in Colorado; the Grand Canyon in Arizona; New Mexico, the Land of Enchantment; but the one to cap them all, for me, was the view of the island of Catalina, just off the coast of California, owned by the chewing gum king, William Wrigley. On Catalina the Chicago Cubs did their spring training, while people like ourselves, who could only chew gum, sailed about in glass bottomed boats gazing at schools of exotic fish and mermaids. Of all this grandeur, until I came to Chicago, I had heard nothing. Two long and bitter winters in Chicago had greatly enhanced my interest.

On Sunday mornings, the only time we spent together, my father would tell me of the many ways Chicago had failed his expectations. They were not large, but they frequently led him to the Want Ad section of the *Chicago Tribune*. It was there that he stumbled on flight as form of advancement and adventure. The ad went something like this

Motoring to California. Will share expenses with two, three people. Warm, southern route all the way.

In this way the window that opens into space accommodates the changing needs of the viewer – in the Platte Valley of Nebraska it had opened on the east, in Chicago it had moved around to face the west. A song with the refrain *California Here I Come!* was in the air. In my father's opinion too many travelers were sharing expenses out of Chicago, so we went to Kansas City where the warm southern route all the way to California really began. A bit of research indicated that nine people could be seated in a seven passenger Big Six Studebaker touring. We left Kansas City a few days before New Year's, one of the passengers being a one-legged actor on his way to the Passion Play in Los Angeles. I often wonder if he made it. Several weeks later the Studebaker was abandoned in the outskirts of Albuquerque, and my father and I continued the journey in the side car of a motorcycle. The return trip to Chicago, less than six weeks later – the land of milk and honey also having failed my father's expectations – will provide the scenario for *My Uncle Dudley,* my first novel, written in Los Angeles in 1941, where the window of my room near Echo Park opened out on the open road of the past.

I have sketched in this incident to suggest the way the windows occur in my own house of fiction: events insert them, but time will pass before I get around to looking through them. The house itself appears to sit in open country, with unbroken views in all directions. One novel is explicit in this matter –

Come to the window. The one at the rear of the Lone Tree Hotel. The view is to the west. There is no obstruction but the sky. . . .

At a child's level in the pane there is a flaw that is round, like an eye in the glass. An eye to the eye, a scud seems to blow on a sea of grass. Waves of plain seem to roll up, then break like a surf. Is it a flaw in the eye, or in the window, that transforms a dry place into a wet one? Above it towers a sky, like the sky at sea, a wind blows like the wind at sea, and like the sea it has no shade, there is no place to hide. One thing it is that the sea is not: it is dry, not wet.

Now windows, as women have known for centuries, make ideal view framers. These lines from *Ceremony in Lone Tree* frame the windows that I seem to find the most congenial. Just recently, in *The Fork River Space Project,* the author speaks of a hole in space through which a piece of the highway, a filling station, and sections of a roadside motel apparently disappeared. Can we describe that as a new twist on the flaw in the glass through which dry places appeared to be wet ones?

The narrator goes on to ask, why is it that some places accommodate so easily to bizarre perspectives? Mammoth creatures once grazed the plains, and tiny dog-sized horses, as well as saber-toothed tigers, crouched on the rim rock. Red men speared their fish, white men set their traps, horse thieves, scoundrels, and buffalo hunters looked up the ravines and gullies to the sanctuaries of their imaginations. On the veined lids of our eyes the whirling globe gathers into its vortex assorted flying objects, not all of them identified. On seeing planet earth rise on the chaste moon's horizon, the author is still subject to seizures of longing for how things once were in Fork River. *Really* were, that is. Assuming, of course, there was such a place.

Is the confrontation that is now a public wrangle over the question of land use and its conservation a sign of the apprehension many Americans feel at the loss of our repositories of longing, those sanctuaries where we salt down our dreams?

The experience of writing fiction – a way of redeeming time – is one way the writer opens windows in the time in which he is captive. Let me give you an example.

As late as 1943 I was trying to assemble the disparate and unrelated parts of my own past. I knew little or nothing about my own people. My father's eyes had been set on the future; my mother had died at my birth. Shortly afterward, her father had gathered up his family of girls and moved to a Seventh Day Adventist colony in Idaho, out of my life. On these windows essential to my house of fiction, one opening to the east, one to the west, the blinds were drawn.

In 1943, driving from New York to California, I stopped in Chapman, Nebraska, at the barber shop of Eddie Cahow. My mother had been born on the bluffs south of the Platte. My father had been an apprentice station agent in Chapman. They had first met, so Cahow told me, in his barber shop. According to his story, my father had leaped from the barber chair to help my mother down from a buggy. It made a good story, and who was I to contradict it? What Cahow told me, and what I was able to guess, opened holes in the sky over Chapman and windows in the mirror where we exchanged glances. In Chapman I had found a place on the map, to which mail might be delivered, with windows that opened in the necessary directions. The views agreed with the blueprints for which I had been wired.

That following winter, in California, I wrote a novel with the title *The Man Who Was There*, the man himself predictably missing. In this novel I made the first effort to assemble the raw materials necessary to a start on my house of fiction. The far west, the midwest, even a vision of the new west, are interleaved with snapshots of the Wiener Wald, near Vienna, and a boat trip on the Danube to Buda-Pest. In an unguarded moment, having written very little, I admitted that everything I had written had the stamp of an object made on the plains.

I should have added that once it was made, it often turned up somewhere else.

Being somewhere else has resulted in a strange medley of fiction, *Man and Boy*, followed by *The Deep Sleep*, are concerned with life – we might say of all places – on the Main Line in suburban Philadelphia. Seasons in Mexico resulted, in due time, in the bullring setting of *The Field of Vision*, and *Love Among the Cannibals* in Acapulco. A stay in Venice led to *What a Way to Go,* and return to Schloss Ranna, in Austria's Wachau, resulted in *Cause for Wonder.*

On the evidence, which accumulates, my fiction derives from the need I feel to relate my private, imaginary preoccupations, with the actual world in which I am living. Let me give you an example.

Ceremony in Lone Tree had its origins in the Starkweather murders in Nebraska, a prime-time news event in the mid-fifties. This crime made a profound and disturbing impression on two Nebraskans who were living at that moment in suburban Philadelphia, myself and my friend Loren Eiseley. We pondered and discussed this incident over a long summer and into the fall. Since I had been dealing with Nebraskans in *The Field Of Vision,* and all my dealings result in unfinished business, I felt the need to accommodate these new facts to the world of my fiction. In this manner, and no other, I made my own accommodation with the crime.

A similar, but more explicit accommodation, occurred in the writing of the novel *One Day,* that day being the Friday in November John Kennedy was shot in Dallas. This had occurred at the moment I was well into a new novel. When I was able to return to it, five days later, I could not recover my previous involvement with the fiction. Brooding on this impasse it occurred to me that the event itself – rather than ignored – should be incorporated into the novel, just as I was obliged to incorporate it into my life. I no longer have the faintest notion what I had in mind for the original fiction. It became the novel where the shots fired in Dallas caused the earth to tremble in Escondido, California.

In May of 1965, on a visit to Oberlin, Ohio, my wife and I arrived the morning following a series of disastrous tornados. For several days we lived with tornado warnings. This will prove to be the seedbed of the novel, *In Orbit,* published two years later. I believe this indicates the way the windows in my house of fiction adapt themselves to my life in the world.

In January, of the coming year, Harper & Row will publish *Plains Song for Female Voices,* which some of you will acknowledge sounds like another Morris novel. We all have hopes it sounds like one a lot of people will want to read.

To return to my first question – where does the west begin, and who is a western writer – my feeling is he is one, wherever he is, whose fictive windows open on wide spaces. The west is the window on those chronic inclinations that congeal into longings, and the longings into expectations. Great expectations – in their flux and reflux, their alluvial deposits and their tidal shiftings – have got us to wherever we now are west of the first Missouri crossings.

If we once more put our eyes to that flaw in the pane, the one that is round like an eye in the glass, waves of plain may appear to roll up and break like a surf. The tall corn may flower or burn in the wind, but the west is still a metaphysical landscape where the bumper crop is the one we harvest through a hole in space.

Fred Astaire's Hands

C lear days. Memory of weather. We're driving aimlessly west on 104, along The Ridge – a shelf of land about twenty miles deep that runs for over two hundred miles along the southern shore of Lake Ontario. The land here is flat, so flat that sky meets field with a slap. Illinois. Or Kansas. On either side, apple orchards tell us it is upstate New York. All summer we've watched: blossom, white headdress, nubbin, pale green moon. It takes a lifetime of learning to distinguish darkest fruit from darker leaves. The eye adjusts and suddenly there they are: brilliant, burnished red.

But now the fields are going to gold. Turning south on an unmarked road, we drive past fields of spent corn. Some farmers will cut their fields, leaving sharp stubble to poke through early snow. We'll hear geese, their wintry chatter. Others will let their fields stand as stalks turn paper-thin and dry to the color of parchment. If we kept going, we would cross into Livingston County where much of the country's onions are grown. Black dirt sucking in the light. Farther south, potatoes. But here, on the first Sunday in October, cabbage smothers the ground with that particular gray-green color – dusk-color of muted silk – that you can only refer to, when you see it somewhere else, as the color of cabbage.

These landscapes are not beautiful, exactly. They withdraw into themselves, sealed in silence like old men who know more than they will tell you. Even the prosperous farms sprawl across the land with a cluster of ugly sheds and rusted equipment. Raw umber. When you learn to love a land like this, you don't want to be fickle. You take your time, season after season, driving the back roads, letting them tug you forward into the mystery of where people settle.

Or they tug you back to the Southern Tier where you grew up in hills that stretched forever, into Pennsylvania and beyond, Appalachia beginning in your back yard. That's how far you've come: ninety miles north, to where the land is flat and boring. It took you years to do it – years and two foreign countries and several states – but now you're home. You know you're home because the sumac and milkweed pods and burdock feel so familiar you could walk out into the brush and climb back into the car picking off the sticktites of your childhood.

And when does the "you" – the person who inhabited that childhood – become the "I" of the present, the one who sits, now, in the passenger seat? Here she is, as the fields drift by. Here she is: here I am. But I am passive compared to the child who lifted and touched, who fingered the milkweed and let it fly. I open the window to let the cool air remind me of the day, the hour, the season we've entered, the one that's yet to come.

Suddenly we're bombarded by signs for tax-free cigarettes. Kools. Lucky Strikes. And a diner – at least it looks like a diner – called Sah-Da-Ko-Nee's. Of course we have to stop. Of course we have to discover where we are.

Where we are is the Tonawanda Indian Reservation, one of several small areas of land across upstate New York set aside for what is left of the Iroquois. Inside the diner (which the menu tells us translates to "The Eatin' Place"), the specials are listed in red crayon on a bulletin board. Tomato soup and grilled cheese sandwich for $1.95. Who could resist?

Who eats here? Look around. One man, dressed in a gray suit, green shirt, and bright purple bow tie, moves from table to table, talking to those he knows like any good politician. Another wears jeans, saddle shoes, army cap. A woman in her sixties with dyed red hair wears a Buffalo Bills sweatshirt over her white dress. Who are they in the rest of their lives? What do they think of us?

We are served by a woman with short curly hair. A permanent. Has to be. In fact, all the other waitresses have short hair too, though the men behind the counter (and those who come through the door marked "ciga-rettes") all have long hair in ponytails. The food is vintage 1955. Camp-bell's soup. Hot cheese. My grandmother's sturdy black shoes. Her apron. Stan's lunch is more interesting, at least on the menu – "Indian Taco, with Fry Bread." It comes, heated in a microwave. Even the lettuce and tomatoes are steaming.

Outside, there are three black-haired children, each carrying a leash, trying to let three puppies out of their pen. The dogs push open the door and spew into the road in a yipping tumble of fur, children swirling after them. I catch one puppy, holding him until one of the children can hook a leash to the collar. Their mother stands on the porch above us. She does not say thank you. She does not smile.

Cattaraugus. Tuscarora. Tonawanda. On the map, these three reservations ring the city of Buffalo in space clearly delineated, set apart. On the ground, they are in the middle of nowhere. There is no distinction between here, on the outside, and there, where Sah-Da-Ko-Nee's seems to be the center of life. All I know is that one Sunday afternoon I am back in Painted Post and my grandmother Mayme has fixed a lunch of soup and sandwiches. Forty years have disappeared, swallowed by a landscape that never seems to change, for all the WalMarts and Kentucky Fried Chickens and aluminum siding and satellite dishes.

But everything has changed. Time proves that. Long ago my father fought the Army Corps of Engineers when they decided to move the Cohocton River, and then, years later, in 1972, the river reared up to prove him right. It plunged over the new highway built in its former bed and right down the main street, six feet of water in the old house on Hamilton – a house that had survived since 1804. It survived again, but not intact. They ripped out the built-in bookshelves, the dining room cupboards. There were the same blue goblets – on a new wide windowsill – sun streaming through, painting the carpet as though nothing had happened at all.

Funny, that landscape – yellow house, treed yard, hovering hills – is only external, at best a memory stilled to photograph. What lives inside, stirs and wells up in the least expected moments, is a field of poppies. English Yorkshire farmland with its dark stone walls, its green-glass fields, sky a fury of cloud. And the poppies flickering in the field. A moment of pure peace, contained, as in a bowl, though the only person in sight was myself. A loneliness so complete it felt like living more than one life.

Sometimes landscape settles inside you and makes room for nothing else. Each emotion is weighed against that inner scene to determine how it fits, whether or not it has a rightful place. Whole ranges of possibility have been discarded in the face of one flaming field.

Now it's early summer. Black caps ripen in our backyard. I pick them in memory of my father, his careful garden. They're large and unruly, falling into the fingers without resistance but leaving a stain like a bruise. The day is brimming. Heat shimmers up from the sidewalks and nothing moves. Memory itself is a stagnant pool, a pockmarked surface.

Easy to warp and ruin the built-in bookshelves. Harder to wash away the sound of my father's axe on a weekend afternoon. Chunk. Pause. Chunk. The growing stack of wood. His god was science – dispassionate science. He was the only person I have known whose daily vocabulary included the words *premise* and *proof*. I'm still learning how to say *was* instead of *is*. It's not yet a month since he died and he still comes to me in dreams as a voice on the phone. Sheer sound. A voice split and stacked against the cold.

The State Anatomy Board would like to express its sincerest condolences to the family and friends of Robert B. Randels and acknowledge our appreciation of the donation for the advancement of medical education and research study in Maryland. The gift of his body provides a legacy for the improved health of generations yet to come. On behalf of the Board and those medical programs, I would like to express our deepest gratitude.

He wasn't alone. The world will remember Jacqueline Kennedy Onassis. Sir Stephen Spender. Jonas Salk. Mickey Mantle. Ginger Rogers. Ginger Rogers – her fluid body, flinging itself out into a life of its own, then drawing back again, following Astaire's lead. I've read that Fred Astaire was embarrassed by his hands, his too-long fingers. Who ever looked at his hands? All we remember is the feet, the perfect synchronicity of his polished shoes, a blurred landscape of metallic motion like a hummingbird at the feeder. Who ever noticed his hands, the two middle fingers pressed down into his palm so that only the other two pointed upwards, jaunty and optimistic, objectified and oddly self-conscious in the stilled shot where the dance stops in mid-air?

I am left with the singular first person, poised on the brink of knowing something about myself. "Hi there," he says, his voice brightening over the thin wire that holds us up. But it fades into voicescape, a sea of sounds, scarves I'm trying to buy for Christmas, a lost house suddenly sprouted in the middle of the night, darker than dream spun out of control. I know the dreams will fade, the voice will lose the clear, familiar tone. Inside, poppies will stir in a breeze I've almost forgotten, spring to wiry life in blood-red fists.

I suppose we all have something we think others will notice. Something we press into the palm of secrecy. But no one ever does. No one sees the baseboards the hostess scrubbed with a toothbrush. No one looks for the crooked tooth. What worries me is the other side of that thought. What is it we think no one sees that is evident to everyone but ourselves? I touch each bitten fingernail, listen to each grumpy note of frustration. Too obvious. Maybe it's the rough sole of the bare feet I tried too late to scrub each time I went into labor. The rough sole gone deep until it is a part of personality.

In my father's eye there is a river. It bends and twists for thirteen miles until, as the crow flies, it comes to a spot only four miles from his home. In the winter, he and his friends can hitch a ride on the runner of a sleigh for those four miles, hop off, put on their skates in late afternoon light and then head back, hugging the curves of the bank on ice that glints ahead of them. I look back for whatever it was he worried about, whatever he wanted to hide. But the road to his death seems so straight, so plainly marked. He signs his Living Will on recycled paper. He leaves us three thousand empty Styrofoam cups. He laughs out loud when his medical student first pulls back the sheet. "Mine has a red beard," he hears him shout.

How do you push past the imagined *fact* of your father's death? So many times he relished the moment in prospect that it seems necessary to let him relish it in reality. But in reality he will not know his medical student, will be nothing but whatever the body is without its fire. So you put it on the page, where it can live indefinitely. Something my father didn't understand.

My son William recounts an argument with his grandfather that lasted the length and duration of a 1,000-mile trip – about the meaning of the phrase "metaphorical truth." My father could not comprehend a truth that did not contain the words *theorem, therefore, by extension* – the gods of logic. How would he have internalized the latest scientific vocabulary, the way physicists now postulate without expectation of final results? There are other ways of knowing. Ways the word or image drills through the surface to unfurl beneath the skin.

Look at what Plath did with what I think of as my poppies. "Little poppies, little hell flames, / Do you do no harm?" "I put my hands among the flames. Nothing burns." "If my mouth could marry a hurt like that!" July again on the page, but July tinged with the mad desire for the colorlessness of death. July brought to life in pain. Lucky I saw the poppies before I saw the poem. It would have changed them forever.

And even Plath could see the shifting nature of metaphor, the way it is true one minute and not the next. A truth to counteract dispassionate curiosity. By October she was calling them a "love gift." "Oh my God, what am I / That these late mouths should cry open / In a forest of frost, in a dawn of cornflowers."

Does she open herself to the landscape? Does she open her landscape to us? Where does the truth reside? Sometimes I think metaphor is the magic of electricity, flick of the switch. Sometimes it's osmosis, slow seepage, transaction. July to October: day lily to marigold. Orange, tinged with copper. Rust. The flames are burning elsewhere, in a field in Yorkshire – a field most likely now a tract. Row houses, fenced yards, roses. Central heating. Mod cons.

It all gets lost in time. Or time gets lost when there's no way to share it. The other day, in the line for ice cream at Friendly's, a boy who said he'd seen the fireworks "yesterday – a long time ago." How long has it been since time was so fluid, so filled with *space?* The banks of the Cohocton grew wide as the water shrank to a shallow stream. Tadpoles. Slippery, moss-covered rocks. Stepping stones. Whole hours filled with the slow passage of water. Dragonfly wings. The way they sometimes catch the light, skittering iridescence over the convex surface. The sun dragging its heels over the sky, hot on your shoulders. Your hair wispy in the breeze. Your feet tough. How did you finally pull yourself back from the earth, retrieve your bicycle and pedal home? When did the leaves form their arch overhead, the street a canopy of shade? And where is your mother's voice, calling you in, past the potted geraniums and the yew, up the gray steps, through the heavy front door?

Nostalgia could make of anything the perfect moment, and those moments were only the fabric of the days, ordinary and incomplete. Metaphor completes the process. Perfection was saved for the screen where Hollywood told us what we wanted from our lives. Provided the perfect, carbon-copy metaphor. Not that you ever felt you could dance that way – the two of them in perfect pitch, as though their minds were in tune, not as though they had practiced and practiced, behind the scenes, off screen, day after day, to reach for this illusion. They did not so much personify desire as create it.

No, you never thought you were the dancer, but knew the dance could stand for something else. For what you feel when you watch the dance. Fred Astaire looks down at his hands and they repel him. They betray his inner sense of self, reveal him as gawky and adolescent. He puts one behind his back, or tips his hat, anything to keep people from looking at his imperfection. He presses the middle two fingers into his palm to divert the eye and make a visual deception. All he is conscious of is his hands; his feet do what they've been trained to do since childhood. His feet – they are so much a part of his interior that he never thinks to think of them. It's only his hands that flicker, tentative as dragonflies, extended between himself and the world he's always wanted.

MIROSLAV HOLUB
TRANSLATED FROM THE CZECH BY
DANA HÁBOVÁ AND DAVID YOUNG

Otters, Beavers and Me

When I was sojourning in Tucson, Arizona, I was an absolutely happy sojourner. I don't know why it is, but the stony desert, the heat, and the saguaro cacti – which compared to our homely cacti are like dinosaurs compared to somewhat dispirited green lizards – appeared to me to be a pleasant place to sojourn, even appeared to be a home, although nature-wise I come rather from the Sumava mountain forests. For me, the Mojave Desert is something like a tonic, giving a feeling of good arrangement and anchorage, despite the fact that the Indians whom you meet on the desert roads, driving their station wagons straight at you, remind you rather strongly that without the assistance of indigenous deities residing on the peaks of Santa Rita, you can take your good feelings and stuff them.

My feelings, however, were affected by Lewis Thomas, who was in Tucson before me, and who announced in his book, *The Medusa and the Snail*, that for a few minutes, in this place, he lost his sense of being a scientific and habitual reductionist and delighted in directly observing the beavers and otters kept in the Tucson zoo. Naturally, thanks to the car of a friend who undoubtedly had buddies on the Santa Rita peaks, I hurried to the location given by Thomas; it is in fact called The Desert Museum, but is nevertheless also a zoo.

A deep path cuts through the grounds, and from it beavers can be seen on the right and otters on the left, depending on your direction, first from above, on the bank of a narrow water tank, and then in a tunnel behind a glass wall, from below, hence underwater, and then once more from above. Beavers on the right, otters on the left, or vice versa. Lewis Thomas observed: "Within just a few feet from your face, on either side, beavers and otters are at play, underwater and on the surface, swimming toward your face and then away, more filled with life than any creatures I have ever seen before, in all my days."

Having seen them, Lewis Thomas gains an insight about himself: ". . . I am coded, somehow, for otters and beavers. I exhibit instinctive behavior in their presence, when they are displayed close at hand behind glass, simultaneously below water and at the surface. I have receptors for this display. Beavers and otters possess a 'releaser' for me, in the terminology of ethology, and the releasing was my experience. What was released? Behavior . . . standing, swiveling flabbergasted, feeling exultation and a rush of friendship . . .″

With Thomas's words at heart, I approached the passage between the otters and the beavers, brimming with the same sense of expectation I might have if a beautiful girl were to emerge from a pool and sit down at my table, or come out of the bathroom, in a white dressing gown if possible.

Alas, I am not Lewis Thomas.

On the left, on a sandy bank, three otters were lying around, obviously bored by the desert museum, the water, the sand, Tucson, the visitors, the fish, and life itself. After a long time, an otter got up, in the manner of a shop assistant who isn't being paid for working overtime, and slipped into the water. But it did not swim toward my face; on the contrary, it disappeared behind a stump and later wiggled back to its original place, where it slumped down with a manifest skepticism about an otter future that contained nothing but tree stumps.

There were no beavers on the right, just one, a very obese beaver, lying hidden from sunshine in the tunnel but out of the water, on concrete, and it was shivering, with its paws turned up. If it did release something in me, it was the memory of a room in the psychiatric ward in Kateřinky, where, according to a plaque on the wall, Smetana died, and where deeply depressed patients got electric shock treatments.

Later, talking to experts, I asked why an obese beaver would lie on a concrete platform on its back and shiver; it turned out, however, that zoologists know a lot about beavers but very little about shivering, physiologists know a lot about shivering but next to nothing about beavers, and pathologists refuse to have anything to do with anything that can't be embedded in paraffin.

Following the footsteps of Lewis Thomas, I did not learn whether I was coded for beavers and otters, and learned nothing about my distinctive behavior. If I accept his metaphor, then I am fatally related to otters and beavers which are fatigued by the sight of water that is too small to live in and too large to die in.

Ruminating In Tucson the following night, after seeing the film *The Unbearable Lightness of Being* in those "stereotyped, unalterable patterns of response, ready to be released" with which we are stamped, as Thomas says, I came to the conclusion that my patterns were Czech. Through them I readily accept the fact that creatures seen as full of life by an American are apt to be seen as fatally lost when faced by us Czechs, even when we are in an otherwise quite atypical state of bearable lightness of being. It is not just our habit of cyclic heaviness, which probably in itself brings on more cyclic heaviness and which might be infectious and contagious to rodents, even through glass. But maybe Czechs have receptors for creatures in distress, and perhaps some chemical signals for distress imperceptibly guide our steps through zoos, desert museums, and possibly through life. Thus it is that, unmistakably, we come upon otters and beavers at the moment when their pavilion is conspicuously reminiscent of the state of the Central European pavilion.

While both types of pavilion share a profound similarity, there is not much choice in either of them.

In both of them the process of self-realization, the fulfillment of existence by essence, as Mr. Sartre would put it, is rather more limited than it appears to be to people outside the pavilion. In pavilions there is a little less freedom, fewer facts, and a little more communicable suffering. It is not so much that hell is others, but rather that the bars and glass are, for a small nation, both essential and existential. If anything, we are condemned not to freedom but to a pavilion, without which we might not survive anyway. Neither we, nor the beavers and otters in the Mojave or Sonora deserts.

And in particularly inspired moments we can have freedom furnished, or even organized, but always with the sense of restriction somewhere at the bottom of our minds.

The visitor from a different world can feel at moments that both kinds of pavilion are full of life and elegant, marvelous movement, just behind the glass, on land and underwater, corresponding to the visitor's receptors for play, creativity, and lightness. He can feel that they make him lose habitual reductionism and facilitate direct observation.

Maybe sometimes we offer just such good sights as the otters and beavers in Tucson did when Lewis Thomas came to see them.

I think he should, as soon as possible, try to come to Prague. And to Bratislava, of course.

Excerpts from *The Low Road*

LEGACY
1953 – New Jersey

My brother Larry and I sleep with Mommy in our parents' bedroom. I love the friendly telephone and the sweet dark scent of old mahogany bureaus. We never speak about periodic bloodstains on the big sheet. After all, we are used to Grandma's daily bandages, dark with pus as well as blood.

When Daddy is gone and the house is quiet, one of us snuggles up on each of Mommy's sides. In the morning, later than most mothers, she fumbles into the kitchen to make toast. Larry and I stay in bed and play house under the top white sheet.

Once or twice we talk about Mommy's death. We always know it is coming. We know she will leave us.

So we squabble, as siblings often do – over the inheritance. Who will get her arm bones? Who will get the legs?

VIEW FROM THE ESCALATOR
1954 – New York

Just the two of us (and a dozen silent strangers) speeding into the gleamy city. In companionable silence, we sit together on the old Bergen County Transit bus to Manhattan. Along snowy streets. Over the George Washington Bridge. Our bridge.

As the bus ducks beneath the black-gray web of wires, I think how much I hate this ugly part. (Later "sinister" is the word I use about these innards, these urban life support systems.)

When we finally enter the big Port Authority Terminal, this different world is full of possibility, safer, darker, taller, faster, my kind of place. Mom and I hold hands along 42nd Street to Fifth Avenue. There, on our favorite street, each revolving door opens to a bright foreign galaxy.

Together we hunt, careful not to lose one another. Always careful. Our family is continually losing parts of itself. I know this before I understand which parts have dropped off, which have sloughed away, which have evaporated. I see the danger if not the remedy. But here in New York, all we have to do is keep an eye on each other. This kind of getting lost is a real fear, easier than the anxieties at home.

Store basements are the most fun: dim, hot, smelly, crowded with people in unbuttoned overcoats who are pushing, pulling, shoving, buying. Mom has warned me to be careful. Some of them are not our kind. Not so honest. Not so clean. You can't tell them by sight, she says, you just have to stay alert. Indeed I have inherited her radar. Heroically we persist, finding a shirt for Larry, socks for Daddy, and clutching our booty as we ride the escalator up to the ground level.

Never take the elevator because you might miss something: a new style, a lady spraying perfume samples, a sale, clearance, discount, closeout, special. It is in a department store that I first grasp the concept of synonym.

First floor. Second floor. Pajamas, I remember, are on the fourth floor. Then, maybe we can go up one more flight to look at the dolls. After Christmas each year, I bring my gift money and buy a new doll from the sale rack. During the fall, I like to drop by for a visit, to inspect the newcomers. In a way, to welcome them.

Suddenly we see Stuart Erwin, the TV star. We notice him riding down to the second floor as we are riding up to the third. I spot him. Them. Stuart and June Erwin, TV and real life husband and wife. Stuart and June, she agrees. Oh, how I wish I had said something.

"Go ahead. Go on back down," she nudges me.

But what would I say? I watch him standing there in front of the men's shoes. June beside him, helping, nodding like on the show. I've always envied their TV daughter Jackie.

"Go ahead," she says. "Tell them you like the show."

"Really?"

"Really."

"Come with me."

No, she shakes her head and lightly touches my shoulder wings. "You go ahead, by yourself."

Alone, I think. Then, heart racing, I ride the escalator down from sportswear to men's shoes. Looking back, I find her watching. Carefully.

Here they are. Headed to a different department when I say in an embarrassingly childish voice, "Are you Stuart and June Erwin?"

They could flee. They could ignore me.

Instead, each of them takes one of my hands and smiles.

Jackie, I wonder, has something happened to her, do these safe people need a new daughter?

"Nice to meet you, Valerie," he is saying.

I come to my senses. Say something else.

They are both smiling, glad I like their show. Even thank me for thanking them.

They wave, walking slowly into socks and belts and I watch until they disappear. Then I ride the escalator triumphantly filled with a story for my mother.

Childs Restaurant is her favorite. Today, we get a booth.

She orders pancakes for lunch. With butter and maple syrup. A little too rich, but I would never say so. This meal is a treat, an extravagance that will be savored for weeks. It's not every day you meet a TV star.

Cold air on our faces afterward, we hold hands as the crowds gather around us at the corner. This is one of my favorite parts of New York life, the way people walk from east to west in huge gangs. Together, with the human train, Mom and I travel across the streets, her hand tightly gripping mine.

The first passengers on the homebound bus, we claim the next-to-the-last seat, which is higher than the others and better for viewing.

Our packages around us, she says, "This is a good kind of tired."

I nod contentedly.

The dark outside is spotted with yellow lights, tiny golden sapphires. Silent now, we watch together for signals from a thousand lives we will never know.

'NEATH THE PALE YELLOW MOON
1956 – New York and New Jersey

We are driving home in the dark from cousin Ginny's. I am thinking about poor, plain cousin Jane, who never married. My brothers are fighting in the back seat. I feel cold in the front, seated between my parents. Dad's at the wheel, smelling of that last Scotch.

He swerves and Mom grabs my arm.

Dad winks at her, in safe control of the wheel, of his family.

"Let's sing," she says, gently releasing her grip.

He groans good-naturedly.

"She wheeled a wheel barrow / through streets wide and narrow. . . ."

He joins us. "She was a fishmonger / And small was the wonder / Her mother and father were fishmongers too."

He quickly tires, stops singing, stares at the road ahead.

She turns to "A roamin' in the gloamin' / On the bonny banks o'Clyde. . . ."

I am puzzled about fishmongers and gloamins, but this is not the time to ask. She's just got started.

Now the car is warming up. My father lights a cigarette, spicing the whiskey smell. We are a family, I tell myself, safe from the cold, singing our way home. Together.

" 'Abdul a Bull Bull,' Mommy, sing that one," I plead.

My brothers, still tussling in the back seat, couldn't care less.

Again, I have no idea who Abdul a Bull Bull is, but I love his name and I understand my friends' families don't sing these songs. I know this is something special from my mother.

"The sons of the prophet are brave men and bold / And quite unaccustomed to fear / – But the bravest of these in the ranks of the Shah / Was Abdul Abulbul Amir."

Daddy laughs at her squeaky voice. I am frightened she will fall silent.

Instead, she joins him, laughing. "My father scoffed too." She likes to talk about her father. He was a wonderful man.

"Vile Infidel, know, you have trod on the toe / Of Abdul Abulbul Amir."

He is laughing louder.

Mom pauses. "Father would look at me and say, 'Mae, your voice! How is it earthly possible?' "

She is laughing, singing again.

My brothers have grown quiet.

We all listen to the final verse.

"They fought all that night 'neath the pale yellow moon / The din, it was heard from afar, / And huge multitudes came, so great was the fame, / Of Abdul and Ivan Skavar."

Too soon, Daddy pulls into the garage and we are home.

RITUAL MEALS
1977, 1989 – California

Mom and I are eating lunch in my cute new Berkeley apartment. Finally, things between us feel almost balanced. We are developing a friendship. I am mature enough now to admire my mother. She is beginning to understand me, or at least beginning to relinquish some expectations. Shopping, of course, is a major bond. I visit her in San Francisco where we scout out sales at the big stores; she takes the bus to Berkeley to hunt with me through the quirky boutiques. Today we have been talking about our jobs, her customers at the Yum Yum Room and my students at U.C. Berkeley.

The perfect setting for a good talk: sun pouring through the big living room window, comfortable chairs. Heaped in a basket on the table are French rolls, her favorite bread. I have prepared Salade Nicoise, something simple, healthy, elegant. For dessert, I've bought chocolate truffles.

"You seem a little nervous," she says.

"Oh, no," I answer, spearing a piece of tomato and putting it in my mouth. But I am nervous, because this is the day I have planned, with excruciating care, to tell Mom about Pat, my lover, to tell her I am a lesbian. I want an honest relationship, a solid friendship with this wonderfully brave and witty and vulnerable mother. Months have gone into the planning of this lunch: the salad, the rolls, the truffles, the gentle conversation.

I breathe deeply, reminding myself that I have done everything right, for once. Finally, at age thirty, I am living back home. I am publishing stories and essays, working on a novel. She still urges me every three or four months to consider a more secure job at the Telephone Company. She holds up successful Cousin Billy as a model. But she likes the idea of her daughter teaching university, even if only as a lecturer.

"It really is a lovely apartment," she says, looking around, happily, from her perch on the chair, "and so convenient to the buses."

"Yes," I smile. I am renting my own apartment, after years of what were to her morally dubious housing collectives. This year I have had my ears pierced, learned to drive, and even bought a secondhand car. I should know that for her this is enough. She doesn't need any more news.

She picks around the funny little olives, but is enjoying the rest of her salad.

I take another breath, look out the window for courage. We need to talk about this.

"That was lovely," she says, filling the silence, putting down her fork.

Serving tea in the flowery china cups I have bought second – or sixth – hand at the Leeds Market and Covent Garden Market in my adventurous youth, I begin tactfully. "I have something to tell you."

She sips the tea.

"I want us to be friends, to share our lives. But well, this is something that might upset you."

"Then don't tell me," she suggests, shrugging her small, sturdy shoulders.

But I have spent all week preparing, shopping, cleaning, practicing my disclosure, getting advice from friends. I have spent all my life preparing. I hate her denial, can't see it as just a different approach to truth.

"Where are we shopping this afternoon?" she asks.

I roll my eyes at her deflection, feeling both guilty and angry. I don't yet understand that one difference between us is that while Mom negotiates difficulties, I believe in conquering them.

Suddenly the chocolate truffles feel like a stupid, gross idea.

I sit back on the couch, inherited from Mom's recently dead friend, Mrs. Decoto. Honesty, I remind myself, is the only passage to trust. Then I reveal yet another thing she does not want to hear about my life. When I come out to her, do you know what she says?

My mother, cashier at the Yum Yum Room, looks at the ceiling and says, "There are more things in Heaven and Earth, Horatio, than are dreamt of in your philosophy."

Then Mom puts her head back against the chair and asks, "Is it my fault? Is this because of something I did wrong when you were growing up?"

1989

We're having a drink at the Claremont. One of her favorite things to do on a Saturday night is to take BART from her stop in San Francisco to my stop in Oakland, go out to a cocktail lounge overlooking The City, her city, have a meal at Norman's (taking half of it home in a doggie bag) and watch *Golden Girls* and *Empty Nest* on TV before going to sleep in my spare bed.

I like this view of San Francisco Bay from the Claremont Bar. I love watching the sun set over the ocean and witnessing my mother loosening up over a margarita. I don't like the smoke or the executives visiting from Los Angeles. Or the jars of tasty, fattening pretzels-seaweed-nuts marinated in soy sauce. We both enjoy the broad-hipped, no nonsense waitresses and like to think that Martha and Monique and Molly – are they hired for their names? – remember us, although it's such a busy place, they probably don't.

On this hectic, crowded night, I curse myself for not planning better. We're too late for our usual window table. I'm not sure which of us is more disappointed, but Mother will never show it, will never indicate directly that I have failed. *Mom*, she prefers me to call her Mom and I try to remember.

Here in the middle of the bar, we can look past the two thin young men sipping Heinekens, out to the butterscotch ball dipping slowly, irrevocably, toward the Pacific. What is it like for her to watch the sun set over an ocean she could only imagine as a Scottish child? I was shocked to learn that she never saw the Atlantic Ocean either, never knew waves larger than those of the Firth of Forth, until she was already on the ship from Glasgow. She had read about waves, of course, she thought she had read about everything.

Now I want to ask if she finds this confusing, distressing, magical, the idea of day dropping into Asia. But she will look disturbed or impatient at yet another oddball query. Lately she has given me to understand there isn't time for silly questions. She's not interested in "theorizing," prefers to spend her time remembering our life: family Christmases; the delinquent dog, Friskie; fabulous sales at Magnarama. Or recalling fragments of *her* life – those first thirty-seven years before I was born.

Abruptly, the sun disappears, leaving a yellow haze over the water, just below the slate sky. Off to the south, a jet streaks its white trail of possibility, contradicting the day's surrender. I imagine myself on that plane now, heading away.

"Days like this remind me of Peggy," she muses.

"Who?" I ask.

"Peggy," she repeats impatiently.

"Who's Peggy?"

"My sister," she answers, sipping the margarita pensively. Then a strange expression crosses her face, a new look that has come to Mother in her late seventies, a face of shame and relief that another secret has slipped from the war chest.

"Who is she?" I am alarmed, excited. "Whose side of the family – your mother's or your father's?"

"Peggy, my sister," she is annoyed with me, with herself, with the whole unwieldy experience of family. Making herself even smaller, she pulls in her elbows tightly. "No *side*. She was born between Colin and me."

As she explains, I wonder if it is impertinent to believe these stories are mine as well? How can it be that I am forty-two years old and have never heard about my aunt, who is not even a half-aunt like Bella and Chrissie, but an aunt who was born of both my grandparents, who lived in the same apartment with Mom for ten years?

"You never mentioned her. Ever."

Mom pauses to fish for a cashew from the jar of marinated goodies. "Oh, you've just forgotten. Remember the family who wanted to adopt me?"

"Yes."

"Well, Peggy went instead," she says matter-of-factly.

I watch this small woman picking the cuticle on the side of her corrugated thumbnail and I wonder how many other secrets she has. When she dies, will I discover answers in the bureau drawer, or carefully slipped into that cardboard box between old bills and Christmas cards? Whom has she been protecting with this silence? Perhaps for years, she did manage to forget her sister Peggy, her closest sibling. Mom's secret-making has shaped and fortified her optimistic keep-on-keeping-on-with-the-world view. She has constructed a story of the cosmos as intricate as Milton's theology, a universe in which she is both innocent and sinner, a life in which what you don't remember can't hurt you.

"But, well, did you stay in touch?" I finally ask.

"No," she stares at the last yellow shimmering. "I never saw her again."

A familiar, awe-filled sadness silences me.

She barely knew her mother; her father would "always be with her," and her sister has just disappeared for sixty-eight years. Mother is losing a grip on her imagined life. The characters are beginning to seep back. So much for the power of fiction. The family history is deep in her body.

"Enough of that," she wipes her hands on the small magenta paper napkin. "I'm getting hungry. And I don't want to fill up on these silly nuts."

I am tempted to explore this new opening, press another margarita on her, but I can tell she will admit no more questions.

"Dinner, madame?"

She looks out at the dimming sky, then smiles coquettishly, takes my arm.

No time for reminiscing. I leave a big tip for Martha.

And we hurry out the door, because Mom is right, we don't have much time left. We might miss our reservation.

DAVID HAWARD BAIN

Camden Bound

Figure One:
'Bird's Eye View of Camden, N.J. In the Centennial Year 1876,"
Thaddeus Fowler (Fowler & Bailey, 1876), Camden County Historical
Society.

*You're hovering in the air a mile above the Delaware River and looking
down across the eastern bank – at least in your mind's eye you are, sitting
actually on terra firma at a drafting table with your stack of notes and
photographs and old street maps and waiting pencils and pens and a fresh
pot of ink – and as you look down on the river from a gull's prospect, a
ferryboat closes in on its slip at the Camden & Philadelphia Ferry Company,
just as another emerges from the adjacent West Jersey Ferry Company, its
pilot with his eyes on the goldleaf roof of Independence Hall and then
perhaps at the skyspeck overhead that is your imagination. A sidewheeler
chugs upriver with a three-masted schooner in its wake. Many vessels
crowd the river, but other movement on land catches your eye: across the
city grid of red brick rowhouses and the occasional matchbox relic, of nine
church steeples and numerous mercantiles, a Camden & Atlantic Railroad
engine pulls its tender and four passenger cars past the newly-constructed
Cooper Hospital, tooting its whistle at a passing dinky of the West Jersey
Railroad. Smoke rises in a southerly breeze from the engines, and from the
tall stacks of the Camden Woolen Mill, the Camden Brass Works, the
Camden Tool and Tube Works, from the Anderson & Campbell Canning
Factory, the Wood & Haslane Cotton Manufacturing and Bleaching Factory, the United States Fertilizer and Chemical Company, the Jos. D. Reed
Hide and Tallow Works, the Doughton, Son & Co. Lumber Yard, Door, Sash,
and Box Factory, and all the others, the smoke trailing into the sky as the
effluvia pours into the Delaware and into the Cooper's Creek. Up from the
C & P Ferry Dock you let us go, up Federal Street to Third and then right,
across Taylor, Bridge, and Mickle to Stevens Street, and with our most*

fulsome thanks, Thaddeus Fowler, you deposit us on the doorstep of a red-brick rowhouse, 431 Stevens Street.

It is the home of George Washington Whitman, inspector at the nearby Camden Tool and Tube Works, but it is in George's brother, who has boarded with George and his wife Louisa for nearly three years, that we are interested. Let's say for a moment that it's January 26th, 1876, morningtime, and a boy has just flung a copy of today's *West Jersey Press* against the jamb of #431, and a large, blue-eyed, gray-bearded man is now stiffly leaning out the doorway and retrieving the newspaper. He seems older than fifty-six, his true age, due to one serious paralytic stroke suffered in Washington three years ago and a subsequent milder episode some eleven months before the present. But he is somewhat on the mend. He finds the article he's seeking; it's about himself, entitled "Walt Whitman's Actual American Position." It's unsigned. "Whitman's poems in their public reception have fallen stillborn in this country," it says. "They have been met, and are met today, with the determined denial, disgust and scorn of orthodox American authors, publishers and editors, and, in a pecuniary and worldly sense, have certainly wrecked the life of their author." And further down: "Whitman has grown gray in battle. Little or no impression, (at least ostensibly,) seems to have been made. Still he stands alone." And further: " 'Old, poor, and paralyzed,' he has, for a twelvemonth past been occupying himself by preparing, largely with his own handiwork, here in Camden, a small edition of his complete works in two volumes, which he himself now sells, partly 'to keep the wolf from the door' in old age – and partly to give before he dies, as absolute expression as may be to his ideas." The words please the Good Gray Poet – as much for their sentiment as for their fidelity to the uncredited author's original draft, with which Whitman is familiar because he himself wrote it. Later that morning he will walk over to the West Jersey Press building and purchase an armful of issues that he will send out to supporters around the world with suggestions that they see to the article's reprinting in newspapers and magazines. This will be done. It will touch off a great controversy on both shores of the Atlantic. Inflating the myth of neglect and abject poverty, it will aid the Centennial publication of *Leaves of Grass*. It will rachet the Good Gray Poet upward in the literary scheme of things. It will be good.

Pen and inkwell are still busy. Two short blocks away, the Pennsylvania Railroad tracks run up Bridge Street, the thrum of the cars coming up through his soles as he sits in his abysmally littered bedroom up on the third floor, and he scratches out "To a Locomotive in Winter" – "Thee in the driving storm even as now, the snow, the winter-day declining, / Thee in thy panoply, thy measur'd dual throbbing and thy beat convulsive," he scrawls. The "steadily careering" engine is "Type of the modern – emblem of motion and power – pulse of the continent." And, he will continue, "For once come serve the Muse and merge in verse, even as here I see thee, / With storm and buffeting gusts of wind and falling snow." Smoothly, as if negotiating a track switch, the leviathan merges too with the poet: "Fierce-throated beauty!" he effuses. "Roll through my chant with all thy lawless music, thy swinging lamps at night, / Thy madly-whistled laughter, echoing, rumbling like an earthquake, rousing all, / Law of thyself complete, thine own track firmly holding" . . . . He holds to his own track and the echoes of his lawless music, his madly-whistled laughter, float rousingly past us. The *New York Tribune* will publish it in a few weeks.

Out on the streets of the city as winter finally begins to give way, there is ample inspiration and reason to look ahead – especially to the spring, when the Centennial Exposition will open up across the river in Philadelphia. The fathers of Camden hope for much, with all traffic from the north passing through its streets, alighting from trains at its wharfside. "The shapes arise," Whitman wrote twenty years before (the Brooklyn of his brawny heyday finding its simulacrum now in the Camden of his decline), "shapes of factories, arsenals, foundries, markets, / Shapes of the two-threaded tracks of railroads." Mechanics are swarming over the new Centennial terminal at the Pennsylvania's railhead. Buildings – hotels, stores, factories – rise from vacant lots. And up Stevens Street a few blocks, workmen – carpenters, joiners, lathemen, plasterers, plumbers, and finishmen – are smoothing out the insides of Cooper Hospital toward its opening. No stranger to medical environments, believing, in fact, that his toils over the war wounded and dying in the Washington military hospitals had planted "the seeds of the disease that now cripples him," as he has written in the anonymous article, Whitman will mark the hospital's progress with great interest.

Figure Two:
Newborn's Footprints, The Cooper Hospital, Camden, N.J., 23 February 1949.
He weighs less than an almanac – four pounds two ounces – and he hardly makes a sound as you hold him and press his tiny inky feet against a

white sheet of paper and then gently lay him down to wash him, swaddle him, and then place him in an incubator, and perhaps it all seems a little hopeless, him being born prematurely at six months, and it may seem likely that his big toe – is it even a quarter-inch long? – will have a tag wired around it before long, but you wipe off your hands, adjust your uniform, look at him scrawny and red and unfinished as you lower the lid of the incubator, and you write next to the drying impression of his little right foot, "2/23/49 – Male babe Bain – Born @ 9:05 P.M.," and you turn to the more promising infants in the ward.

They had just moved East from Kansas City – promotions within the Radio Corporation of America often came with a change of venue, and for him this was a good one, from a circuit of tending radio station clients across the Midwest between Chicago and Kansas City to more time behind a managerial desk in the home office, within a few hours' drive of an ocean she'd never seen. Rosemary Haward (of Kansas City) and David Bain (born in Wilmington, North Carolina, and raised in Jacksonville, Florida) had been married just six months and were lodging now at the Benjamin Franklin Hotel in Philadelphia while the apartment complex they'd found in Haddonfield, New Jersey, was being finished. Through January and February, 1949, while Dave worked in Camden, Rosemary – who was pregnant now – walked around Philadelphia shopping for furniture and household items in the big department stores. On weekends there were parties out in the Jersey suburbs, RCA parties; for them the corporation was truly an extended family where employees worked and then relaxed together. Dave, with his salesman's jokes, his Jolson imitations, his stories about the prewar days in five-watt radio stations across the South, had no trouble fitting in, nor did Rosemary – who, at twenty-eight, upon her marriage, had left her professional career in a Kansas City radio station, WHB, where she had written shows and "continuity" and hosted her own celebrity interview slot. Xavier Cugat, Sigmund Romberg, you name it. If the RCA wives' lot seemed a trifle tame to her, with the men disappearing after dinner and the women chattering about home and children as they tidied up, then there were at least the glittering, laugh-filled moments of poker and charades (at both of which she excelled), martini glasses clinking and cigarette smoke spreading, when the groups reunited.

Perhaps it was all the walking in high heels through Wanamaker's and Best's and Macy's. Perhaps it was the Camels, the occasional beer or martini – *how little people knew then! we say with the smugness of hindsight.* Perhaps it was that they were still very much newlyweds, enjoying each other athletically in their suite at the Ben Franklin. But nevertheless, on Sunday, February 20th, they were present at a television party (*was it Milton Berle's fault? Ed Sullivan's?*) in the home of Dana and Eunice Pratt, in Earlton, New Jersey, everyone transfixed in the gray glow of the still-rare tube set. Dana was Dave's boss, a lifer at RCA. Suddenly, Rosemary felt an embarrassing wetness and took Eunice aside and to Eunice, an experienced mother, it sounded like leaking amniotic fluid. She called her obstetrician – Rosemary had not yet consulted one in the East. Ordered immediately into bed, Rosemary stayed overnight at the Pratts'. (*She stayed in the cowboy-pennant-and-boy scout-decorated room of the Pratts' ten-year-old, Larry, who, forty-seven years after his displacement onto the living room couch, would achieve some notoriety even in Gingrich Republican circles for his enthusiasm for militant racist and nativist causes.*) In Larry's room Sunday night, Monday, Monday night, Tuesday, with Eunice keeping her prone and staying in touch with her doctor, Rosemary finally began to feel contractions – strong ones, although she had no way of comparing – on Tuesday. And so she took her first and only ambulance ride from Earlton to Camden. And the baby was born on Wednesday. After the drugs wore off (it seemed routine to sedate her during childbirth), in a haze of pain, confusion, and naïveté, she wrote to her mother in Kansas City on a scrap of paper: *they brought him into my room and it was hard to look at him, he was so little and weak and red – surely it can't last.* Touch and Go. At that moment she could not bring herself to refer to me by name.

For most of my life my birthplace, the city of Camden, has been a point of irony, worth a wince and often a hasty explanation that though I was *born* in Camden, we didn't actually ever *live* in Camden, but in a succession of pleasant South Jersey suburban towns – Haddonfield, Collingswood, and finally splitlevel Westmont (during my father's second tour of duty at the home office, after an interregnum in Washington DC), a place out near the Cooper's Creek, new enough that suburban streets with signs and hydrants ran improbably through the unpopulated forest behind our house (developers could not keep up), and the summer air always smelled of newly-cut pine boards and was filled with the sounds of new shingles being pounded onto virgin roofs. The few miles between the Camden city limits and Westmont (or even Collingswood, for that matter, just over the Camden line) was the width of a continent, with industrial Camden, home office Camden, workingclass Camden, *slum* Camden being – well, as wags had been saying in Philadelphia for four or five decades, *Camden? that's the place over behind the Victor and the Campbell's Soup factories.* As I moved through life, occasionally being called upon to fill out license forms insurance or loan applications, I would write out the name *Camden* (I'm ashamed to name my shame now) with a shudder. Only briefly, in college, at Boston University where I studied writing and politics and sometimes put down my literature texts and journalism assignments in order to play piano in a succession of blues and R&B bands, did I allow myself anything resembling comfort (let's not go so far as to say pride) at having emerged into the world in the smoky industrial haze of Camden, New Jersey. Among my set – musicians, mostly white boys from the suburbs, playing with joy and imagined cultural affinity the music of the black urban postwar workingclass – we affected more proletarian roots, seeking authenticity. Bonnie Raitt (who was then at Radcliffe, rooming with someone I knew in high school, and who often did solo sets on either side of the Charles) could say she was "from L. A." and make it sound like the tough part of town, omitting her singing star father and private schools; David Epstein, guitar picker from the Main Line, could cock an eyebrow and claim "Philly"; James Montgomery, harmonica and vocals, of Grosse Point (whose father was a General Motors' P.R. executive) could just intone gruffly, "Dee-troit" and leave it at that – *perhaps the neighborhood of John Lee Hooker? Big Maceo?* We all did it. We can laugh at it now: *kids.* And when I said "Camden," dropping Haddonfield, Westmont, Chevy Chase, the maple-shaded-quarter-acre-and-Colonial in Port Washington on Long Island, people looked at me with respect. Camden? *Whoa, got us beat!*

Years and years later, after some time in publishing and after I'd begun to negotiate a fulltime writing life, the very notion of Camden began to intrigue me: what to do with it? How to use it? How to fit it in? The feeling intensified after 1984, when my father died. He had remade himself on Long Island representing a raft of broadcast equipment manufacturers, calling on radio and television stations all over the metropolitan New York area, trying to rely on all the old contacts and associations, trading on his long experience and knowledge within the industry that allowed him the privilege of wearing the tie tack and cufflinks of the Broadcast Pioneers of America, competing with just about everyone, and alas doing only moderately at it. Getting his kids through college. But years beyond, borrowing on life insurance close to the end. Before, there had been short stints at Fairchild and Muzak (*we had a Muzak tuner in our house when I was in high school!*), but the really vivid time in his postwar professional life had been the fifteen years at RCA, during which time he had met his wife, married, had four kids, secured some of the best friendships of his life, and made something of himself. For me, as a writer, after Dad died in 1984 he waited invisibly somewhere on my writing desk. His time would come someday on paper – and so would, separately, the city of Camden. Until that latter event my memory of the place would be straight out of early childhood – sitting in the backseat of our Mercury, driving down to the tollbooths of the Ben Franklin Bridge and then up, up, over the city toward the Delaware River and the Philadelphia skyline, me peering out the window to glimpse the huge, illuminated round stained-glass tower portrait of the RCA Victor dog, Nipper, and the legend below, *His Master's Voice*, and all of a sudden through Dad's open window would come the overpowering aroma of tomato soup cooking in the huge vats of the Campbell's factory, just below, and almost at eye level would appear the gigantic rooftop soup cans, and then we'd be out over the river and Camden would be behind us.

Very recently, Camden began to also seem ahead of me, most particularly after my mother was sorting through some papers and found a sheet of hospital stationery with my premie prints and a nurse's hurried, not altogether hopeful scrawl upon it. I began to peer into the whorls of the inkstamped footprints at odd, ruminative times, wondering, *Just where do they lead?*

Figure Three:
Aerial View, Camden, N.J., 28 March 1996.
It's all in a haze, a vague mist of low-hanging clouds, riverfog, and vaporous discharges from the lofty stack of an incinerator on the Delaware shore, but abruptly as the southbound U.S. Air Boeing 737 descends directly over the wide river, the Philadelphia skyline leaps into view at starboard, and passengers on that side of the jet crane to see Independence Hall, while those on the port barely look up from their magazines. You, however, among the indifferent rows, are squashed against the seethrough plastic, taking in the long-denied city of your birth: incinerators, sewerage plants, empty wharves, dead factories, shanty rows off toward the horizon, entire blocks of brick rubble, and the devastating headline of a recent Time *magazine article on the city swoops like a bat into your brain – "Who Could Live Here?" – and some of the righteous indignation of Jonathan Kozol's diatribe on the state of public education,* Savage Inequalities, *seethes from that paperback on your lap as if from a hot brick out of the ruins, but then – wait – there's*

the RCA *tower and the dog still there, thank God, and you're like an excited kid at your birthday.*

"I DREAM'D in a dream I saw a city invincible to the attacks of the whole of
    the rest of the earth,
I dream'd that was the new city of Friends,
Nothing was greater there than the quality of robust love, it led the rest,
It was seen every hour in the actions of the men of that city,
And in all their looks and words."

from Calamus, *Leaves of Grass*

The words, written some thirteen years before Whitman even so much as paused to tie his shoelace in Camden, are inscribed on the twenty-two-story Art Deco–style City Hall; the first two lines have been annexed by the city, with no discernable irony, as its unofficial motto. I'm driving slowly down Market Street toward the river just after glimpsing and identifying those proud words – "city invincible" – and despite it being a weekday morning, there is hardly any traffic in sight, and very few parked cars, and only an occasional pedestrian here in the center of town – no "city's ceaseless crowd." Nonetheless I am driving with extreme caution, like a stagecoach driver past the Hole in the Wall, the admonitions and warnings of friends in Philadelphia still fresh in my ears. Too many newspaper headlines crowd my brain – "Camden Hopes for Release from Its Pain"; "In Struggles of the City, Children Are Casualties"; "Camden Forces Its Suburbs to Ask, What If a City Dies?"; "A Once Vital, Cohesive Community Is Slowly, but Not Inevitably, Dying." And that devastating question from *Time*: "Who Could Live Here?" There are, the statistics repeat across recent years, more than 3,000 vacant houses in Camden. The unemployment rate is higher than twenty per cent. Half and more of Camden's 87,000 citizens are on some form of government assistance. It has been called the poorest city in New Jersey, and some have wondered if it is the poorest in the nation. Adult men and women stand or sit in front of their shabby two-story brick houses, stunned by purposelessness. In abandoned buildings, drug dealers and their customers congregate. On littered sidewalks, children negotiate through broken glass, condoms, spent hypodermics. I have driven past them on my way downtown, and now, taking a left onto Third and over to

Stevens, to a block of rundown three-story brick rowhouses with marble steps and lintels, intent on finding the Italianate style house built for George Whitman in 1873, I find a blankness: no #431. "Burned down," a passing man explains in an accent from the Indies, "by the dealers, mon." He walks on, shrugs, looks back, joins a knot of men on a facing stoop, and accepts a paper bag from which a greennecked wine bottle protrudes. They are apparently used to pilgrims appearing on their street, looking for something no longer there. They offer me nothing. I dare not ask.

Figure Four:
Detail, "Bird's Eye View of Camden, N.J. In the Centennial Year 1876."
You eye the waterfront from your lofty imagination, Thaddeus Fowler – the dredgers and derricks, the barks and sloops and cutters, their sails furled and stowed at anchorages or billowing in in the northerly breeze as the ships enter the current, the wharfs, piers, docks, ferry slips, the sprawl of merchandise and Jersey produce awaiting the grunting stevedores, and you render them with all of your draftsman's art, and precisely you print the names of the Delaware's attendant streets: Bridge (there will be no bridge for fifty years), Point, Beach, Water, River, Port, and you take care in capturing the cavernous new ferry terminal at the foot of Federal Street, it being more or less at the focal point of this bird's eye view.

The river's edge is the city's *raison d'être*, and there are blissful moments when he feels the same after riding the omnibus down the few blocks from George's to the Federal Street ferry (with its preponderance of human cargo) or to the nearby Bridge Street ferry (more mercantile, with the delight of joshing with and admiring the laborers at their tasks, just as, indeed, "one of the roughs."). He gets out more in 1876 than he did in '73–'75, and the waterfront with all of its particularities allows his imagination an even greater mobility – "the great arrogant, black, full-freighted ocean steamers," he'll catalogue them from a bench or even a packing crate on a similar April morning in exactly three years, in *Specimen Days*, "an occasional man-of-war, sometimes a foreigner, at anchor, with her guns and port-holes, and the boats, and the brown-faced sailors, and the regular oar-strokes, and the gay crowds of 'visiting day' – the frequent large and handsome three-masted schooners . . . some of them new and very jaunty, with their white-gray sails and yellow pine spars – the sloops dashing along in a fair wind." And of course there are the ferries – "What exhilaration, change, people, business, by day," he exalts.

"What soothing, silent, wondrous hours, at night, crossing on the boat, most all to myself – pacing the deck, alone, forward or aft. What communion with the waters, the air, the exquisite *chiaroscuro* – the sky and stars, that speak no word, nothing to the intellect, yet so eloquent, so communicative to the soul."

Franklin Benjamin Sanborn, of the Concord group and literary correspondent of the *Springfield Daily Republican,* will in a week's time stroll up the "still, Philadelphia-looking quarter" of Stevens Street, "of long rows of brick houses with white marble doorsteps and white wooden shutters," and spy Whitman through a bay window on the side street, and the Good Gray Poet will answer the door himself, leaning on his cane, dressed in gray clothes, a white scarf around his neck, and a blue waistcoat – "altogether a picturesque and befitting attire," notes Sanborn, "careless but effective." The journalist finds him "as one would wish to find such a person, master of himself and superior to his circumstances," of good cheer despite the lingering tinges of paralysis and the nagging digestive slowdowns. He speaks warmly of Emerson, Bryant, Longfellow, and Whittier, remembers pleasant visits from Alcott and Thoreau, and recalls Miss Alcott in the wartime hospital camps and wards. He waves a good-natured, dismissive hand at the current controversies over his neglect and poverty, at the sometimes hostile reactions to Whitman's poetic intrusion of "the fleshly and generative forces out of which human life springs," as Sanborn will put it, "but of which the human soul is reasonably a little shy." Perhaps his interlocutor will discreetly mention the recent, scathing anti-Whitman screed of Peter Bayne in the *Contemporary Review* (Sanborn will dismiss it as "dull abuse"), and if the journalist is feeling voluble (he does tend to inject himself into his work) under the poet's kind, encouraging eyes he may deride the disgusted "virtuous people" who listen long enough to the "cheap and nasty poets in England" who "rave a little too much about Whitman's genius (attracted by this very whim of his)" – will Whitman raise an eyebrow at "cheap and nasty"? Never mind. Sanborn will opine that "In sober fact, his verses are cleaner and his life incomparably more praiseworthy than Burns's," and he will close out the account of his visit with precise directions for Centennial visitors to find the poet's home, and an endorsement of the fine new edition of *Leaves of Grass* – "two volumes of about 700 pages in all, with three portraits of the author, and his autograph signature, finely bound, and sold for $5 a volume." And Whitman will pat him on the back and wave him down the street toward the river.

Figures Five, Six, Seven:
Aerial Photographs, Camden, N.J., 1922–1938, Victor Dallin and Aero Services, Inc.

You aim your biplane at the attentive dog in the Tower overlooking the blocks of factory buildings as you bank toward the Delaware, and you adjust for a level horizon and get a momentary aesthetic thrill of the perfect lines of Cooper Street and the Tower and the Victor power plant smokestacks at wharfside in the upper left field, and yes, even the Campbell's stack in the foreground, soupsteam wafting northwest in a light breeze, and yes, yes, the old four-masted schooner at the Elm Street dock in the upper right, and you press the shutter release, and sail over the Victor factory complex and the river, and like an Escadrille dogfighter you joyously loop around and head back for another pass – plenty of afternoon light and fuel left, and Campbell's and then the Esterbrook Pen building, await. . . .

Between Linden and Federal, where nineteenth-century lumberyards and machine shops stood at river's edge, lies the triad of city industry, world renowned. Look it up in the 1938 New Jersey guide published by the wpa. Marvel at the figures. Two hundred million pens annually pour out of the five-story Esterbrook factory on Cooper Street; founded three years before the Civil War by an Englishman, Richard Esterbrook, who imported fifteen countrymen to Camden, the firm will, by 1938, employ two hundred and fifty. With Market Street as its center, Campbell's has grown to forty-two buildings over eight blocks, with the landmark rooftop water tanks painted in soupcan red and white. Joseph Campbell and Abraham Anderson built a preserves factory there in 1869 – *it is visible in the 1876 Bird's Eye View* – but in 1897 a chemist, John T. Dorrance, was hired at $7.50 a week; his experiments at condensing soups for canning made Campbell's something rather more than a household name. Dorrance, president of the company from 1914, founded a dynasty that would lead the company almost to the end of the century. "Dorrance amassed a fortune of $117,000,000," we are informed by the Jersey writers who've found a temporary respite from the Depression with the wpa guide project. "On his death in 1935 the State inheritance tax amounted to $15,000,000, which temporarily solved the problem of raising funds for relief."

And as Dorrance was waiting for his first week's paycheck in 1897, another tinkerer down the block was working out of a tiny machine shop behind the Collings Carriage Company on North Front. It was Eldridge R. Johnson, a Delaware native who specialized in fabricating working models of inventions; he had earlier patented a bookbinding machine to no discernable commercial interest, but in the year before, in 1896, a customer had walked into the shop with a Berliner Gramophone, a hand-cranked talking machine that employed a flat disk. "The little instrument was badly designed," he recalled many years later. "It sounded like a partially educated parrot with a sore throat and a cold in the head, but the little wheezy instrument caught my attention and held it fast and hard. I became interested in it as I had never been interested in anything before." Johnson was given the challenge of producing a spring motor to make the sound more consistent, and after building a motor and improving the gadget's delivery of sound, he won a contract from Berliner to manufacture parts and assemble the complete machines. Johnson's ties to the company's founder, Emile Berliner, continued to solidify even as his inventions and improvements within the field gave him his own presence. By 1901 the two had survived an expensive patent infringement and lawsuit and combined into a new business – the Victor Talking Machine Company – the name coming from famously vanquishing the infringer – and Johnson became president. And Berliner sold him an intriguing trademark acquired a year earlier from his London business associate: it was a painting of a fox terrier confronted by the gleaming horn of a talking machine, cocking his head in puzzled recognition. The artist, Francis Barraud, had inherited dog Nipper and phonograph from his brother, and Barraud noticed the terrier's curiosity over the machine. In his inspired first painting, dog and phonograph rest on a highly polished wooden surface which, once shadowy handles are discerned, reveals itself as a coffintop; the legend, "His Master's Voice," thereby exhibited a flowery Victorian sentiment quickly excised by the businessmen who purchased Barraud's first painting and copyright for £100 and set him to painting copies for the rest of his life.

Johnson would spend over $24 million between 1901 and 1926 to popularize his trademark, the company's official history by Frederick Barnum says; the dog and horn would appear not only on the Victor machines with their brass-belled tin horns and on the improved model with horn concealed in a handsome cabinet called the Victrola, and on the disk labels, but also in advertisements all over the world. Victor's exclusive artists would include Caruso (he would be the star vocalist among a distinguished list, recording at New York's Carnegie Hall and even in Camden); John Phillip Sousa, "The March King," would be on the list too, and all artists' portraits and signed recommendations would be prominent in Victor advertisements. And the Victor company would expand across entire city blocks in Camden over the next ten or fifteen years, becoming completely self-contained: twenty-two buildings in 1911 – cabinet factories, metal manufacturing, matrix departments, research laboratories, record factories, printing plants, recording studios, shipping general offices, power plants. Sales by 1911 had reached 731,523 instruments and nearly forty-seven million records. And the Victor complex continued to grow and grow, often with overhead walkways connecting buildings. In 1916, the newest cabinet factory, sprawling, six stories high and designated Building #17D, rose on Cooper Street; it was topped by a seventy-five-foot tower (built to enclose water tanks), in which four stained-glass windows, 14.5 feet in diameter, were set, illuminated from inside, to display the dog and the horn and the trademark words, "His Master's Voice." The windows had been designed and built by the famed D'Ascenzo Studios of Philadelphia, which had also adorned the National Cathedral in Washington, the Cathedral of St. John the Divine in New York, and chapels at Princeton and the University of Pennsylvania.

Throughout the late teens and early twenties, the company grew even more. It bought the old Trinity Church on North 5th Street in 1918 and converted it to a sound-recording studio for records (and later, motion pictures, including the Academy Award–winning *Wings*, the film music augmented by recordings of swooping and landing airplanes over at Camden field). "The Victor-Victrola brings to you the greatest array of talent ever assembled," trumpeted the ads – "the greatest opera artists, the greatest instrumentalists, the greatest bands and orchestras, the greatest comedians." Add Paderewski. Add Harry Lauder. Add Kubelik and Martinelli. Add the Boston Symphony, the Philadelphia Symphony, and of course add Stowkowski. Add Heifetz, that sixteen-year-old Russian prodigy. Add Caruso again, for a highly-advertised twenty-five-year extension to his contract (he would die with fourteen years unfulfilled). Add the Vatican Choir and the La Scala Orchestra with Toscanini. Add Rachmaninoff. Add some oomph: add Paul Whiteman, Jelly Roll Morton, Fletcher Henderson, Bennie Moten with Count Basie, Fats Waller, all strolling up the Camden streets from the ferry and into the Trinity Church of Recording.

And, in the mid-twenties, add electrical recording and the revolution it caused. Add radio – and the temporary slump in Victor sales, until it formed an alliance with the Radio Corporation of America to produce Electrolas and RCA Radiolas in the same cabinets. Add more artists – Casals, Tibbett, Horowitz. And subtract Eldridge R. Johnson, who since 1919 had been in poor health and out of direct contact with the company's management; in 1927, his interest in the company he'd founded – 245,000 shares valued at $115 per share, or more than $28 million – was acquired by a Wall Street banking firm. Then, as a publicly-traded company with increased capital to $53 million, Victor continued to expand until March 1929. Add RCA – which bought its partner Victor (31 buildings on 58 acres in Camden, and worldwide facilities) for $154 million, becoming known as the RCA Victor Company. Nipper, gramophone, and "His Master's Voice" were – of course – retained.

Figure Eight:
Walt Whitman Cultural Arts Center (formerly Cooper Branch Library), Friends of Johnson Park, Rutgers University, 1996

You're sitting on a bench in Johnson Park in front of the eerily familiar old Cooper Library, with the merest tendrils of memory of having been here long ago – perhaps in a stroller with your mother, in the city to meet your father who was just about to get off work at RCA. The bronze statue of Peter Pan would have caught your eye then – he is standing as if he's just alighted on a tall tree stump, at the base of which among entwined roots you could see rabbits, mice, squirrels, and even fairies. There would have been water splashing in the pool fountain, and there would have been the smell of hot dogs and the sounds of many children, for this is the only patch of green in this part of the city, and the Cooper Library's specialty is children's literature.

The neoclassical sandstone building with its six fluted, towering ionic columns and crowning parapet, built by Eldridge Johnson as a gift to the children of Camden and dedicated in 1919, presides today over a dry wading pool, empty benches, unattended sculptures; the sycamores, their new leaves stirring in the same breeze that drives litter across winter-killed grass, shelter a new generation of scampering squirrels, which provide the only mammalian movement around the edifice. There is no one within sight. (If the horror stories from Philadelphia are to be believed, one *wants* to remain alone.) Some of the original bronze sculptures, such as the battling duck and turtle (Albert Laessle) are here, but others have been stolen, recovered, and are presently stored inside the building, their feet sawed off by plunderers. (In the furor after the statues' theft, the owner of a metal scrapyard, who had paid cash when the hooligans appeared at his gate with the seventy-year-old bronze sculptures, returned them.) I have been assured over the telephone that someone is inside the building. Up the wide granite steps and past the columns, I'm presented with an extraordinary mosaic frieze of opalescent glass over the doorways (100,000 pieces, I later learn) – *America Receiving the Gifts of the Nations* by Nicola D'Ascenzo, the same studio responsible for the "His Master's Voice" stained glass towering a block or so away. There's America in the center, flanked by her son, Opportunity, and daughter, Equality. There's Moses with the tablets, Arabia with an abacus, Raphael with his Madonna, Greece with a temple, and Japan, Persia, Babylonia, India, and England (it's Tyndale and his translation of the Bible) and Germany (Gutenberg, of course); there's Christopher Columbus, Michelangelo, George Washington, Dante, Moliere, and – yes – there's Walt Whitman. Beneath the frieze are three large metal doors. Locked tight. But a buzzer and a puzzling conversation over an intercom (*"Are you sure you've come to the right place?"*) gets me inside the building.

The books are gone – the city had taken over the library after it was deconsecrated, and since 1986 park and building have been owned and tended by the Camden branch of Rutgers University, which also runs an art gallery not far away. As the Walt Whitman Cultural Arts Center, the organization sponsors exhibitions, lectures, poetry readings, concerts, and dance productions, nearly all appropriately for Camden with an African American flavor. Among all attending, about 10,000 children visit the center annually. Upstairs, in a crowded little office, I am confronted by the most unusual sight of a young black man in a towering white ten-gallon hat; he has a full beard; a large red bandana around his neck; a handsome fringed buckskin vest over a capacious white shirt; well-worn blue jeans tucked into a pair of gleaming hand-tooled cowboy boots. "Hi," he says. "Howdy," I say. "Where's your horse?" "Left him at home," he replies with a grin, "but I brought m'saddle." He is Robert H. Miller, the author of mid-grade readers, "The Black Cowboy Series" and the "Stories of the Forgotten West Series." He gives me a handbill with his picture on it. He is here to address a group of young excursionists, second and third graders given the morning off from one of the city's dreary elementary schools. He disappears downstairs to retrieve his saddle from his locked car.

I turn to look around the office walls. Nicely-rendered pastel portrait of Whitman. Camden Cultural Center Poster – Ralph Ellison, Maya Angelou, Sun Ra, and "Carrie Smith's Blues & Jazz Storybook." Color photo of actor in Whitman beard and clothing posing in front of tomb – eerily as if the stone has just been rolled back. Rene Huggins, the center's executive director, ends a phone conversation and emerges from her sanctum to tell me about their Saturday Family Theatre Series offerings (movement, mime, cultural, and historical presentations) and their Sunday Mainstage Events (jazz, gospel, R&B, and a tribute to "Camden's other great poet," Nick Virgilio). We talk about the much-vaunted "turn-around" of Camden as visualized by hopeful politicians and residents exactly ten years ago – the bulldozing of dozens of blighted industrial blocks in the waterfront district; the construction of an immense New Jersey State Aquarium at the foot of Federal Street, and a three-acre public park and waterside promenade not far from a new marina, all now a reality; the recent completion of an outdoor, 25,000-seat amphitheater, which is to house the Southern New Jersey Performing Arts Center, the Papermill Playhouse, and the Haddonfield Symphony, along with visiting blockbuster acts. The waterfront revitalization began during the Republican administration of Governor Thomas Kean, but it was given added momentum in 1989 when Jim Florio, a Democratic politician from Camden County (it encompasses not only the blighted city but comfortable suburbs like the one I grew up in), was elected governor of New Jersey. There was much talk of job training for Camden's unemployed, and of more money to be pumped into the schools, so that the impoverished could share even a measly part of the anticipated boom. Now, in the hard reality of the nineties, with welfare, jobs training, and education under fire, and with a Republican back in the State House in Trenton with no charity in her heart for the state's cities, the hoped-for improvement in city residents' lives is fading rapidly. "And on top of all that," Rene Huggins says to me, "we get that headline in *Time* magazine – 'Who Could Live Here?' Why not just give us a lot of shovels and bury the place?" She snorts in disgust.

Suddenly there is the sound of a hundred children's indrawn breath, and oohs and ahhs, and the applause of little hands, cascading into the office from the downstairs auditorium built in the old central reading room and galleries. Robert H. Miner with his ten gallon hat and furry chaps has ambled onstage to tell them the amazing news that there were once real black cowboys in the Wild West, and black soldiers actually fighting for freedom during the Civil War, and black pioneers beyond the Mississippi and Missouri. He twirls a lariat and tells them of their history, and – kids being kids – there is a good chance that the anecdotes he shares will make more of an impression than what their teachers told them yesterday in class. These are likely the younger siblings or even the children of the children who thronged the broken-down halls of Camden elementary schools, and its high schools, when Jonathan Kozol passed through town in the spring of 1990, researching his book *Savage Inequalities: Children in America's Schools*. "The city has 200 liquor stores and bars and 180 gambling establishments, no movie theater, one chain supermarket, no new-car dealership, few restaurants other than some fast-food places," he writes. "City blocks are filled with burnt-out buildings. Of the city's 2,200 public housing units, 500 are boarded up, although there is a three-year waiting list of homeless families. As the city's aged sewers crumble and collapse, streets cave in, but there are no funds to make repairs. What is life like for children in this city?" He found Pyne Point middle school to be in a neighborhood of factories and rowhouses, many abandoned, and "roughly equidistant from a paper plant, a gelatine factory and an illegal dumpsite" – noxious outside, and inside, in battered, broken-down, crowded rooms, teem the youth of Camden, with dysfunctional fire alarms, outmoded books and equipment, no sports supplies, demoralized teachers, and the everpresent worry that a child is going to enter the school building armed. White bastions Cherry Hill and Haddonfield are minutes away. Desegregation will never happen. And suburbanites wonder why they should pay to help alleviate the city's misery. "The world is leaving us behind in Camden," a teacher tells him. Campbell's has closed down here and moved. RCA has been bought, absorbed, dismantled, and taken elsewhere. "Before us, over the darkened water of the Delaware," Kozol writes, "are the brightly lighted high-rise office buildings and the new hotels and condominiums of Philadelphia. The bridges that cross the river here in Camden bear the names of Whitman and Ben Franklin. History surrounds the children growing up in Camden, but they do not learn a lot of it in school. Whitman is not read by students in the basic skills curriculum. Few children that I met in Camden High, indeed, had ever heard of him." Kozol rails at the terrible contrasts between the schools of Cherry Hill and Princeton and those of Camden and Paterson, and at "the dread that seems to lie beneath the fear of equalizing. Equity is seen as dispossession. Local autonomy is seen as liberty – even if the poverty of those in nearby cities robs them of all meaningful autonomy by narrowing their choices to the meanest and the shabbiest of options."

As Rene Huggins and I continue our chat about the Cultural Center's brave and useful program for city residents, touching for a moment on the dire chapter in Kozol's book, gales of childish laughter flow up to us from downstairs as the Black Cowboy jokingly parries a question about guns from an intensely curious boy in the audience – my son would ask the same, were he here. I remark that several people I met in Philadelphia – white professionals – are aware of what some politicians and real estate speculators have called "Camden's Renaissance" on the waterfront, although the Philadelphians I met have never been to Camden, and each has mused that perhaps it would be a wise and prescient thing to buy a Camden brickhouse, or even a block, as a good investment. There's more laughter from below, as if to punctuate the irony of it all. *The attentive, quiet children, the loud, proud, restive base of the streets.* . . . Rene and I pause, sharing delight in the sounds of kids having a good time, and as she smiles, bemused, and shrugs at what I have just recounted, it is abundantly clear that it is not the politicians nor the developers nor certainly the real estate moguls, but that it is the teachers, the cultural servers, and the exhausted, beleaguered social workers of Camden who are the true heroes of the city.

Though Kozol's dire observations are unchanged in the few years since his trip, some lighter news regarding Johnson Park, at least, has appeared, which in tangible and intangible ways will affect the 10,000 schoolchildren who visit the center. The park, a state and national historic site, is the object of an enthusiastic fundraising effort toward a three-year restoration. Some $115,000 in federal, corporate, and private donations was raised, and a matching grant from the New Jersey Historic Trust, to a ceiling of $186,000, would be awarded not long after my visit. In a further burst of fortune, investigators discovered a long-lost trust for park upkeep, donated in 1921 by Eldridge R. Johnson, which had sat undisturbed for decades in city coffers. Principle of $44,500, and accrued interest of more than $100,000, would, by the end of 1996, be transferred to Rutgers University to benefit Johnson Park. A three-phase plan, to restore the mall and library plaza, to rehabilitate the pools and stone fountain, and to refurbish the bronze sculptures and restore landscaping and perimeter walks, seems finally to be moving ahead. If so, the children of Camden will at least have one oasis in their difficult lives. "The children love the park," says Rene Huggins. She is hopeful that no snags will appear.

Rene Huggins says that as the morning's sole visitor I will be one of the last to see the photography exhibition of Milt Hinton, the celebrated jazz bassist who has carried a camera around nearly his entire life. Down the hall in a bright gallery hang fifty of Hinton's black-and-white photographs, taken between the late thirties through the seventies. An integral part of jazz history, Hinton has captured thousands of relaxed, unguarded, and intimate moments of the great music people he's encountered. Washed over with regret at not being here three weeks ago, when Milt

Hinton graced the exhibition's opening cocktails, signed books, sold CDs, and lectured, I peer into the photographs: there's Dizzy Gillespie puffing out his cheeks for some little neighborhood boys in Nice; there's Louis Armstrong, Ben Webster, and Lester Young; there's Sarah Vaughan, Pearl Bailey, and Ella Fitzgerald; there's Lionel Hampton and Jay McShann. There's Basie consulting over a piano with Billie Holiday – it's from 1957, in a New York television studio, and the Count smiles while Billie leans toward the keyboard, looking perplexed: she'll be dead in two years. The photo reminds me of a Basie-in-Camden anecdote. In the early thirties, Basie was playing with the Bennie Moten band out of Kansas City and on the verge of going out on his own. During a tour East, the band was booked into the Pearl Theatre in Philadelphia – "our first big theater date of that tour," Basie recalled in *Good Morning Blues*, the memoir written with Albert Murray. "We had ourselves a ball all that week, playing those shows and wining, dining, and partying the chorus girls. We really lived it up." Many of the members ran up huge tabs at the hotel, and by the end of the week they had moved into the tour bus down the street – "the big headliners of last week out there sleeping in the goddamn bus!" Unfortunately, when they went to draw their pay, the band members found that they had no money coming to them: it was going to pay back their booking agent for advances for new uniforms. Moreover, they learned the bus was about to be confiscated. Bennie Moten was as shocked as anyone. Visits to the local pawn shops got them out of the hotel bills, and meanwhile, Moten found a local promoter, Archie Robinson, who hustled another bus and booked them into the Victor recording studio in Camden. On empty stomachs, during a long recording session they made, Basie says, "one of the best batches of records any of Bennie's bands ever made" – "Moten Swing," "Toby," and "Imagination," and a number of others, all classics. "Then," he continues, "when we got off around six o'clock, old Archie had gone somewhere and rounded up something for us to eat, and he took us into a pool hall, and there was a big pot of rabbit stew and a pot of beans and hocks and a big old pan of corn bread all spread out on that pool table. So we all gathered around and ate. I can still taste how good it was."

Thinking of his words, hearing "Moten Swing" in my head as it must have sounded inside the Trinity Church recording studio – and outside the brick walls and stained glass on the busy Camden sidewalk – I'm drawn to a gallery window overlooking the park. Above, to the right and north, it's the Ben Franklin Bridge stretching out over the Delaware; it stood above the vanished but once sprawling, vigorous shipyards which gave employment to tens of thousands of Camden residents. Ahead, it's the brown-brick Victor executive building (1916), from basement to roof built more like a sumptuous hotel than an office building, particularly in Eldridge Johnson's seventh-floor president's suite with its Circassian walnut paneled walls, old Italian marble mantel, and teak floors. To the left, and south, past the city block that had once held the Victor record-pressing plant, there's the Tower of Building 17 – the round stained glass panel of the dog and the gramophone. That's the view from the old library window. What's not gone is empty. Dead. But like Lassie leaping in a daring rescue across the brick rubble, like Rin Tin Tin dashing from the fullness of the past to the vacancy and neglect of the present, little Nipper tugs me toward Building 17.

It was built in 1915 (the year my father was born; for some reason that date has trailed me across many endeavors) and it opened for business in January of the next year, and the brick and terra-cotta cabinet factory boasted of many industrial innovations for air and water quality, temperature regulation, insulation, noise reduction, and it featured an interesting new safety feature, employing an internal ramp system as opposed to fire escape stairs – during fire drills, nearly five thousand workers could exit in fifteen minutes. *The American Architect* featured Building 17 in a 1916 issue and praised Victor's "intelligent liberality" for providing humane working conditions for its woodworkers and assemblers of gleaming Victrolas, Electrolas, and Radiolas – *Olé!* And of course the building's two greatest features were at its bottom and top – first the portals on the sidewalks with their massive, ornate wrought-iron gates (with the proud, overlapped iron initials, vtmc) which gave delivery trucks access to the building's interior courtyard and loading docks; and then the seventy-five-foot tower with its terra-cotta trimmings, its tenth-floor balconies, and of course the four stained-glass panels of Nipper, visible for up to five miles.

The building is now, most certainly, deserted, and as I walk down the street, dozens of hopeful, unattended parking meters rising at the curbs, I look above, glass crunching underfoot, and see that all of the big industrial windows are blasted out. Fragments of wall partitions are visible inside. Cables and wires dangle. Electric fans, hanging from ceilings, turn windmill-like in a stiff easterly breeze flowing unimpeded through the building. The tower, an elegant five-story water storage machine with its eight immense interior water tanks and its central circular iron staircase all the way up to the rooftop flagpole, stands, a dead sentry still at his post. And although rca is now gone, Nipper remains. Eldridge Johnson had paid Nicola D'Ascenzo $25,000 for the four stained-glass panels in

1916, and as the corporate historian, Frederick Barnum, has noted, "for the next 53 years, Nipper faithfully sat high above the Camden waterfront." In 1969, suffering from amnesia, RCA actually removed the four panels and replaced them with a block-style logo, "RCA," deaf to the resulting furor. The corporation donated one window to the Smithsonian, one to Penn State University, and one to Widener College in Pennsylvania. None to New Jersey – until belatedly, the fourth was given to the Camden County Historical Society. (One can stand on tiptoes there, peering over an obstruction, and see it still inside its large wooden packing crate.) But ten years after the tower desecration, RCA came to its senses and commissioned replacements, which were dedicated on April 10, 1979, a day proclaimed "Nipper Day" by New Jersey Governor Brendan Byrne. RCA itself, bought by General Electric, in turn absorbed by Lockheed–Martin Marietta, is now as gone as the Victor Talking Machine Company – its consumer electronics division sold to an outfit in the Midwest, which markets televisions and VCRs made in Korea with the RCA label attached and a "modernized" Nipper logo printed on the cardboard cartons; its record division – Caruso, Jelly Roll, Fiedler, Elvis, and all – went to BMG Music Service, catalogue merchants of CDs and tapes in Indianapolis (it is a subsidiary of the privately-held German communications giant, Bertelsmann AG), whose copyright now anchors any use of the Nipper image. Still, in South Jersey, there are fond, family-like, nostalgic monthly lunches of ex-employees of RCA, though their central identity is long gone. The older members may have known my father from the days when the breakup and abandonment were absolutely unthinkable. And today, despite occasional declarations that the owner in concert with the Cooper Waterfront Development Authority will someday turn Building 17 into a six-story shopping mall and professional office space, many observers feel it's more likely that Nipper from his high vantage point will up and bark. I've talked to people who've climbed the circular iron staircase in the open, unguarded building past the seventeen-year-old stained glass. They say that pieces are already falling out.

Across the street from vacant, decrepit Building 17 is a new and handsome building owned by Martin Marietta, builder of spaceships and weapons systems (*"Unscrew the locks from the doors!* I seem to hear on the wind. *Unscrew the doors themselves from their jambs!*). Its architects have used the building's shape, brickwork, and terra-cotta to echo the old Victor edifice; there are even bands of green at cornices, reflecting the stained glass field behind Nipper and the gramophone. One would be surprised now to learn if any of the people who work here actually live in

Camden. Landscaped parking lots, attractive sidewalks of brick and cobble, stretch around and behind the new place, some of the lots covering the old Campbell's blocks, for of course Campbell's is all but gone from the region despite periodic denials and promises; the last factory closed in 1990 with a loss of nine hundred jobs. John Dorrance's famous international collection of soup tureens – once a tourist stop at the Campbell's Museum, with lavish crockery such as Catherine the Great's drawing sixty thousand visitors a year – was donated to the Winterthur Museum in Delaware. The four huge red-and-white soup can water towers that stood atop an eight-story factory, their water fed down into the big soup vats, were blown up along with the building by thousands of dynamite charges in 1991, to make way for aerospace corporation buildings and parking lots, although one water tower was subsequently salvaged and placed in storage until funds could be raised to restore it somewhere on the waterfront.

And it is to the waterfront itself that I am now drawn, hoping, implausibly, for a little "revitalization" myself. Some several blocks across the empty blacktop lots is the attractive New Jersey State Aquarium, home to "nearly 4,000 animals of 300 species," says a brochure, "over 36 sharks, with daily dive shows in the 760,000 gallon Open Ocean tank." I am too tired to go inside and shuffle with a crowd past all the glass windows, so I find myself a bench on the new promenade. A shiny office tower built out of material resembling yellow, blue, and gray Lego blocks for the development authority rises behind me, manufacturers' decals still on some of the windows. The Delaware flows by – seagulls dive, a freighter stands to out in midstream, and a sleek, modernistic helicopter vaults over the river and lands some wealthy businessmen or visitors at a pier on the Philadelphia side. Golden Independence Hall gleams over there. On the Camden side, a tourist family of Japanese, all in new blue denim outfits, take solemn snapshots of one another leaning against the esplanade railing. Another group, strolling down in the spring sunlight from the aquarium, is Filipino – I hear Tagalog on the Delaware and can look directly across the river to Admiral George Dewey's flagship, anchored there as a museum, with a pair of brass footsteps welded to the bridge where he stood, looking over Manila Bay, about to order his gunner, Gridley, to begin to devastate the decrepit Spanish fleet. Joggers pass – a trim mother encouraging her slightly overweight teenaged daughter: "handsome, welldrest Jersey women and girls," the Good Gray Poet noted in *Specimen Days* while sitting in the bustling Camden ferry waiting room, not far, certainly, from where I sit now, "the bright eyes and glowing faces, coming in from the air. . . ." Two men in shirttails, with children perched up on their shoulders, stroll by – they are black, not from Camden but from Africa, judging by the language in which they converse. One can imagine Whitman's utter delight and unsurprise were he to see this panoply of internationalism at riverside, even in the face of dispiriting change. At least after many years of absence, there is a ferry again at the foot of Federal Street, although it is for Philadelphia tourists to experience the New Jersey State Aquarium or the Blockbuster–Sony Music Entertainment Centre without having to venture very far into New Jersey's Camden. The ferry is not running at this moment as I send my thoughts out over the river, watching a flock of seagulls as Whitman did many a time on the Delaware landing or out on the crossing – "I never tire of watching their broad and easy flight," he wrote in the spring of 1879, "in spirals, or as they oscillate with slow unflapping wings, or look down with curved beak, or dipping to the water after food." Across many loafing days and many solitary evenings, he kept going down to this spot, and in the diary entries recording the people, the riverine wildlife, the scudding clouds and reassuring constellations, one sees as much of a source of solace for the aging poet as were the Jersey countryside woods and farmland of his occasional repair. "For two hours I cross'd and recross'd, merely for pleasure," he recorded in a typical note, "for a still excitement. Both sky and river went through several changes. The first for awhile held two vast fan-shaped echelons of light clouds, through which the moon waded, now radiating, carrying with her an aureole of tawny transparent brown, and now flooding the whole vast with clear vapory light-green, through which, as through an illuminated veil, she moved with measur'd womanly motion." Transported to more places than mere opposing riverbanks, studying the stars another night, he finally went ashore – "I couldn't give up the beauty and soothingness of the night," he wrote, and "as I staid around, or slowly wander'd, I heard the echoing calls of the railroad men in the West Jersey depot yard, shifting and switching trains, engines, &c.; amid the general silence otherways, and something in the acoustic quality of the air, musical, emotional effects, never thought of before. I linger'd long and long, listening, to them."

Later, I stand in the wind atop the five-story Camden Waterfront Parking Garage – it, like other new buildings in this district of revitalization, is built of brick and terra-cotta and it quotes from the Victor derelicts a few blocks away – and I turn my back on the extraordinary view of the Philadelphia skyline and the Ben Franklin Bridge to look out over Camden. From here I can see the smokestack of the old powerhouse, with the word "Victor" still visible in faded paint on its vanquished bricks; I see two faces of the Tower on Building 17 – Nipper looks south, Nipper looks west; I see the Cooper Library and Johnson Park, in which my father might have loafed for a couple of extra minutes, leaning back on a park bench with his face upturned toward the sun after a two-martini lunch at Kenny's steakhouse, some time in the late fifties, until the one o'clock whistle would summon him back to his office at RCA; and, finally, from this high parking garage vantage, I look across the empty black lots toward Mickle Street, where, at the age of sixty-five, Whitman bought his first house, largely from book royalties, and began living there, in the spring of 1884.

Figures Nine, Ten, Eleven:
Mickle Street Photographs; Walt Whitman and Warren Fritzinger on Camden Wharf, July, 1890, John Johnston M.D.

You have made a pilgrimage from England to meet the Good Gray Poet, and you have spent hours conversing with him. Your devotion – and that of your circle of friends in Lancashire – borders on the religious; after your American pilgrimage, which will include visits to old Whitman haunts in Brooklyn and Huntington, your weekly discussion group of men and women will grow into nothing less than a church with Whitman as its messiah. And yours is not the only group of believers. Now, here in Camden, you have sworn that you will record everything he says to you, that you will note every detail of his living conditions, that you will take photographs, and this you've done. The block on Mickle Street, with maples and sycamores at curbside, seemed rural in character despite the city bustle nearby; a delivery wagon halted two doors down from his house; another approached; two ladies beneath parasols strolled in the midsummer heat: you snapped a picture. Then it was a view of the two-story frame house itself, with his housekeeper, her adopted son, and their dog posing on the front stoop; upstairs, Whitman's windows were tightly shuttered. just now, though, in the early evening as you lounge outside your hotel, he's conveyed down the sidewalk in his bentwood, rattaned wheelchair by his nurse, Warren, and Whitman invites you to accompany them down to the river's edge. "How delicious the air is!" he exclaims, and you pose him and "Warry" before a tugboat and its barge of firewood. You have already noted his "physical immensity and magnificent proportions," his "picturesque majesty," his leonine head, his streaming white hair and beard "like a cataract of materialized, white, glistening vapour, giving him a most venerable and patriarchal appearance." Hours of conversation later, you walk them back home. Every-one seems to like him. He salutes nearly all he passes – the car drivers he accosts by name; he says, "How do, boys?" to the young men, and to the women sitting on doorsteps with babies on their laps, "How do, friends, how do? Hillo, baby!" The workingmen standing idly on corners salute him with, "Good evening, Mr. Whitman," and they bow respectfully or take off their hats. After another half-hour of talk, about his health (you are, after all, a physician), he allows you to take his pulse. It is fairly full and strong and quite regular.

The wheelchair is necessary now – since early June, 1888, when he had three paralytic strokes, he is unable to get around by himself – but he continues to take pride in the measure of independence given him by home ownership ("a little old shanty of my own") and the generous attentions of his helpers. Chiefly, there is Mrs. Mary Davis, a sea cap-tain's widow, who had begun her association with Whitman by taking in clothes for mending, and who had moved into the Mickle Street house in early 1885 as housekeeper (bringing all her furniture; Whitman had none) after taking pity on the poet watching him shamble down the street one day, looking lost and alone. There's also Mrs. Davis's adoptive son Warren Fritzinger, a nursing student who is engaged to be married, whose parents Mrs. Davis had cared for until their deaths. With Warry, with Mrs. Davis, and with Mrs. Davis's modest furniture and curios and many pets – she has a dog, a cat, a canary, some turtledoves, a robin, and several chickens – Whitman will live an agreeable domestic life, in, as he will write, "the early candle-light of old age." Visitors appear in a steady stream. There is a certain amount of travel, near and far. For a time the poet had the use of a horse and carriage paid for by a group of supporters, including Mark Twain, John Greenleaf Whittier, and Oliver Wendell Holmes, and he enjoyed "taking the breeze" around Camden and en-virons; there were a number of highly publicized trips to other cities for readings and lectures. The strokes have put an end (with rare exceptions) to all but simple wheelchair jaunts down to the river, but not an end to his work, which he continues to perform in bed or in a large rocking chair with an old wolfskin robe draped over his shoulders. His poetry and prose appears in newspapers and magazines all over the country, and in 1888 the new work, titled "Sands at Seventy," is annexed to *Leaves of Grass*. A new annex grows in 1890 and 1891, "Good-bye My Fancy," continuing the backward glances, the musings on advancing death, the panoply of a full life. One late afternoon he sits in his overheated bedroom, "in twilight late alone by the flickering oak-flame, / Musing on long-pass'd war-scenes – of the countless buried unknown soldiers," and the countless brief truces when "grim burial-squads" were permitted to go out and do their jobs before the carnage resumed, and the war returns, even to Mickle Street in Camden: "Even here in my room-shadows and half-lights in the noiseless flickering flames," he scrawls, "Again I see the stalwart ranks-on-filing, rising – I hear the rhythmic tramp of the armies." He embalms the unknown in his love.

His friends have no use for workingclass Camden with its noise and smells. Edmund Bucke, the visionary Canadian psychologist, argues that the poet should move to a Baltimore nursing home he knows – the ramshackle house on Mickle Street is "the worst house and the worst situated." Jeanette L. Gilder, editor of the *Critic* and occasional publisher of his writings, thinks that "there is that about Camden which dissipates any poetic preconceptions one may have in visiting that Jersey town. One would as soon expect to find a bard in Long Island City. Even the poet's house has no outward appearance of sheltering any but an ordinary tenant beneath its roof. A two-story-and-a-half frame building, painted a dark brown, with the upper shutters closed and the edges of the loose-fitting lower window-sashes stuffed with newspapers to keep out the wind beating down from the north greets the searcher. . . ." "Poor but respectable," says William Roscoe Thayer of the neighborhood, "with a suggestion that unrespectability was just around the corner." John Burroughs proposes that he resettle near him in a cottage in Esopus, New York. "How I wish you were here," the naturalist writes in 1888, "or somewhere else in the country where all these sweet influences of the season could minister to you. Your reluctance to move is just what ought to be overcome. It is like the lethargy of a man beginning to freeze." To J. W. Wallace, another visiting Lancashire enthusiast, Whitman turns away the friends' concerns, saying that he finds Camden and Mickle Street tolerable enough, with his attendants' ministrations: "Every cock likes his own dunghill best."

Figure 12:
Mickle Boulevard, 1996
Nipper is still listening up in his tower, a half mile away, as you pull onto Mickle Street – correction, it's now Mickle Boulevard, urban renewal having swallowed a double row of houses encompassing the north side of old Mickle and everything that was Bridge Street, the four resulting lanes of asphalt now divided with concrete urban renewal planters – the same used

to keep terrorists away from public buildings – and the planters are empty. Half of Walt's side of the block is also missing, gone to bulldozers, and the rubble has largely been scraped smooth; you'll steal an old Mickle Street brick when you leave. And what's this directly across the street from Walt's little gray two-story clapboard house and its three remaining companions? A county jail. Hulking, formidable, concrete. Behind razor wire in a compound are squad cars and a blue and white Tastykake delivery truck, which looks like a swat *vehicle and probably is one. Up the street a new court-house stands to keep the jail full. "You felons on trial in courts, / You convicts in prison-cells, you sentenced assassins chain'd and handcuff'd with iron," he wrote in 1860 about Manhattan's Tombs, "Who am I too that I am not on trial or in prison?"*

A police car is hugging the bumper of my rental car as I drive slowly up and down Mickle Boulevard. When I innocently, self-consciously stop across from the Whitman house to sketch the four old buildings left on Walt's block, the officer flashes his lights at me. In my rearview mirror he is pushing at the air over his steering wheel and brandishing a fat ticket book. Time to move on. I do, and make sure I don't commit a U-turn when I head back on Walt's side and stop at a parking meter in front of his house. I am generous with my quarters.

No one answers my knock. I have been warned that the Whitman house has been renumbered by the Post Office to number 330 Mickle Boulevard, and there is no mistaking the house: two stories, peeling gray clapboards, shutters removed from the facade. Several blocks down the street, past a boarded-up brick tavern called "Harbor Place," and a store-front Iglesia de Dios Pentacostal Fuente de Vida, and a wig and beauty shop, and an opened-early bar and grill near the courthouse called "Off-Duty Lounge," I find a working public phone, stand in line with a couple of dealers and a woman in a pair of Guess jeans who speaks briefly with a bail bondsman's answering service, and finally I reach Margaret O'Neil, the Whitman House curator. "Where did you go?" she asks. "By the time I got down to the door you were driving away. Just ring the bell this time." And then I am admitted.

For years after Whitman's death, the little house was rented out to boarders by George Whitman – until, in fact, 1923, when the city bought it and began a museum. Until then visitors on pilgrimages would find the street address, knock on the door, and ask if this was Walt Whitman's place. "He doesn't live here!" the renter would shout and slam the door. But now he is most assuredly here. Off a dark, narrow hallway are the two connected parlors in which he entertained visitors until he could no longer manage the steep staircase – "comfortable enough," recalled his *Critic* editor, Jeanette L. Gilder, "but suggestive of anything rather than poetry." In his time, flowered wallpaper ran busily up from floor to wainscoting, and the upper walls were festooned with sconces, bricabrac shelves, mirrors and portraits in gilded frames – his parents', notably, and his own – and on either side of an old German mantle clock countless unmounted photographs and cards stood or leaned together or began a tumble toward the floor. Plaster statues, busts, a ship's model, and a stuffed bird stood on bookcases or on the bare floorboards. His rattan wheelchair was one of many chairs in the parlor, most of them, and the overstuffed easy chair and sofa, supporting stacks of opened books, magazines, or newspapers. Now the rooms are still filled with ephemera, artifacts, curiosities, and paintings, including a recent copy of the famous portrait by Thomas Eakins. A guestbook records present-day visitors' homes – Las Vegas, New Mexico; Tempe, Arizona; Nagano, Japan; Appleton, Wisconsin; Deposit, New York; and Brunswick, Georgia. I add Orwell, Vermont. In back, a dilapidated, water-stained and gape-holed chamber stands where Mary Davis's kitchen was; one can nearly peer through the ceiling (from which once hung the housekeeper's four birdcages with their deafening, voluble occupants) into the overhead room. Upstairs from the front hall are the two bedrooms; Mrs. Davis's, in back, is empty, structurally damaged, and unsafe to enter, but Whitman's, overlooking Mickle Boulevard, its shutters now removed to let in the bright light, is furnished in approximation. There is his heavy old bed and some old bookcases, mostly empty; pictures cover the walls. It was remarkably different in the old days – Whitman only opened the shutters to peer out onto the street, so it was always dark and stuffy – in wintertime, his old bones easily chilled, he kept a stove going full-blast. And the place resembled a rubbish pile. "I was more and more struck with the disorder on all sides," recalled Elizabeth Leavitt Keller, who attended his latter days. "My first glance had been of bewilderment; I now looked with deliberation and amazement at my surroundings. Confusion, dust and litter – it seemed the accumulation of ages. I afterwards learned that for over two years no books, magazines, or manuscripts had been removed from this, Walt Whitman's peculiar sanctum. There were no bookcases, large shelves or writing-desk; there was no receptacle for newspapers, and apart from the two overloaded tables, the floor had received all of them. Upon this general table the daily papers had been dropped when read; the weeklies had followed, and in their turn the monthly magazines. An immense number of periodicals and pamphlets had been received in the course of two years, and all were still there. Almost everything was yellow with age and soiled with the constant tramping of feet." It was two feet deep across much of the room with the notable exception of the left side of his bedstead, where it was four – although after investigation Mrs. Keller found a buried lounge. "The tables stood like cows in a meadow with the grass up to their bodies," she added. In the litter she found "innumerable letters; thousands of requests for autographs; poems that had been submitted to his criticism; friendly letters from home and abroad; all his business correspondence; postal cards, notes of congratulations, invitations, envelopes unnumbered, visiting cards, wrapping papers of all brands and sizes, a variety of string of all lengths . . . several pieces of rope, coins, pins galore, countless pictures, many photographs of himself. . . . And under all, some little crusted brown worms had made their home. Moths flew around the room in perfect security, and industrious spiders had curtained the corners and windows." Ernest Rhys, of his British publisher, once visited and observed that "out of this sea of paper he always seemed able to fish up any particular print he wished to mention," but nonetheless items disappeared for years at a time.

There has been talk, Margaret O'Neil tells me, of restoring this chaos to the bedroom, with velvet ropes to keep visitors from venturing too far into the room. As I contemplate this, wondering if moths and cobwebs will be included, I stand at the window and look out past a sycamore tree's upper branches onto the boulevard. Across the street, a man in a gray windbreaker and jeans stands on the sidewalk next to the jail, gesticulating wildly as he looks to an upper story. There is a Camden jail sign language; the man is carrying on an urgent, not altogether private conversation with an inmate within.

Figure 13:
Coat of Arms, Camden, N.J. (1907)
"The design is a shield, the dexter half containing the arms of Lord Camden, the sinister half an antique ship in the stocks ready for launching, indicative of Camden's shipbuilding industries; supporters personifying industry and knowledge, the old locomotive that first ran into Camden, emblematic of the city of to-day, the great railroad centre of West Jersey, Lord Camden's crest, and the pine tree springing from it, typifying the primeaval forest that covered so much of Camden's territory and recalling the origin of its first name, Pyne Poynte." – Howard M. Cooper, "Historical Sketch of Camden, N.J.," 1909. Virtus et Industria: *At left she stands, books at her*

feet and cradled in her arm's nook, the light of learning at hand; at right
stands he in his laborer's apron and printer's cap, a wrench in one hand and
a maul in the other, with a large cogwheel behind. Above the shield floats a
crown. Above the crown grows a pine.

Dutch and Swedish explorers investigating the Delaware River in the first half of the seventeenth century noted at a deep bend in the river the thickly growing pine forest above a bold bluff, near a stream with a remarkable number of deer about; William Cooper, an Englishman who like other Quakers had been drawn to the area around Philadelphia, settled there in 1681, finding with the abundant pines "peach trees and the sweet smelling sassafras tree." He called it Pyne Poynte. Showing gifts of diplomacy and fairness, he not only secured a British deed to the place but paid a good sum to the Delaware tribe for their title. A few other enterprising Quakers located there, and soon enough a ferry to Philadelphia was established; for more than one hundred years the settlement would be known as "Cooper's Ferry." The names of those earliest settlers – notably William Cooper, John Kaighin (from the Isle of Man), Archibald Mickle (from Ireland), and Elizabeth Haddon (England) – are enshrined nowadays on important thoroughfares; their many descendants remained in Camden into this century. The settlement did not grow much, but in 1773 it acquired the dignity of a formal survey under the auspices of Jacob Cooper, a merchant. He named the town Camden to honor Charles Pratt, Earl of Camden (1714–1794), the vociferous defender of the American colonies' rights whose name was similarly given to twenty other towns in the nation. "The British Parliament has no right to tax the Americans," he had thundered in the House of Lords in 1765, "Taxation and representation are inseparably united. God hath joined them; no British Parliament can put them asunder. To endeavour to do so is to stab our very vitals." Soon after its naming, the Revolution broke out, and Camden was often overrun by British and Hessian troops; two skirmishes there occurred, in which the colonial heroes Mad Anthony Wayne and Count Pulaski figured.

Two other famous names of the era are included in Camden's early history, that of Franklin and Washington. Benjamin Franklin had been but a teenager when he left Boston for Philadelphia seeking work as a printer, in 1723. He found an evening boat for Philadelphia at Burlington, New Jersey, and was forced to take up an oar along with all other passengers when the wind failed. At midnight, midstream in the Delaware, the voyagers became convinced they had rowed past the unlighted town and put in at the New Jersey shore where they built a fire of fence rails. At daybreak they found they had camped at the mouth of Cooper's Creek, just across from their destination, and with this inauspicious event young Benjamin Franklin crossed the river about where a bridge would much later be built and named in his honor, and began his new life. George Washington, while serving as President and living in the then-capital city of Philadelphia, often took Cooper's ferry to Camden for a horseback jaunt in the West Jersey countryside. Howard M. Cooper, the best chronicler of the city's early history, whose "Historical Sketch" (1909) has yielded most of the stories in this section, relates the story of Washington's last ride there, in 1797. "He nearly frightened out of his wits a Dutchman, a Hessian deserter at the battle of Trenton," Cooper writes, "who said to him, 'I tink I has seen your face before; vat ish your name?' The President, reining in his horse and bowing said, 'My name is George Washington.' The Dutchman, thunderstruck, cried out, 'Oh, mine Gott, I vish I vos unter te ice. I vish I vos unter te ice. Oh, mine Gott.' Washington reassured him and smilingly rode on."

After Independence, the city as ferry-port and concentrator of mercantile goods and Jersey produce was free to grow, especially from the 1830s when the railroad era commenced. The Camden and Amboy Railroad, the state's first, chartered in 1830, was to stretch from the Camden ferry slip to the Amboy city ferries carrying passengers and goods to Manhattan. For a while, at least, the Camden and Amboy would be the longest rail line in the country; the nation's first locomotive, made in England, was named the *John Bull*. Understandably in that innocent time, the appearance of the railroad – even during its construction – was an occasion of great excitement. Cooper recounts that "people kept watch to see the trains arrive . . . going to the tops of their houses to view the novel sight." While the line was still being built, around 1831 or 1832, a congressman from Kentucky by the name of David Crockett interrupted his trip to Washington to stay at a Camden hotel on Federal Street, just up from the ferry. He and some friends went to a shooting match within sight of a completed stretch of the Camden and Amboy. He was squinting down his rifle barrel toward the faraway target when a great clanking roar rose up behind him. Shaken, he whirled to behold the *John Bull* – all noise, smoke, and cinders, pulling a work train – advancing up the track toward him. As it passed he was dumbstruck. Finally, in wonder he exclaimed, "Hell in harness!"

The combination of Delaware ferries and railroad terminii (two lines eventually joined the C&A in the city) sealed Camden's financial success for a century; after the Civil War, as the 1876 Bird's Eye View attests, there was an explosive growth of factories along the entire waterfront, and when every site was filled, says the WPA Guide, "the shops and mills overran the town." A tremendous influx of laborers from abroad and from the American South swelled population. Throughout the Gilded Age, across the turn of the century, and well into the 1930s, with all this industrial expansion there was a concurrent interest in civic affairs; up rose churches, free schools, public libraries, charitable and cultural institutions, a prize-winning sanitary waterworks (it beat out Philadelphia's typhoid-breeders for years), hospitals, three successive city halls, and three successive courthouses (each monumentally reflective of those architecturally ambitious times). To be sure, such reliance on industrial plants coupled with the cheap neighborhoods necessary to sustain a large labor force gave Camden a less than elegant appearance, though there were exceptions. Even the WPA writers of the New Jersey state guide of 1938 – usually, as in all volumes in the Federal Writers' Project, trying their best to put a positive spin on what they saw and described – could muster only half-hearted praise. Camden, they wrote delicately, "is utilitarian in architecture and arrangment of streets. . . . [It] represents a job and a home. It might be called a two-story brick town, but there is beauty as well as naked utility in its brickwork." There were, to be sure, blocks of rowhouses resembling the prewar high-rent gentrification of Greenwich Village, and occasional grand houses, but "there are also rows upon rows of tight boxlike houses without space between," of red or yellow brick, with the other colors of Camden described as a universal "utilitarian brown," or a variation, brownstone brown, with the occasional mansard's slate, or the "peculiar yellow-green" of serpentine building stone. However, conceded the guidebook writers, "unlike many other industrial cities, Camden seems to make a point of keeping streets and sidewalks neat and clean." Faint praise, that.

If anything signaled the beginning of the city's demise – decades before the postwar decline of the predominately nineteenth-century industrial base, or the white flight of the fifties, or the bulldozer blade of urban renewal in the sixties, or the long, drawn-out, drying-up of federal and state educational, job-training, and welfare aid, and the desperate deepening of poverty – it was the construction of the Delaware River Bridge (later named after Ben Franklin when the Walt Whitman Bridge was raised downriver). Completed in 1926 after it became apparent that Camden's many ferries were still unequal to the burgeoning automobile traffic, the bridge and its approach obliterated a beautiful residential section and sent most of its citizens of means out to the Jersey suburbs. But more significantly, it encouraged the lifeblood of commerce to speed past the heart of Camden, high over the river and into Philadelphia. Terse, businesslike President Calvin Coolidge cut the opening ceremonial ribbon of what was at the time the longest suspension bridge in the world. Also in attendance at the opening was Will Rogers, who spoke on less lofty matters; Philadelphia, with its history of blue laws, closed its taverns at midnight on Saturdays, giving Camden establishments the drinking trade. "Week-end parties in particular," admitted the WPA guide, "are longer and more enjoyable on the New Jersey side of the river," but then celebrants had to time their return to Philadelphia with night-running ferries; sometimes they were stranded. "Now we have a bridge," crowed Will Rogers to the gleeful multitude at the ribbon-cutting, "we can get out of Camden when we want to."

Figure 14:
Pencil Sketch, Tomb at Harleigh Cemetery, 1890, Walt Whitman
For that of you which is to die. It will summon the image of King Solomon's temple, some of your more extravagant friends will say, but they are wrong for it will be anything but ornate. You take a scrap of paper and make haste with the sketch, having in mind a Blake engraving, "At Death's Door"; your rough rendering makes it look like a simple woodshed but its final form is clear in your mind: above, the triangular pediment will simply bear your name, and it will sit massively over a plain entablature and two great supporting stones flanking the door. In your hand: "Harleigh Cemetery Camden Co., New Jersey. Walt Whitman Burial Vault . . . 20 x 30 feet on a sloping wooded hill . . . surrounding trees, turf, sky, hill, everything crude and natural . . . vault [of] heavy undress'd Quincy, Mass. grey granite — unornamented." The door will be six-inch-thick granite, and it will remain open so that your soul will be free.

In the summer of 1887, the Whitman enthusiast William Sloane Kennedy of Boston returned from a visit to Camden, finding the city torrid, Whitman's house airless, and the poet's demeanor fatigued though good-humored; during a previous pilgrimage in midsummer, Kennedy had heard the old man vent about the irritating habit of neighborhood women going out two or three times a day with their brooms and stirring up the water in the gutters, lowering dust, hastening absorption and evaporation. "If they would only leave it alone," Whitman had complained; he thought it caused malaria. Kennedy determined to join the ranks of supporters pulling for Whitman's release from the city, even if for just the

sweltering months. He and a few friends, including the journalist Sylves-
ter Baxter, began to put away money. "Our original project," wrote Baxter
later, "was to raise the money quietly, build the cottage, and have somebody drive Whitman out there and take him by surprise." They hoped to
build the cottage at Timber Creek in the Jersey countryside where Whitman had repaired body and spirit in 1876 and occasionally thereafter. But
the project leaked out to the press and subscriptions poured in, one from
Mark Twain, who disliked *Leaves of Grass*, but sympathized with the
situation of the Good Gray Poet. "What we want to do is to make the
splendid old soul comfortable," Twain wrote, "and do what we do heartily
and as a privilege." An architect and an artist contributed plans and
appointments, and Whitman's host out at Timber Creek pledged the
property. "But," recalled Baxter afterward, "when we raised the money,
we sent it to Whitman for him to build how and where he pleased,
thinking he would take delight, as an old builder, in looking after the
matter himself. He intended to do this, but he never got round to it. I
think the lethargy of age was creeping over him fast, and he lacked the
energy to make a beginning."

Another admirer's gift intervened when the owners of Harleigh Cemetery, on the Camden outskirts, attempted to attract business by giving a
prominent local person – Whitman – a plot of his choice. The park lawn
cemetery had opened its gate in August, 1886, borrowing its landscape
design from the Parisian Pére La Chaise, Cambridge's Mount Auburn,
and Philadelphia's Laurel Hill, and its circular drives, open lawns, and
manmade lakes, and requirement that there be no internal fences nor any
monument copying another, gave the cemetery an open, bucolic, intriguing, even cheerful affect. Showing the same lethargy noticed by Baxter,
Whitman hesitated for a year before accepting, but he picked a pleasant
hillside spot on Christmas Day in 1890; it must have reminded him of
Timber Creek with its "primitive solitudes, winding stream, recluse and
woody banks, sweet-feeding springs, and all the charms that birds, grass,
wild-flowers, rabbits and squirrels, old oaks, walnut trees, &c., can bring."
He thereupon became happily preoccupied with the tomb's construction,
in part using the money from his supporters' cottage fund. Afterward, in
the few occasions that he got out in early 1891, he liked to take visitors
there. "I was once taken for a ride in [Whitman's] carriage," recalled
Harrison S. Morris, a friend, and "Walt said: 'Where shall we go?' I had
no preference. He then said . . . 'You have not been to the tomb!' . . . and
he called out, 'Same place, Harry,' as though the tomb were his common
resort."

On May 31st, 1891, his seventy-second birthday, at Mickle Street,

Warren Fritzinger carried him downstairs to a banquet in his honor. Some thirty of his most ardent friends crammed themselves at long tables squeezed into the two small parlors. He could not walk and he could barely see, but the champagne was iced and the food was rich, and amidst the gouty, over-caloric speeches and adoring declarations, Whitman's own quivering, tenor voice could be heard, trying to explain to them something about poetic inspiration: "Equip, equip, equip from every quarter," he said in self-definition, from "science, observation, travel, reading, study." Then "turn everything over to the emotional – the personality."

Late summer and all of autumn were devoted to preparing the "final" edition of *Leaves of Grass.* "I have probably not been enough afraid," he wrote in a kind of preface, "of careless touches, from the first – and am not now – nor of parrot-like repetitions – nor platitudes and the commonplace. Perhaps I am too democratic for such avoidances." To his readers he was unabashed in his frailty but capable still of a little wry humor – he was "much like some hard-cased dilapidated grim ancient shell-fish or timebang'd conch (no legs, utterly non-locomotive) cast up high and dry on the shore-sands, helpless to move anywhere – nothing left but behave myself quiet, and while away the days yet assgn'd. . . ."

Soon after he finished the publication process and received his first copies of what would be called the "Deathbed Edition," Whitman began his final slide. His "last deliberate composition" (his executor's words) was dated December 1891, and it was titled, "A Thought of Columbus." The dying old man's creative thought leaped across the time and tumult of the ages and linked to the navigator's.

The last collapse began on December 17th. In his cluttered little room on an unremarkable street in the clamorous, smoky city, his final miracle would be that he took so long to die. "Now he lay on a decrepit bedstead," writes Justin Kaplan, "in a shabby bug-ridden room with paper peeling off the walls and the ceiling plaster beginning to fall. He subsisted mainly on milk punch and month after month lingered on, but so tuberculous, wasted, congested, atrophied, abscessed, tumored, collapsed, and obstructed that his body, like that of Poe's M. Valdemar, was a carnival ground of decay, and his survival evidence of the countervailing force of constitution and unconscious will."

With that power of will he lived until March 26, 1892, when, in the company of five friends including Mrs. Davis, he breathed his last. "There was no sign of struggle," recalled Horace Traubel. "The light flickered, lowered, was quenched. He seemed to suffer no pain. . . . He passed away as peacefully as the sun, and it was hard to catch the moment of transition. That solemn watch, the gathering shadow, the painless surrender, are not to be forgotten. His soul went out with the day. The face was calm, the body lay without rigidity, the majesty of his tranquil spirit remained. What more could be said? It was a moment not for the doctor, but for the poet, the seer."

Figure 15:
Statue of Walt Whitman (1992) by John Giannotti
You are standing in Whitman's upstairs chamber looking at a brochure, at a picture of an eight-foot bronze statue by the Camden sculptor, John Giannotti. It is patterned after the legendary Phillips and Taylor photograph of 1883, taken in Ocean Grove, New Jersey, in which Whitman is seated on a rustic bench, his right hand upright, with a butterfly balanced on his forefinger. The photograph became the frontispiece of the 1889 edition of Leaves of Grass. *"To the romantic-minded," writes Gay Wilson Allen in "The Iconography of Walt Whitman," "here was a poet so close to nature that he could draw a butterfly to him and induce it to light on his finger." The romantic-minded would have been disillusioned to learn that a cardboard butterfly, wired to fasten on the finger, was discovered among Whitman's notebooks in the Library of Congress. The Whitman statue is to be placed in a vestpocket park down Mickle Street from the house, one dedicated to the citizens of Camden and designed by neighborhood residents in conjunction with professional architects "to bring neighbors and visitors together to experience the commonality of America," says the brochure, which also predicts the imminent opening of a state Walt Whitman museum in the two rowhouses alongside number 330 Mickle Street. As you read this you notice that the handsomely-designed brochure is five years old, with the completion dates nearly four years past, and the site is still as the bulldozer left it.*

A hole has been knocked through the upstairs wall between Whitman's dwelling and the three-story house next door, which at this point is restored with new wiring, lighting, and wallboard and is mostly empty but for a bare bones curator's office for Margaret O'Neil and a museum restroom for visitors. One can see where the gift shop might be, and one takes cheer from the thought of "interpretive displays" and "historical artifacts of and about Whitman," some of which are currently in storage and some of which sit randomly around the poet's house, awaiting funds for a reverent restoration. Another house beyond, presumably to be inwardly coupled to these, is the Walt Whitman Association office and library, headquarters of a private, nonprofit group dedicated to preservation of the house and promotion of his works and repository of a private collection of Whitman materials. All is not good in New Jersey culture-land, alas, the brochure's dated predictions notwithstanding. For in these budget-cutting hard times, with a Republican in the state house, the Whitman house is in trouble – certainly not helped by its administrative place within the state's Department of Environmental Protection and Division of Parks and Forests, a prime target area. Overall the state will cut six jobs from its historic sites budget – for a savings of just $150,000. The state plans to discharge the Whitman house's full-time curator in four months, end its educational and cultural programs, and reduce the facility's open days from five to two per week, Margaret O'Neil tells me. That the Governor of New Jersey is named Whitman – she is, assuredly, no relation – seems a particular irony. (A month later, during state legislature deliberations, staff funds for New Jersey's historic sites was restored to the year's budget, after a flood of calls and letters from individuals all over the country. The Whitman house will remain open full-time next year, although year by year it will continue to be vulnerable to political raids.)

Downstairs again, and in a somber mood thinking about the halted restoration project and the threatened cuts, I pause in the entryhall, where there is framed the doctor's notice of Whitman's death, which had been nailed to the poet's front door on the evening of March 26th, 1892. One hundred and four years later (and three days before I would stand here in Whitman's front hall), Margaret O'Neil tells me, the Whitman Association commemorated his death with a well-attended gathering; participants read from his poetry and from accounts of his death. Attendees were also treated to a singular literary reading, that of Dr. Henry W. Cattell's autopsy report, which of course left no area of the corpus unexplored, and which pronounced that the cause of death was "pleurisy of the left side, consumption of the right lung, general miliary tuberculosis and parenchymatous nephritis." "It is, indeed, marvellous," concluded the physician, "that respiration could have been carried on for so long a time with the limited amount of useful lung tissue found at the autopsy. It was no doubt due largely to that indomitable will pertaining to Walt Whitman. Another would have died much earlier with one-half of the pathological changes which existed in his body."

Out on Mickle Boulevard, with the doorlock of Whitman's house clicking behind me as I descend two steps to the brick sidewalk, I see there are now three correspondents across the street at the jail, waving hands, whirling arms, patting the air for the benefit of inmates within. A police cruiser advances slowly and the correspondents busy themselves getting elsewhere. Me, I head to the cemetery.

There is time, though, for a detour to Pomona Hall in a gentler neighborhood of Camden, a stately dwelling of the Cooper family for two centuries and now the home of the Camden County Historical Society. There I find exhibits of Camden's settlement and colonial days, of the shipbuilding era, of its industrial past and relics of its glory days, with Campell's and RCA Victor standing in the forefront just as they did in the waterfront of old; there I find a Victor exhibit, with photographs and gramophone and arcana only steps away from a huge flat wooden crate which holds the last original stained glass Nipper window from Building 17; there I find an excellent little library of local history, presided over by the capable and generous librarian and historian Paul Schopp; there I find, in a large ornate frame, the yellowed "Bird's Eye View of Camden in the Centennial Year 1876" by Thaddeus Fowler, into which my imagination allows me to fall – like a skydiver leaping from the present and being suddenly catapulted back through time to an era when giants like Whitman walked the earth – and there I am, floating, like the artist Fowler above a city of smoke and sounds and smells, and the form of this essay becomes suddenly clear. Paul Schopp will take my eagerness without understanding it exactly, and indefatigably procure me a copy of the Bird's Eye.

There are other reasons to put off the cemetery – a Camden County Historical Society pamphlet, with its self-guided tour inside, will lead me around the city where I will see, at mile 0.8, the site of Camden Central Airport with its boast of being the first rooftop landing by an auto gyro (the forerunner of the helicopter) in 1938; at mile 1.0, the site of Weber's Hof Brau nightclub (where comedian Red Skelton began his career); at mile 1.1, the site of the nation's first drive-in movie theater, where in 1933, a businessman named R. M. Hollingshead Jr. noticed that with the Depression the last things people were willing to give up were their cars and their movies, "so he decided to put the two together;" at mile 1.3, the site of another Depression fancy, the "Automobile Roller Coaster," where for a quarter daring motorists could drive their cars on a big wooden U-shaped structure with fifteen or twenty hills; at mile 3.3, the site of the vanished Walt Whitman Hotel, which featured a large lobby mural, which, as Gay Wilson Allen has noted, "was highly symbolical, presenting Whitman as a semidivine figure silently 'charging' the men and women of various occupations with his spiritual power;" at mile 4.5, the site of the Temple Theatre, in whose stock company the young actor Francis X. Bushman launched his career in 1910. The meandering drive will also take me back past Cooper Hospital, the Whitman House, the waterfront, the RCA Victor plants, the Cooper Library, and, unerringly, it will lead me in a final straight line to the gates of Harleigh Cemetery.

I always find much that is interesting in burial grounds, from the iconography of gravestones to the terse stories told by occupants' recorded life spans to the epitaphs carved therein: *Mary B. Bowden, 1845– 1903 / "She hath done what she could."* Harleigh is no exception, with its towering Celtic Cross wrought by Alexander Stirling Calder (father of the mobilist) for the Sewell family plot, and its lifesize bronze elk presiding over a hundred members of the Elks Lodge #293 BPOE but of course Harleigh's most famous feature is the Whitman tomb, tucked down a dell and into a hillside, not far from the fence separating the park cemetery from Our Lady of Lourdes Hospital, where my sister was born.

Surprisingly, nothing has prepared me for the beautiful simplicity, the utter finality, of this particular granite structure with the name *Walt Whitman* carved into the triangular pediment. Everywhere there is the springtime odor of decaying leaves, moist soil, reawakening ivy. On the flanking hillsides, beneath overhanging trees and freshly-planted rhododendrons, are several dozen strewn blocks of granite, all with deliberate chisel marks – spoiled gravestones among clumps of daffodils. A pond lies nearby. Crow caws sound overhead. On the sidewall of the tomb, three albino pigeons sit contentedly and regard me. I can see numerous names carved into the tree trunks above me: *Pete '83 / Carol & Maria '68 / Jim Morrison / Niki & Lori / I love you Walt.* Beyond the tomb's open door, beyond its locked iron gate, there are the seven crypts of Whitman and his family members, mother, father, stolid brother George and his wife Louisa, poor feebleminded brother Eddie. Walt. Water drips into a puddle of water and sycamore and oak leaves inside the tomb. And behind me, a few feet away, rises a modest new commemorative stone with a relief portrait of the poet and some of his most famous words:

I depart as air, I shake my white locks at the runaway sun,
I effuse my flesh in eddies, and drift it in lacy jags.

I bequeath myself to the dirt to grow from the grass I love,
If you want me again look for me under your boot-soles.

Boot-soles and a newborn baby's footprints somehow merge. Somewhere an attentive dog barks and a father waits patiently. But now my faraway children beckon, as does the rest of my life, which began in this home soil beneath my boot-soles, and it is time to pay my respects and to depart. The words beyond Whitman's carved words in "Song of Myself" spill off the edge of the granite stone and into my mind: *You will hardly know who I am or what I mean, / But I shall be good health to you nevertheless, / And filter and fibre your blood. / Failing to fetch me at first keep encouraged, / Missing me one place search another, / I stop somewhere waiting for you.*

A jet flies far overhead. Tomorrow I will be on one just like it and it will be rainy and foggy as the plane ascends, and I will get one more bird's eye view of my birth-city as it breaks up and obscures in haze, and I will be the only one on the craft to look there as we rise and then the only one to look down to my lap where *Leaves of Grass* sits, and in a cloudburst of inspiration I will turn to "The Voice of the Rain," where I read:

And forever, by day and night, I give back life to my own origin, and make pure and beautify it.

And when I look back out the porthole, the city is, of course, gone.

A Room with a Bath

W e chose the room with the bath instead of the room with the view. To be sure the chamber overlooking the Latomia gave access to a rickety bower which the optimistic and the courteous would call a balcony, yet we declined it without reluctance. We selected an utterly inadequate sleeping space whose size made us marvel anew at the ingenuity of the race which had managed to insert a bed therein. The one window of this architectural afterthought commanded a striking prospect of shed-top and chicken-yard but its intimately adjoining bath-room was palatial. We could not see the mimosa and almond blossoms but we could smell the cinnamon pungency of our carnation soap.

Everything has a price and the inevitable rooster among the neighboring good fowls had the delusion, common to all poultry residing in the vicinity of hotels, that he was a cuckoo-clock. He crowed all the hours, halves and quarters, with a faithfulness which another might have found touching. This is not by way of complaint. It is only idle comment, though there may be those who prefer to consider it a justly material retribution.

Syracuse, we soon discovered, is a central point for tourists because it is necessary to stop over at least two days to do the town conscientiously – the Greek theatre and the Roman amphitheatre and the Catholic cathedral, not counting forts, fountains, and public buildings. English tourists, especially, rally in hordes at Syracuse and we see them loitering in neutral silence on the outskirts of popular ruins, or in adenoidy conversation at tea.

Although we encounter them often, we are not yet inured to the appearance of the female of the breed. The middle-class Englishwoman-on-tour resembles nothing else on earth. We see her unwavering and uncomplaining in hotel foyers, as mutely desolate as a hitching post in Times Square. Her face is a weary blur of mottled flesh, the features aimlessly and unpleasantly arranged about a nose of singular patina. Her lower jaw hangs down in a relaxed fashion, exposing teeth.

We are unable to find words adequately descriptive of the structure which is skewered upon her head; so we consider the garment which covers her meagre body. It is a coat draped loosely, save where it is belted an impartial and sexless distance between knee and neck. About the coat's upper edges is a weird fringe of vegetation suggesting fur. It projects in spiky clumps and whorls punctuated by long feelers, which vibrate gently when anyone passes. The lady is mounted on bony legs quite devoid of contour. They terminate in shoes of such construction and dimension as to explain her economy of movement. She grasps a bulging bag still bearing traces of native bead work and she is well hung with devices, some ornamental and studded with garnet and cat's-eye, others utilitarian and suggesting an imminent departure to remote unexplored regions.

We wonder what she pursues in her hurried and unrewarded peregrinations about the globe, or, at least, the flatter parts of it. She interests anyone who finds in observing others an anodyne for the binding discomfort of being only one person in a lifetime. For an individual like this Englishwoman, imaginative detours are, mercifully, almost impossible. She goes about in a world of guidebooks, views, and decent-places-for-tea.

We say that we travel to see new places and old things. We pretend that traveling is a voyage of discovery when it is really a flight: a flight from ennui and duty and the usual, a flight from persons and localities reminiscent of too much, a flight from reality. As city succeeds city and country follows country we lose ourselves in a sequence of places and events. We feel the past and present mingled in us; we sense the involved relationship of all things to time. Our personal world acquires a sort of fourth dimension, and we know the security of being infinitesimal.

As nowhere else, in the Latomia Cappuccini – quarries which date from the Athenian supremacy – one's own personality is torn away by the combined forces of an impressive setting and historical association. It is incredible that these great pits could have been gouged from the earth by any human agency. Their rough, grand conception – or, rather, their superb planlessness – makes them seem the work of an original cause. We wander under blundering archways into caverns and rock-crowded shafts in which it seems as if the walls must shut upon us like a fist clenching. The sky is only a jagged strip of blue incised brutally by the cliff-tops. Harsh shadows settle about everywhere, split by surging shafts of gold, strange and unexpected.

Here seven thousand captive Athenians were starved to death. The foliage is luxuriant, contrasting strongly with the gaunt walls. Perhaps the bodies of the ignobly dead have enriched the once sterile soil and find an unsatisfactory reincarnation in this restless, omnivorous plant-life. One leafless tree, borne down by rattling gray twigs, is tortured into growth between two giant rocks, the symbol of a very bitter frustration. All about it are the sprightly entwining branches of lemon trees.

What can cast shadows where nothing obstructs the sun? What is the secret of the seven thousand? We decide to postpone reflections until we have managed a tub in the handsome bathroom, and then, with our corporeal self on a comfortably material level, the incorporeal remainder – unhampered by the need for a bath and a change – may go where it damn well pleases.

Contributors

DAVID HAWARD BAIN is the author of four books of nonfiction including *Empire Express: Building the First Transcontinental Railroads* (Viking 1999). His essays have been published in *Smithsonian* and *American Heritage*, and he reviews regularly for *The New York Times Book Review*. "Camden Bound" appeared in the fall 1998 issue of *Prairie Schooner*. He teaches writing at Middlebury College.

STEPHEN K. BAUER's work has been published in the *Louisville Review* and *Sewanee Review*. "Reading the Currents" appeared in the fall 1996 issue of *Prairie Schooner*. He teaches writing at Babson College.

JO ANN BEARD's essays have appeared in *New Yorker, Story,* and *Iowa Review*. Her first collection of essays, *The Boys of My Youth*, was published by Little, Brown in 1998. "Cousins" appeared in the winter 1995 issue of *Prairie Schooner*.

JUDITH ORTIZ COFER has published several books of poetry and fiction in English and Spanish. Her recent books are *Woman in Front of the Sun: On Becoming a Writer* (U of Georgia P, 2000) and *The Year of Our Revolution* (Arté Publico, 1998). "*Casa*" appeared in the fall 1989 issue of *Prairie Schooner*. She is the Franklin Professor of English and Creative Writing at the University of Georgia.

VIRGINIA FAULKNER (1913–80) was a novelist, screenwriter, and internationally respected scholar on the works of Willa Cather and Mari Sandoz. She served as editor-in-chief of the University of Nebraska Press from 1959 until her death, and she was also a professor of English at the University of Nebraska–Lincoln and an associate editor for *Prairie Schooner*. "A Room with a Bath" was Faulkner's first published work, appearing in the summer 1932 issue of *Prairie Schooner* when Faulkner was a nineteen-year-old student at the University of Nebraska (the essay was also reprinted in the winter 1981 issue).

ROBIN HEMLEY is professor of English and creative writing at Western Washington University and editor of the *Bellingham Review*. He has published a novel, three collections of short stories, and most recently, *Nola: A Memoir of Faith, Art, and Madness* (Graywolf, 1998). "Jinx" appeared in the spring 1997 issue of *Prairie Schooner*.

JONATHAN HOLDEN has published collections of poetry and essays and books of criticism. His latest books are *Knowing: New and Selected Poems* and *The Old Formalism: Character in Contemporary American Poetry* (U of Arkansas P, 2000) and *Guns and Boyhood in America: A Memoir of Growing Up in the '50s* (U of Michigan P, 1997). "Tea and Sympathy" appeared in the fall 1995 issue of *Prairie Schooner*. He is University Distinguished Professor of English and Poet-in-Residence at Kansas State University.

MIROSLAV HOLUB is author of several collections of poetry and essays, translated from Czech, including *Shedding Life: Disease, Politics and Other Human Conditions* (Milkweed Editions, 1997). "Otters, Beavers and Me" appeared in the winter 1992 issue of *Prairie Schooner*.

JUDITH KITCHEN teaches creative essay writing at the State University of New York at Brockport. Poetry reviewer for *Georgia Review*, she is the author of a collection of essays, *Only the Dance* (U of South Carolina P), and coeditor of *In Short*, an anthology of short nonfiction (Norton). "Fred Astaire's Hands" appeared in the fall 1997 issue of *Prairie Schooner*.

TED KOOSER is the author of several books of poetry, including *Winter Morning Walks: 100 Postcards to Jim Harrison* (Carnegie Mellon P, 2000) and *Weather Central* and *Sure Signs*, published by University of Pittsburgh Press. Winner of the Stanley Kunitz Prize for Poetry and the Society of Midland Authors Award for Poetry, his latest book, *100 Postcards to Jim Harrison*, will be published by University of Pittsburgh Press in spring 2000. "Lying for the Sake of Making Poems" appeared in the spring 1998 issue of *Prairie Schooner*.

MAXINE KUMIN received the Pulitzer Prize for poetry in 1973 and is the author of eleven books of poetry, the latest being *Connecting the Dots* (Norton, 1998). She recently published an animal rights murder mystery, *Quit Monks or Die!* (Story Line P, 1999), and she received the Ruth Lilly Poetry prize in 1999. *Inside the Halo and Beyond: The Anatomy of a Recovery* (Norton, 2000) is an account of her nearly fatal horse and cart accident. "Jicama, without Expectation," which appeared in the spring 1994 issue of *Prairie Schooner*, was selected for inclusion in *Best American Essays 1995*.

VALERIE MINER is a novelist, essayist, and professor of English at the University of Minnesota. Her seventh novel, *Range of Light*, appeared in spring 1998 (Zoland). She is also author of *Trespassing and Other Stories* and *Rumors from the Cauldron,* collections of essays. Excerpts from *The Low Road* appeared in the fall 1998 issue of *Prairie Schooner.*

Novelist, photographer, and native Nebraskan WRIGHT MORRIS (1910–88) wrote thirty-three books, including *Field of Vision,* winner of the National Book Award. His groundbreaking novel of words and photographs, *The Home Place,* was reprinted by the University of Nebraska Press in 1998. "Where the West Begins" appeared in the summer 1980 issue of *Prairie Schooner.*

LINDA PASTAN's poetry has been nominated for a Pulitzer Prize. She has ten collections of poetry, most recently *An Early Afterlife* (1995), and *Carnival Evening: New and Selected Poems* (1998), both published by Norton. "Washing My Hands of the Ink" appeared in the winter 1991 issue of *Prairie Schooner.* She has taught at the Bread Loaf Writers' Conference and served as Poet Laureate of Maryland.

ALBERTO ALVARO RÍOS is author of four volumes of poetry, including *Whispering to Fool the Wind,* winner of the Walt Whitman Award. His first collection of stories, *The Iguana Killer,* won the Western States Book Award; his newest collection of stories is *The Curtain of Trees* (U of New Mexico P, 1999). "Translating Translation" appeared in the winter 1994 issue of *Prairie Schooner.* Ríos is professor of English at Arizona State University.

NANCY WILLARD has published novels, collections of stories and poems, books of criticism, and more than a dozen children's books, and she has been a recipient of a Newberry Award for Children's Literature. Her most recent books are *Swimming Lessons: New and Selected Poems* (Knopf 1996), and *Step Lightly: Poems for the Journey* (Harcourt Brace, 1998), a collection of poetry for children which she edited. "Something That Will Last" appeared in the winter 1991 issue of *Prairie Schooner.*